Winning in Tough Hold 'em Games

Short-Handed and High-Stakes Concepts and Theory for Limit Hold 'em

By

Nick "Stoxtrader" Grudzien

and

Geoff "Zobags" Herzog

A product of Two Plus Two Publishing
www.twoplustwo.com

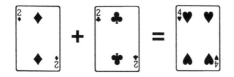

FIRST EDITION
FIRST PRINTING: APRIL 2007

Printing and Binding
Creel Printing Co.
Las Vegas, Nevada

Printed in the United States of America

Winning in Tough Hold 'em Games
Short-Handed and
High-Stakes Concepts and Theory for Limit Hold 'em

Copyright © 2007 by
Two Plus Two Publishing LLC

For information contact: **Two Plus Two Publishing LLC**
32 Commerce Center Drive
Suite H-89
Henderson, NV 89014
www.twoplustwo.com

ISBN: 1-880685-38-8
ISBN13: 978-1-880685-38-9

Table of Contents

About Nick "Stoxtrader" Grudzien

Nick worked as a Wall-Street trader for ten years before taking a hiatus to play poker "professionally," write this book, and spend time with his wife and two children, ages four and two. He currently spends his time playing high-stakes, online cash games, and traveling to a few of the bigger WPT and WSOP tournaments. He splits his time evenly between limit and no-limit play, and continues to study the game intensely.

Nick started playing poker seriously in the fall of 2003. He rapidly moved up in limits until the spring of 2005 at which point he reached, and has continued to play in, the highest cash games online. As Nick moved up in limits, he had the luxury of a stable job and considered poker to be recreation, at least initially. Bankroll requirements and risk objectives can be much more lax when the limits you play are small relative to your current earning potential, and this is a big reason Nick was able to move up in limits so quickly. Once Nick started playing $100-$200 limit hold 'em online, bankroll considerations started taking a somewhat more serious perspective. Since then, he has always had 1,000 big bets in his poker designated bankroll for any limit hold 'em game in which he has played.

Nick is one of the featured bloggers at Stoxpoker.com and regularly posts entries and produces instructional videos there. He also posts frequently under the name "Stoxtrader" at twoplustwo.com.

About Geoff "Zobags" Herzog

Geoff received undergraduate degrees in mathematics and economics from Colorado College where he and Nick were fraternity brothers. After college, Geoff worked briefly as an actuary before enrolling at Harvard Law School. Upon graduation, he moved to Miami to work for a big law firm that specialized in defending financial services companies in multi-million dollar, class-action lawsuits. While there, he met his wife, Laura, who was also an attorney at the firm.

After one year of practicing law, Geoff decided it was time for a change and moved to Jacksonville, Florida to work for a small venture capital company which invested in technology start-ups. Eventually, he became the Chief Legal Officer for one of the firm's portfolio companies. About this time, Geoff got interested in online poker when Nick explained how lucrative it could be. After many hours of coaching from Nick, and in less than one year, Geoff was able to move up in limits, going from $0.50-$1.00 to $50-$100. During this time, Geoff realized he could make more money playing poker than practicing law, so he "retired" to focus exclusively on poker. Since then, Geoff has had success grinding out a large number of short-handed limit hold 'em hands, usually playing 6 tables at a time.

With the free time Geoff gained from playing poker for a living, he decided to pursue his other dream of being a professional hockey player. Even though he had not played competitively since college (8 years prior), Geoff was able to play a few games for the Jacksonville Barracudas of the Southern Professional Hockey League during the 2006-2007 Season.

Geoff is also a CFA® (Chartered Financial Analyst) charterholder. He frequently posts at stoxpoker.com and twoplustwo.com under the name "Zobags," and coaches a number of students on their limit hold 'em game.

Acknowledgments

There are many people whose support and effort made this book possible. We would like to thank David Sklansky, Mason Malmuth, Charmaine Malmuth, and Mat Sklansky for their help in reviewing and editing this book. We thank Mark Werner from mw2design for designing our cover. Hopefully our words are worthy of your art. Thank you to the members at twoplustwo.com and stoxpoker.com who have engaged us in thoughtful debate, helping to refine our understanding of this great game.

We thank Andrew Prock for his development of PokerStove which has been a great help in writing this book and our poker careers. Hopefully, our words are worthy of your art. We would also like to thank Pat from pokertracker.com for creating such a useful tool and offering great support.

Nick would like to thank his wife Kelly for everything she does, especially being a great mother to their two children. He would also like to thank his parents, Ed and Wendy, who have been unwaveringly supportive throughout his life, his poker confidant and foil, Rob P, and his good friend from the south, Jim V.

Geoff would like to thank his wife Laura for her strength and understanding. He would also like to thank his mother, Roxy, and his brother, Derek, for their support, and all members of the Green Monkey Society for being a second family to him. In addition, Geoff would like to extend a special thank you to his co-author, Nick, for spending countless hours teaching him how to play hold 'em.

Together, we would like to thank our fraternity brothers from Kappa Sigma at Colorado College. Finally, we would like to thank Two Plus Two Publishing, LLC.

Why This Book?

The recent boom of Texas hold 'em on the Internet has changed the game drastically, especially at the mid and high-limit games ($15-$30 and above). First, you can play many more hands online, producing much more income per hour. While live play generates 30 to 40 hands per hour at a full table if things go smoothly — sometimes as little as 25 hands per hour when they do not, Internet play yields 55 to 60 hands per hour, even more at short-handed tables — and because the poker rooms make more money from short-handed tables and many players enjoy the additional speed and nuances of a short-handed game, they are becoming the rule rather than the exception. Therefore, while playing 4 to 8 tables, you can easily play 300 to 500 hands per hour. Winning, on average, $1.00 per hand, which many good players do at stakes as low as $30-$60, would produce an income approaching $1,000,000 per year "working" a 40 hour week.

These days, hold 'em games also tend to be more aggressive. Against certain opponents, it may be correct to call down with as little as ace-high, sometimes even king-high. In addition to being more aggressive, the games are tighter, meaning many more pots will be heads up on the flop. Not only does a larger portion of heads-up pots post-flop mean greater variance, it also requires a completely different strategy. "Part Three: Playing Heads-Up Post-Flop" will address this. We should note that whenever we say "playing heads-up" we mean playing heads-up post-flop (i.e. exactly two players see a flop) and not playing at a table with only two players. Not only do we discuss what to consider in various situations, we also reveal specific lines which can be very effective in heads-up play, and explain in what circumstances they should be used. Think of these lines as tools in your poker arsenal, like the different clubs in a golfer's bag.

2 Why This Book?

This book is not meant to replace other great books on hold 'em strategy, rather we hope to build on them and assume the reader is already familiar with the concepts presented in them. Thus, we spend time on more advanced concepts, such as blind defense and stealing, re-stealing, and flop and turn semi-bluffing frequencies.

There are also software tools that can be used with Internet poker which presents good information on your opponents' tendencies. This allows us to discuss certain decisions more in-depth. For example, we are able to recommend specific hand ranges with which to make certain plays based on precise data about your opponents' play. Internet poker also offers the opportunity for "rakeback" deals. Rakeback returns a portion of the rake that you pay to each pot. At the lower limits like ($0.50/$1.00), it can amount to 1.5BB/100 hands, 0.5BB/100 hands at the mid-limits, and 0.25BB/100 hands at the highest limits.

The Internet has forever changed Texas hold 'em. These changes and the strategy adjustments they require are discussed for the first time in this text. We hope you find them useful.

Typical Opponents by Limits

In order to excel at hold 'em, you must adjust your playing style to your opponents in order to exploit their mistakes or counter their overriding tendencies. However, sometimes you will be forced to make a critical decision without a read on your opponent. In that case, it is usually best to assume your opponent is a "typical" player for the stakes you are playing. Below is a brief description of the "typical" play for each group of limits.

Low Limits ($3-$6 and Below)

At the lowest limits, "no fold 'em hold 'em" is the norm. Since it is not uncommon to routinely see 5 to 6 players to a flop, bluffing is far less important and betting for value is far more important. Trying to win without a showdown in these games is like beating your head against a wall — it is only worth doing because it feels good to stop. Knowing the pot odds, calling with profitable draws, and betting and raising for value are the key skills. You will win fewer pots than your opponents, but will take home the money because the pots you win will be larger and you will lose less when you lose. That is unless you run bad, miss all your draws, and get your big hands cracked — which will happen more often than you would like since your opponents will chase you down with marginal draws. You should almost never bluff, but you can bet and raise with your strong draws because you will have an equity edge against large fields. Also, betting for value is key because you do not want to give free cards to players who will pay to chase weak draws.

Middle Limits ($5-$10 to $20-$40)

Most players will have been winners at the lower limits, but you will still find opponents who are new to the game and have enough money to support a losing habit. People correctly play fewer hands pre-flop, and you will see many more pots where there are only 2 to 3 players to the flop. Your opponents will be more aggressive, so making thin value bets can be dangerous, especially against opponents who will semi-bluff or raise for value with a decent (but not strong) hand. If you have mastered the lower limits, moving up to the middle limits can be a big and profitable move. However, it does become more important to know your opponents, and table and seat selection are now a very important factor for the first time.

Upper Limits ($25-$50 to $100-$200)

These games are tight and aggressive. You will find tables full of players that play just like you. You should avoid them. The key is to find a higher stakes table that plays like a middle stakes table because of 1 or 2 loose players. They can be found if you are willing to look. The average player here plays very close to optimally pre-flop, and has probably spent some time studying the game. Bluffing, semi-bluffing, deception, and making thin value bets become more important skills. Pushing your strong draws is still a good play because your bluffing equity will be higher, but your implied odds will be lower. In addition, your reverse implied odds will be worse since your opponents will punish you when given the chance, and your positive implied odds will be lower because you will get paid off less often. But with good table and seat selection these games are beatable, although difficult.

Sky-High Limits ($150-$300 and Up)

Here is where you will find the best players in the world. There will be some variations in style, but for the most part, your opponents' games will be fine tuned, making it more difficult to find exploitable tendencies. For example, some players may play too many hands pre-flop, but they will adjust their post-flop play to partially compensate for their pre-flop disadvantage. Players will battle tenaciously for blinds, and creative play is the rule rather than the exception. Bluff-raising, semi-bluff calling, 3-barrel bluffs, stealing, and re-stealing occur like you have never seen before. Most of the games at these limits are not worth playing, but with a high-level game and the discipline to play only when you have an edge, you can make great money. Variance is huge, and the average player is probably under-bankrolled. (Make sure you are not that player.[1])

---

[1] See the chapter entitled "Bankroll Management and Risk of Ruin Considerations" in Part Five for a discussion of bankroll and variance.

Part One

Pre-Flop Play

Pre-Flop Play

Introduction

In tough, short-handed hold'em games, if you sit around and wait for premium hands before you enter the pot, you will be eaten up by the blinds. You must be willing to steal the blinds with holdings that may seem marginal, especially in the later positions. However, you should still only play hands that are profitable based on your position, your chances of stealing the blinds, and your post-flop expectation. Furthermore, since many of your opponents will be reading hands well in tough games, your opening standards should add some deception to your hand ranges. The chapter entitled "Opening the Pot for a Raise" provides a good set of guidelines for accomplishing these goals.

You must also learn to adjust your pre-flop play to your opponent's tendencies. Failure to do so will likely cause you to get run over. For example, since your opponents will be opening pre-flop with wide ranges, you will have to three-bet with your strong hands (as well as the premium hands). If you are always folding hands like AJo, A9s, and KQo simply because the pot has been raised in front of you, you will be missing too much value. The chapter on "Re-Stealing" teaches how to determine which hands you should three-bet to punish your over-aggressive opponents.

You may also earn extra profit by entering more pots when a loose/bad player is already in. Some of the discussion that follows will help determine when you should take advantage of such opportunities and whether you should call or raise when you enter the pot. In tough/short-handed games, you will be faced with many more situations where everyone folds to the blinds. The chapters entitled "Playing in a Steal Situation" and "Blind Versus Blind" will help you navigate these difficult blind battles.

The Importance of Guidelines

When deciding whether to play pre-flop, it is important to have specific guidelines based on position. Once there are others in the pot, or you are in one of the blinds, circumstances change and the decisions get more complex. But for the easier decisions of what hands to open with when nobody has entered the pot before you, playing by strict guidelines is a good practice. This is because many players may otherwise start to play far too loose, either because they are running bad and feel a need to get unstuck, or because they are running hot and feel invincible. This effect can snowball and cause an otherwise winning player to become a losing one. You should only deviate from these specific guidelines when you have a particular reason. This will also help you develop the discipline required to continually make the correct decisions throughout a hand, session, or year.

Opening the Pot for a Raise

Texas hold 'em is a game of balance. Often times, the correct strategy requires balancing two opposing considerations. For example, if you seem to be getting good enough odds to draw when you have flopped bottom pair, you are usually in a multi-way pot — thus increasing the probabilities that you are already up against a big hand (like top two-pair or a set), or that your hand will be vulnerable to redraws (to hands like straights and flushes).[2] As another example, if you flop top pair in a 3-handed pot, you may want to raise to force out one player, but that same raise may let a third player three-bet. Being able to decide which option carries the best ratio of risk to reward is what makes a successful poker player.

There is also balance in pre-flop strategy. Small suited connectors — hands like: 54s, 65s, 76s, 87s — increase in value in loose games because the pot is more likely to be multi-way. However, tighter games where your opponents are more thinking and observant, tend to be played at the higher limits. Therefore, the small suited connectors have value, even if heads-up post-flop, because by playing them, you make it more difficult for your opponents to read your hand.

Because of this balance inherent in hold 'em, we recommend that when you are deciding whether to open the pot for a raise, you should follow a rote strategy based almost exclusively on your two hole cards and your position. We are basically saying that the many other factors that would change your starting hand requirements offset, simply getting you back to where you started. The largest argument against following a pre-programmed

---

[2] We are not saying that you should never draw when you have flopped bottom pair, but these factors, along with the texture of the flop and your relative position, are important to consider.

strategy is that your hand range is too well defined. This may be somewhat true for your play in the first few positions at a 10-handed table, but aside from that, your range will be wide enough and contain enough different types of hands. In other words, the hand values in a vacuum are more important, on average, than any deception value you may create. There may still be specific cases where deception is warranted, but our opinion is that players tend to overuse this as an excuse to do something they feel like doing, rather than having the discipline to stay the course and be consistent.

The chart below outlines when you should open the pot for a raise based on your position. Each position should be thought of as how far you are from the button. This way the strategy can be easily used in either a full-ring or short-handed game. For example, 7 seats off-the-button refers to what is typically called under the gun (UTG), and 1 off-the-button means what is commonly referred to as the cutoff (CO). On the chart below, each position is listed in the far left column. Each cell represents the weakest hand of each type with which you should be willing to open-raise. For example, if you are 3 seats off the button, you should open-raise with 55+, A7s+, A9o+, K9s+, KQo, QTs+, J9s+, T9s, and 98s. As indicated in the legend, the suited hands are listed in the left column for each hand type, and the unsuited hands are listed on the right.

A few clarifications should be made about the the chart below and any "rigid" set of hold 'em guidelines:

1. It is impossible to encapsulate balancing and metagame considerations in a rigid chart.

2. Early position play in particular can change based on the makeup of the table.

3. Late position play in particular can change based on the makeup of the blind.

Number of Seats off Button	Non Prs	Aces		Kings		Queens		Jacks		Tens		Nines		Eights		Sevens		Sixes	
	Prs	s	u	s	u	s	u	s	u	s	u	s	u	s	u	s	u	s	u
7	99	AJ	AQ	-	-	-	-	-	-	-	-	-	-	-	-	-	-	-	-
6	88	AT	AQ	KQ	-	-	-	-	-	-	-	-	-	-	-	-	-	-	-
5	77	A9	AJ	KJ	-	QJ	-	-	-	-	-	-	-	-	-	-	-	-	-
4	66	A8	AT	KT	KQ	QT	-	JT	-	-	-	-	-	-	-	-	-	-	-
3	55	A7	A9	K9	KQ	QT	-	J9	-	T9	-	98	-	-	-	-	-	-	-
2	33	A7	A9	K7	KJ	Q9	QJ	J9	-	T8	-	98	-	87	-	76	-	-	-
1	22	A4	A7	K5	K9	Q9	QJ	J8	-	T8	-	97	-	87	-	76	-	-	-
0	22	A2	A3	K2	K9	Q5	Q9	J7	J9	T8	T8	97	98	86	-	75	-	65	-

Legend: s = suited; u = unsuited.

Columns under Aces, Kings, Queens, ..., represent hands where the high card is the header for the column.

So entries under the Queens header represent hands, such as queen-ten, where the queen is the high card.

Many would argue that you should always consider more factors, such as, how the table has been playing and your opponents' post-flop play. However, the mood of the table is far less important in high-stakes online games where most of your opponents are playing four or more tables at one time. Also, how your opponents play post-flop is generally balanced by the looseness of the game.

For example, it may seem unnatural to open the pot for a raise with a pair of sevens if you are 5 off-the-button in a very loose game. However, in very loose games your opponents tend to play worse post-flop, so the decreased likelihood of stealing the blinds is balanced by a gain in post-flop expectation.

In other words, if you get many callers behind you, you will be in a multi-way pot with many poor players and a hand that has good implied odds. Moreover, the pot will be large. Thus, your poor playing opponents will be tied to the pot, allowing you to collect a lot of bets when you flop a big hand. This same reasoning holds for opening with a hand like queen-jack suited if you are 5 off-the-button.

The minor exceptions have to do with stealing the blinds (i.e. opening for a raise from 1 off-the-button or the button). Against a player who under-defends his big blind, you should be willing to raise more hands from the button as a pure steal. This concept also applies in the cutoff, but now you need to take into account the playing characteristics of the button plus the fact that he may have been dealt a good hand.

Against an over-defender, you should be less inclined to steal with small suited connectors because they do not play well heads-up. The exception, of course, is if the small blind defends way too often (by calling and not raising) because the pot is now much more likely to be multi-way.

Throughout this book we present real-life data examples from three different players: a high-limit shorthanded player (referred to as "High"), a mid-limit shorthanded player ("Mid"); and a full-ring grinder ("Grd"). The table below shows summary statistics for each of these three players. Note that SD stands for "showdown," and WSF stands for "when seeing the flop."

	Hands	Levels ($)	Avg # of Plys	Hands Played %	Amount Won	BB/ 100
High	317,370	$50-$100 — $500-$1,000	5.36	28.66	$764,793	0.73
Mid	429,555	$10-$20 — $100-$200	5.1	27.68	$11,848	0.04
Grd	673,245	$10-$20 — $100-$200	8.8	17.36	$208,659	0.55
	Folded SB to steal %	Folded BB to Steal %	Att. to Steal %	Won $ WSF %	Went to SD %	Won $ at SD %
High	81.35%	45.57%	39.65%	47.23%	35.02%	58.28%
Mid	85.01%	44.42%	38.55%	45.24%	37.01%	52.20%
Grd	83.41%	57.66%	35.33%	39.63%	33.48%	57.02%

Below is a hand-by-hand chart of results for open-raising from the positions that are 3 or fewer seats off the button (all non-blind positions at a 6-handed table). They are shown for comparison purposes with each other, and you also should be able to compare your own results based on the limits you play. The profitable hands in the tables below should roughly correlate with the opening guidelines that we listed earlier. There will of course be anomalies in the data which are largely due to sample size issues. But even with a somewhat limited sample size, we can begin to see trends in the profitability of certain types of hands adjusted for position. (Negative entries are in parentheses.)

	Trials	Win %	Amount ($)	Avg $/Hand	BB/ Hand	Win % WSF	Went to SD (%)	Won $ at SD (%)
High								
3 Off	3,409	60.72	419,476.19	123.05	0.57	54.4	40.24	60.07
2 Off	6,065	61.15	623,852.61	102.86	0.47	54.70	36.84	61.02
1 Off	8,937	61.43	818,091.60	91.54	0.39	54.25	35.68	59.13
Button	12,408	61.11	952,447.64	76.76	0.35	54.05	33.65	60.20
Mid								
3 Off	3,681	57.92	44,465.43	12.08	0.46	50.89	46.11	54.55
2 Off	7,854	60.15	81,199.79	10.34	0.42	51.04	44.04	54.24
1 Off	11,872	62.18	102,561.70	8.64	0.37	52.59	41.38	53.77

	Trials	Win %	Amount ($)	Avg $/Hand	BB/Hand	Win % WSF	Went to SD (%)	Won $ at SD (%)
Button Grinder	16,854	63.61	122,647.05	7.28	0.32	52.60	39.39	52.40
3 Off	5,914	60.23	226,005.73	38.22	0.47	48.52	38.37	58.76
2 Off	6,708	61.34	263,903.97	39.34	0.50	50.52	36.52	58.98
1 Off	7,513	62.23	251,967.86	33.54	0.38	49.87	35.33	56.41
Button	7,208	63.75	237,419.20	32.94	0.40	51.39	37.31	55.42

High: 3 Off

Hand	Trials	Win %	Amount ($)	Avg $/Hand	BB/Hand	Win % WSF	Went to SD (%)	Won $ at SD (%)
AA	98	89.80	56,832.11	579.92	2.66	87.18	60.26	80.85
AKs	74	67.57	13,925.50	188.18	0.74	62.50	53.13	55.88
AKo	197	68.53	29,828.00	151.41	0..79	61.96	52.15	65.88
AQs	63	68.25	9,374.75	148.81	0.54	58.33	43.75	61.90
AQo	230	66.09	34,613.50	150.49	0.59	58.60	37.10	56.52
AJs	57	59.65	5,781.50	101.43	0.44	54.00	30.00	66.67
AJo	189	61.38	21,512.50	113.82	0.60	55.97	45.28	66.67
ATs	63	60.32	3,378.17	53.62	0.37	52.83	49.06	61.54
ATo	174	59.20	22,366.75	128.54	0.53	52.52	39.57	61.82
A9s	64	56.25	1,682.50	26.29	(0.02)	48.08	30.77	37.50
A9o	2	100.00	799.00	399.50	2.59	100.00	-	-
A8s	67	46.27	1,395.00	20.82	0.22	44.44	26.98	58.82
A7s	80	61.25	14,936.50	186.71	0.77	56.25	46.88	73.33
A6s	29	41.38	(5,573.00)	(192.17)	(0.59)	29.17	37.50	22.22
KK	94	70.21	18,264.50	194.30	0.95	65.43	55.56	51.11
KQs	69	59.42	7,440.00	107.83	0..62	52.54	38.98	69.57
KQo	198	57.07	19,759.02	99.79	0.39	52.05	32.16	52.73
KJs	71	59.15	(978.00)	(13.77)	0.10	49.12	35.09	45.00
KJo	173	52.02	(2,125.50)	(12.29)	(0.07)	44.29	31.43	50.00
KTs	83	62.65	14,415.00	173.67	0.72	55.07	24.64	88.24
KTo	4	75.00	(28.00)	(7.00)	(0.07)	75.00	25.00	-
K9s	59	61.02	5,526.50	93.67	0.62	56.52	30.43	71.43
K8s	25	32.00	(5,666.00)	(226.64)	(1.12)	15.00	30.00	-
QQ	104	80.77	46,547.00	447.57	2.12	78.26	57.61	77.36
QJs	73	54.79	9,975.50	136.65	0.16	44.07	42.37	48.00
QJo	44	38.64	(4,225.73)	(96.04)	(0.55)	38.10	28.57	50.00
QTs	65	46.15	(7,125.00)	(109.62)	(0.40)	41.38	25.86	46.67
QTo	2	50.00	(123.00)	(61.50)	0.10	50.00	-	-
Q9s	5	40.00	(1,933.00)	(386.60)	(1.01)	40.00	40.00	-
JJ	101	66.34	20,729.50	205.24	0.90	60.92	62.07	55.56
JTs	77	63.64	9,297.50	120.75	0.75	56.92	40.00	65.38
JTo	2	50.00	247.00	123.50	(0.76)	50.00	50.00	-
J9s	63	49.21	4,732.50	75.12	0.14	42.86	32.14	61.11
TT	96	63.54	13,075.50	136.20	0.57	57.32	46.34	57.89
T9s	68	60.29	9,627.00	141.57	0.61	55.17	36.21	57.14
T8s	1	100.00	150.00	150.00	0.75	-	-	-

16 Part One: Pre-Flop Play

Hand	Trials	Win %	Amount ($)	Avg $/Hand	BB/Hand	Win % WSF	Went to SD (%)	Won $ at SD (%)
99	100	58.00	4,208.00	42.08	0.17	50.59	38.82	45.45
98s	24	70.83	(1,129.00)	(47.04)	0.41	63.16	31.58	50.00
88	96	63.54	28,701.12	298.97	1.38	58.33	54.76	69.57
87s	4	50.00	1,969.00	492.25	2.30	50.00	25.00	100.00
77	99	60.61	7,393.50	74.68	0.75	54.12	37.65	68.75
66	96	50.00	3,219.00	33.53	0.12	43.53	25.88	54.55
55	85	48.24	6,176.50	72.66	0.27	44.30	31.65	52.00
44	41	43.90	503.00	12.27	(0.06)	32.35	17.65	33.33
Total	3,409	60.72	419,476.19	123.05	0.57	54.40	40.24	90.07

High: 2 Off								
Hand	Trials	Win %	Amount ($)	Avg $/Hand	BB/ Hand	Win % WSF	Went to SD (%)	Won $ at SD (%)
AA	150	86.00	64,103.41	427.36	1.91	83.20	45.60	70.18
AKs	99	65.66	9,687.81	97.86	0.82	61.18	48.24	65.85
AKo	276	69.20	44,428.50	160.97	0.71	63.52	46.78	59.63
AQs	105	72.38	21,422.00	204.02	0.78	67.05	43.18	65.79
AQo	249	68.27	33,474.25	134.43	0.66	62.14	38.84	67.50
AJs	108	56.48	5,917.50	54.79	0.16	48.91	46.74	53.49
AJo	319	56.43	2,828.50	8.87	0.11	48.45	32.56	57.14
ATs	95	69.47	20,252.50	213.18	0.92	65.38	39.74	61.29
ATo	300	60.00	27,850.50	92.84	0.38	53.63	39.11	58.76
A9s	84	55.95	1,212.50	14.43	0.18	48.57	37.14	53.85
A9o	257	61.48	19,500.50	75.88	0.28	54.55	38.28	68.75
A8s	121	62.81	4,729.54	39.09	0.32	57.14	45.92	53.33
A8o	104	60.58	3,085.50	29.67	0.23	48.75	31.25	68.00
A7s	83	57.83	8,520.00	102.65	0.38	51.47	39.71	59.26
A7o	4	50.00	1,044.00	261.00	0.99	50.00	25.00	100.00
A6s	111	57.66	7,633.36	68.77	0.47	49.43	42.53	56.76
KK	143	79.72	55,423.00	387.57	1.86	75.83	61.67	71.62
KQs	99	66.67	18,852.50	190.43	0.89	61.63	39.53	76.47
KQo	254	59.45	12,064.00	47.50	0.22	53.74	32.24	56.52
KJs	88	61.36	7,904.50	89.82	0.37	54.67	37.33	53.57
KJo	288	54.86	11,299.50	39.23	0.21	49.79	30.96	62.16
KTs	78	56.41	8,801.00	112.83	0.32	50.00	30.88	57.14
KTo	34	52.94	(1,842.50)	(54.19)	(0.44)	50.00	28.13	44.44
K9s	80	52.50	(744.50)	(9.31)	(0.10)	47.06	30.88	52.38
K9o	4	-	(740.00)	(185.00)	(2.75)	-	25.00	-
K8s	85	51.76	2,742.11	32.26	0.31	41.43	37.14	57.69
QQ	169	75.15	53,134.50	314.41	1.25	70.63	41.26	66.10
QJs	92	64.13	17,988.00	195.52	0.94	61.25	38.75	67.74
QJo	309	55.34	9,895.50	32.02	0.10	45.94	32.11	56.96
QTs	92	64.13	9,205.50	100.06	0.57	57.89	25.00	57.89
QTo	6	50.00	2,591.00	431.83	1.24	50.00	50.00	66.67
Q9s	74	52.70	(465.00)	(6.28)	0.17	45.16	27.42	70.59

Hand	Trials	Win %	Amount ($)	Avg $/Hand	BB/Hand	Win % WSF	Went to SD (%)	Won $ at SD (%)
JJ	136	61.76	16,305.50	119.89	0.38	55.93	41.53	46.94
JTs	86	62.79	6,458.50	75.10	0.34	55.71	32.86	65.22
JTo	1	100.00	192.00	192.00	3.20	100.00	100.00	100.00
J9s	105	56.19	1,604.00	15.28	0.09	50.00	31.82	46.43
TT	129	70.54	32,670.50	253.26	1.47	66.67	44.74	70.59
T9s	114	54.39	(2,761.82)	(24.23)	(0.11)	46.81	39.36	45.95
T8s	83	59.04	3,255.50	39.22	0.15	49.23	29.23	52.63
T7s	1	-	(150.00)	(150.00)	(1.50)	-	-	-
99	138	65.22	40,237.29	291.57	1.08	59.66	39.50	76.60
98s	97	54.64	5,218.00	53.79	0.38	46.75	28.57	59.09
98o	1	100.00	1,722.00	1,722.00	5.74	100.00	100.00	100.00
97s	26	57.69	(1,159.00)	(44.58)	0.35	47.62	33.33	71.43
88	126	61.90	4,437.00	35.21	0.30	53.85	34.62	44.44
87s	43	41.86	228.50	5.31	(0.43)	32.43	37.84	57.14
77	130	55.38	12,827.50	98.67	0.29	50.85	30.51	61.11
76s	20	45.00	(645.00)	(32.25)	(0.33)	38.89	27.78	40.00
66	147	51.02	979.50	6.66	(0.12)	39.83	29.66	42.86
55	145	57.24	17,539.66	120.96	0.45	48.33	24.17	72.41
44	120	55.83	10,006.00	83.38	0.42	50.93	25.00	74.07
33	57	40.35	(6,912.50)	(121.27)	(0.34)	34.62	23.08	58.33
Total	6,065	61.15	623,852.61	102.86	0.47	54.70	36.84	61.02

High: 1 Off

Hand	Trials	Win %	Amount ($)	Avg $/Hand	BB/Hand	Win % WSF	Went to SD (%)	Won $ at SD (%)
AA	148	89.86	65,898.00	445.26	1.96	86.96	48.70	78.57
AKs	96	73.96	29,257.00	304.76	1.22	70.59	45.88	61.54
AKo	354	71.47	42,018.00	118.69	0.59	64.93	45.83	53.79
AQs	91	70.33	17,995.25	197.75	0.92	64.47	51.32	61.54
AQo	334	67.07	38,117.50	114.12	0.58	58.96	44.78	60.83
AJs	118	67.80	18,200.50	154.24	0.61	59.57	38.30	61.11
AJo	276	65.22	33,932.00	122.94	0.53	58.18	36.82	65.43
ATs	107	63.55	3,947.66	36.89	0.19	55.56	33.33	51.85
ATo	329	63.53	17,124.00	52.05	0.27	53.60	36.40	64.84
A9s	91	64.84	9,003.00	98.93	0.41	57.53	46.58	52.94
A9o	293	61.77	22,517.00	76.85	0.39	53.85	32.05	64.00
A8s	123	57.72	9,374.50	76.22	0.28	51.40	36.45	58.97
A8o	266	54.51	(713.00)	(2.68)	0.03	49.07	32.41	61.43
A7s	98	52.04	(3,289.00)	(33.56)	(0.16)	39.74	28.21	45.45
A7o	267	59.18	12,305.00	46.09	0.09	50.94	29.72	57.14
A6s	90	60.00	5,411.50	60.13	0.14	51.35	40.54	56.67
A6o	115	58.26	12,046.00	104.75	0.34	50.00	36.96	64.71
A5s	102	62.75	16,489.50	161.66	0.46	53.95	22.37	70.59
A5o	1	100.00	75.00	75.00	1.25	-	-	-
A4s	107	62.62	9,982.00	93.29	0.32	50.63	26.58	71.43

A3s	89	53.93	3,349.00	37.63	0.03	46.67	26.67	65.00
A2s	109	52.29	6,010.50	55.14	0.13	45.98	21.84	63.16
KK	167	75.45	57,029.00	341.49	1.64	70.50	58.27	61.73
KQs	96	64.58	10,990.00	114.48	0.71	60.47	34.88	70.00
KQo	276	63.04	27,921.50	101.16	0.44	56.65	32.19	65.33
KJs	100	59.00	8,147.00	81.47	0.19	50.62	30.86	44.00
KJo	314	54.78	2,639.50	8.41	0.06	47.51	31.80	51.81
KTs	97	63.92	9,261.50	95.48	0.28	54.17	45.83	54.55
KTo	308	59.42	28,765.50	93.39	0.36	52.19	39.04	57.14
K9s	94	63.83	5,073.75	53.98	0.30	51.43	22.86	50.00
K9o	4	50.00	60.00	15.00	1.05	50.00	25.00	100.00
K8s	93	48.39	(11,172.50)	(120.13)	(0.33)	43.75	35.00	35.71
K7s	89	59.55	12,626.50	141.87	0.57	52.70	37.84	64.29
K6s	105	46.67	(6,901.00)	(65.72)	(0.18)	36.78	24.14	47.62
QQ	163	77.91	42,103.00	258.30	1.28	74.10	53.24	63.51
QJs	96	60.42	11,362.00	118.35	0.57	54.32	34.57	64.29
QJo	301	57.14	3,888.50	12.92	0.15	51.41	32.93	53.66
QTs	101	62.38	11,647.50	115.32	0.43	54.32	34.57	53.57
QTo	281	58.01	16,815.75	59.84	0.31	50.88	37.72	59.30
Q9s	93	59.14	10,148.00	109.12	0.47	50.67	32.00	54.17
Q9o	1	-	(150.00)	(150.00)	(1.50)	-	-	-
Q8s	83	54.22	(3,347.41)	(40.33)	(0.21)	46.88	28.13	44.44
JJ	150	78.67	46,258.50	308.39	1.47	74.38	47.93	72.41
JTs	79	58.23	8,939.00	113.15	0.36	53.03	43.94	72.41
JTo	272	55.15	(3,023.50)	(11.12)	(0.12)	48.21	30.80	43.48
J9s	103	62.14	13,681.00	132.83	0.49	55.17	32.18	60.71
J9o	2	100.00	450.00	225.00	0.75	100.00	100.00	100.00
J8s	80	57.50	3,932.00	49.15	0.10	47.69	27.69	55.56
J7s	30	33.33	(3,605.00)	(120.17)	(0.29)	26.92	30.77	50.00
TT	152	73.68	32,056.86	210.90	0.94	67.74	40.32	62.00
T9s	104	51.92	(890.00)	(8.56)	(0.04)	43.82	25.84	52.17
T9o	3	-	(1,200.00)	(400.00)	(3.17)	-	66.67	-
T8s	92	54.35	1,649.50	17.93	0.02	49.35	28.57	54.55
99	155	64.52	21,962.00	141.69	0.54	58.33	40.15	60.38
98s	88	56.82	11,394.00	129.48	0.44	52.78	23.61	70.59
98o	2	100.00	1,197.00	598.50	2.25	100.00	100.00	100.00
97s	75	49.33	4,072.08	54.29	0.02	43.75	34.38	59.09
88	150	68.67	23,798.50	158.66	0.73	62.99	43.31	60.00
87s	87	52.87	1,119.50	12.87	(0.15)	42.25	25.35	33.33
77	141	58.87	4,363.00	30.94	0.11	49.12	30.70	45.71
76s	44	59.09	7,269.50	165.22	0.57	51.35	35.14	61.54
66	149	54.36	4,980.50	33.43	0.18	49.25	33.58	51.11
65s	4	50.00	(728.50)	(182.13)	(0.99)	50.00	25.00	-
55	158	52.53	6,130.00	38.80	0.17	44.85	22.79	58.06
44	141	55.32	16,280.50	115.46	0.30	47.06	27.73	69.70
33	155	54.19	7,998.16	51.60	0.38	48.55	31.16	65.12

Hand	Trials	Win %	Amount ($)	Avg $/Hand	BB/ Hand	Win % WSF	Went to SD (%)	Won $ at SD (%)
22	55	50.91	4,048.00	73.60	0.06	35.71	21.43	55.56
Total	8,937	61.43	818,091.60	91.54	0.39	54.25	35.68	59.13
High: Button								
AA	141	92.20	68,421.00	485.26	2.07	90.09	48.65	79.63
AKs	90	76.67	31,133.50	345.93	1.36	69.57	47.83	72.73
AKo	299	70.23	46,373.01	155.09	0.58	63.97	44.94	61.26
AQs	82	67.07	7,375.75	89.95	0.54	63.51	36.49	66.67
AQo	303	67.00	30,592.50	100.97	0.47	61.83	39.69	58.65
AJs	93	68.82	8,089.74	86.99	0.65	61.33	48.00	63.89
AJo	268	73.88	50,741.00	189.33	0.79	66.98	39.15	67.47
ATs	97	73.20	24,979.50	257.52	1.03	69.77	39.53	79.41
ATo	282	61.70	21,846.00	77.47	0.30	54.26	39.01	56.32
A9s	96	68.75	5,109.50	53.22	0.17	60.53	31.58	37.50
A9o	282	63.12	29,071.50	103.09	0.41	54.79	33.79	68.92
A8s	87	59.77	31.50	0.36	(0.04)	53.95	36.84	35.71
A8o	279	57.35	2,855.50	10.23	0.08	49.57	36.64	57.65
A7s	80	57.50	856.00	10.70	0.26	47.62	41.27	57.69
A7o	280	57.86	7,680.50	27.43	0.09	51.46	33.05	64.56
A6s	93	61.29	4,033.00	43.37	0.43	50.00	35.71	60.00
A6o	274	60.95	6,888.00	25.14	0.15	52.51	36.07	54.43
A5s	84	63.10	9,316.67	110.91	0.33	53.85	36.92	54.17
A5o	276	63.04	20,065.75	72.70	0.30	55.56	29.63	73.44
A4s	84	58.33	3,228.00	38.43	0.16	50.00	29.41	45.00
A4o	260	52.69	(14,219.50)	(54.69)	(0.17)	41.06	20.77	53.49
A3s	85	52.94	(4,386.50)	(51.61)	(0.08)	45.21	41.10	46.67
A3o	279	58.42	17,543.00	62.88	0.29	50.90	31.98	71.83
A2s	98	58.16	4,568.00	46.61	0.40	51.81	37.35	51.61
A2o	89	52.81	(2,666.75)	(29.96)	(0.06)	45.83	18.06	61.54
KK	165	82.42	57,061.50	345.83	1.66	79.29	49.29	71.01
KQs	103	67.96	8,039.00	78.05	0.44	58.23	40.51	56.25
KQo	291	63.57	28,967.94	99.55	0.48	55.27	34.18	65.43
KJs	92	68.48	11,649.50	126.63	0.59	62.82	34.62	59.26
KJo	221	61.54	21,317.09	96.46	0.36	54.59	33.51	58.06
KTs	93	64.52	11,919.50	128.17	0.61	58.23	39.24	61.29
KTo	272	59.56	11,192.00	41.15	0.24	53.78	29.33	57.58
K9s	92	66.30	14,152.00	153.83	0.71	59.74	36.36	75.00
K9o	292	57.88	2,175.80	7.45	0.18	50.84	26.89	59.38
K8s	97	53.61	1,277.00	13.16	0.05	42.86	24.68	57.89
K8o	195	49.23	(17,043.50)	(87.40)	(0.28)	43.98	27.11	48.89
K7s	98	50.00	438.50	4.47	0.00	41.46	29.27	66.67
K7o	175	47.43	(12,078.00)	(69.02)	(0.25)	43.14	24.18	48.65
K6s	83	68.67	16,098.25	193.95	0.82	62.12	36.36	79.17

K5s	90	46.67	(1,929.50)	(21.44)	(0.14)	36.99	31.51	52.17
K4s	78	61.54	12,248.41	157.03	0.44	52.46	36.07	54.55
K3s	86	55.81	4,493.00	52.24	0.19	47.06	27.94	47.37
K2s	83	48.19	3,998.00	48.17	0.17	43.06	20.83	66.67
QQ	136	76.47	38,867.00	285.79	1.23	72.65	52.14	65.57
QJs	94	60.64	8,938.00	95.09	0.35	55.42	40.96	52.94
QJo	295	62.37	21,637.50	73.35	0.43	56.73	25.31	64.52
QTs	93	59.14	4,570.00	49.14	0.21	53.66	36.59	46.67
QTo	272	53.68	(7,799.50)	(28.67)	(0.02)	45.13	26.99	54.10
Q9s	97	71.13	19,290.10	198.87	1.06	64.47	39.47	76.67
Q9o	295	55.25	1,757.50	5.96	0.02	48.21	29.88	57.33
Q8s	75	61.33	9,683.00	129.11	0.65	52.54	30.51	66.67
Q7s	85	61.18	226.50	2.66	0.09	50.77	27.69	61.11
Q6s	80	56.25	1,962.50	24.53	0.01	46.67	31.67	42.11
Q5s	57	52.63	1,875.00	32.89	0.31	48.94	23.40	63.64
Q4s	38	47.37	(3,413.00)	(89.82)	(0.48)	36.67	16.67	20.00
JJ	155	72.26	39,279.50	253.42	0.99	66.67	51.94	61.19
JTs	65	58.46	6,829.50	105.07	0.33	53.45	22.41	69.23
JTo	269	57.25	15,838.50	58.88	0.19	50.23	30.52	61.54
J9s	89	52.81	(4,341.00)	(48.78)	(0.02)	46.15	29.49	60.87
J9o	290	53.79	5,174.50	17.84	0.19	46.67	28.75	52.17
J8s	102	56.86	(143.00)	(1.40)	0.01	51.19	36.90	54.84
J7s	74	58.11	1,405.16	18.99	0.14	55.17	29.31	64.71
TT	123	69.11	22,121.50	179.85	0.75	63.46	49.04	64.71
T9s	78	57.69	1,857.50	23.81	0.30	50.00	36.36	50.00
T9o	292	59.25	20,762.50	71.10	0.32	51.28	28.21	59.09
T8s	93	67.74	8,754.50	94.13	0.58	60.53	43.42	51.52
T8o	133	53.38	(382.50)	(2.88)	0.04	42.59	33.33	50.00
T7s	84	50.00	(4,876.50)	(58.05)	(0.22)	42.25	32.39	47.83
99	141	69.50	27,133.00	192.43	0.81	65.60	43.20	61.11
98s	91	48.35	(1,265.00)	(13.90)	(0.17)	44.30	26.58	42.86
98o	234	61.54	17,490.37	74.75	0.29	53.19	30.32	52.63
97s	93	59.14	8,819.00	94.83	0.43	50.65	33.77	73.08
88	146	66.44	19,918.21	136.43	0.52	59.50	35.54	60.47
87s	90	64.44	18,675.90	207.51	0.91	60.00	38.67	72.41
87o	5	80.00	583.00	116.60	0.60	75.00	25.00	100.00
86s	78	64.10	13,363.50	171.33	0.66	59.09	27.27	66.67
77	128	67.19	22,118.50	172.80	0.54	61.11	43.52	53.19
76s	100	59.00	7,135.50	71.36	0.10	50.00	38.75	58.06
75s	80	53.75	2,091.50	26.14	0.02	42.19	29.69	47.37
66	140	57.86	6,473.50	46.24	0.12	50.83	28.33	61.76
65s	94	69.15	18,355.00	195.27	0.97	60.27	26.03	73.68
55	119	49.58	(7,421.50)	(62.37)	(0.22)	40.00	26.00	46.15
54s	20	30.00	(5,071.50)	(253.58)	(1.27)	23.53	17.65	-
44	126	60.32	11,985.50	95.12	0.30	53.27	28.04	63.33
33	139	59.71	23,857.74	171.64	0.71	52.94	27.73	72.73

Hand	Trials	Win %	Amount ($)	Avg $/Hand	BB/ Hand	Win % WSF	Went to SD (%)	Won $ at SD (%)
22	133	56.39	4,828.00	36.30	0.28	49.57	26.96	58.06
Total	12,408	61.11	952,447.64	76.76	0.35	54.05	33.65	60.20
Mid: 3 Off								
AA	101	86.14	7,486.96	74.13	2.25	82.50	62.50	76.00
AKs	70	64.29	648.16	9.26	0.45	58.33	55.00	54.55
AKo	237	56.96	706.13	2.98	0.28	50.72	47.34	53.06
AQs	48	60.42	746.25	15.55	0.17	53.66	51.22	52.38
AQo	221	61.99	4,636.00	20.98	0.69	57.36	53.81	51.89
AJs	62	58.06	1,322.13	21.32	0.43	52.73	60.00	51.52
AJo	229	53.71	989.87	4.32	0.19	45.99	47.06	52.27
ATs	83	54.22	404.50	4.87	0.20	44.12	47.06	53.13
ATo	201	60.70	2,675.50	13.31	0.56	54.32	33.95	60.00
A9s	83	46.99	(1,347.84)	(16.24)	(0.21)	38.89	36.11	57.69
A9o	2	-	(110.00)	(55.00)	(3.25)	-	-	-
A8s	76	60.53	376.50	4.95	0.40	51.61	61.29	52.63
A7s	70	54.29	383.25	5.48	0.23	46.43	37.50	57.14
A6s	2	50.00	(9.00)	(4.50)	(1.45)	50.00	50.00	-
KK	115	75.65	6,087.70	52.94	1.92	72.55	57.84	62.71
KQs	75	50.67	644.00	8.59	0.06	41.27	28.57	44.44
KQo	199	54.77	1,777.25	8.93	0.22	45.96	33.54	50.00
KJs	82	54.88	(141.50)	(1.73)	(0.07)	47.76	43.28	55.17
KJo	144	46.53	(116.00)	(0.81)	(0.17)	39.50	37.82	42.22
KTs	82	51.22	(1,650.68)	(20.13)	(0.03)	47.30	45.95	38.24
K9s	70	45.71	254.00	3.63	(0.03)	39.34	45.90	46.43
QQ	105	76.19	4,253.76	40.51	1.63	70.59	67.06	61.40
QJs	86	68.60	1,041.26	12.11	0.96	60.87	37.68	69.23
QJo	128	57.03	2,854.50	22.30	0.70	51.40	38.32	70.73
QTs	65	52.31	(323.25)	(4.97)	(0.22)	43.64	27.27	40.00
JJ	119	72.27	4,690.00	39.41	1.24	65.63	59.38	56.14
JTs	89	58.43	1,561.50	17.54	0.50	52.56	42.31	54.55
J9s	68	50.00	321.90	4.73	(0.12)	38.89	40.74	54.55
TT	124	54.84	1,879.25	15.16	0.58	46.67	61.90	50.77
T9s	83	57.83	118.50	1.43	0.43	50.00	52.86	51.35
99	119	52.10	448.63	3.77	0.48	46.73	50.47	51.85
88	106	61.32	1,381.70	13.03	0.66	51.76	41.18	60.00
77	125	48.00	130.25	1.04	0.18	39.25	39.25	52.38
66	114	46.49	(841.75)	(7.38)	(0.34)	37.11	41.24	42.50
55	95	55.79	1,174.25	12.36	0.23	48.15	41.98	61.76
44	3	66.67	11.75	3.92	1.11	66.67	33.33	100.00
Total	3,681	57.92	44,465.43	12.08	0.46	50.89	46.11	54.55

Mid: 2 Off								
Hand	Trials	Win %	Amount ($)	Avg $/Hand	BB/ Hand	Win % WSF	Went to SD (%)	Won $ at SD (%)
AA	205	87.80	13,357.75	65.16	2.79	84.85	65.45	79.63
AKs	114	79.82	2,813.26	24.68	1.08	73.56	47.13	73.17
AKo	369	68.02	5,255.50	14.24	0.52	58.45	51.41	56.85
AQs	119	66.39	840.50	7.06	0.44	58.33	51.04	63.27
AQo	391	63.43	5,770.72	14.76	0.48	54.22	53.90	54.82
AJs	119	69.75	3,109.00	26.13	0.86	62.89	48.45	57.45
AJo	371	60.92	3,955.99	10.66	0.32	52.19	44.78	51.13
ATs	112	58.04	1,263.70	11.28	0.42	50.53	43.16	51.22
ATo	393	59.54	1,623.00	4.13	0.30	49.67	48.04	52.38
A9s	137	59.85	1,364.00	9.96	0.31	47.57	39.81	60.98
A9o	350	57.14	2,268.61	6.48	0.20	48.01	41.52	50.43
A8s	134	55.97	401.37	3.00	0.08	45.28	45.28	41.67
A8o	5	60.00	88.50	17.70	0.49	66.67	66.67	100.00
A7s	118	50.85	(58.50)	(0.50)	(0.02)	40.63	40.63	41.03
A6s	106	43.40	53.25	0.50	(0.15)	35.29	36.47	45.16
A5s	105	45.71	(624.37)	(5.95)	(0.13)	32.94	35.29	50.00
A4s	108	54.63	681.25	6.31	0.13	45.35	44.19	42.11
A3s	104	53.85	166.50	1.60	0.00	41.25	38.75	45.16
KK	182	76.92	10,301.80	56.60	1.64	72.00	68.67	63.11
KQs	130	52.31	278.50	2.14	0.11	42.59	39.81	44.19
KQo	353	60.62	2,426.50	6.87	0.39	51.44	37.77	55.24
KJs	119	58.82	2,426.63	20.39	0.48	51.00	43.00	51.16
KJo	352	57.39	1,563.75	4.44	0.20	47.19	36.70	54.08
KTs	102	60.78	1,231.50	12.07	0.32	53.75	35.00	42.86
KTo	9	55.56	44.75	4.97	0.84	50.00	37.50	66.67
K9s	117	50.43	456.55	3.90	0.13	41.24	32.99	53.13
K8s	96	52.08	(467.75)	(4.87)	(0.16)	40.00	30.67	39.13
K7s	128	63.28	2,750.75	21.49	0.75	55.10	39.80	71.79
QQ	191	73.82	6,244.63	32.69	1.44	70.06	64.67	59.26
QJs	117	60.68	519.23	4.44	0.29	50.54	35.48	36.36
QJo	363	53.44	(460.36)	(1.27)	0.08	42.96	37.32	46.23
QTs	119	65.55	696.79	5.86	0.29	56.52	36.96	47.06
QTo	2	50.00	(7.50)	(3.75)	(0.63)	-	-	-
Q9s	118	50.00	210.30	1.78	(0.22)	35.56	34.44	45.16
JJ	171	70.18	3,688.25	21.57	0.96	64.08	57.04	56.79
JTs	116	58.62	644.36	5.55	0.14	48.91	34.78	53.13
JTo	3	66.67	144.75	48.25	0.77	66.67	-	-
J9s	120	62.50	826.51	6.89	0.37	52.22	37.78	52.94
TT	183	72.13	4,995.00	27.30	1.19	63.31	53.96	62.67
T9s	128	54.69	681.74	5.33	0.37	46.23	32.08	64.71
T8s	102	50.00	(756.53)	(7.42)	0.02	40.00	32.94	42.86
99	177	55.37	713.25	4.03	0.15	46.62	49.32	54.79
98s	127	53.54	829.00	6.53	0.25	44.66	47.57	46.94

88	197	55.84	1,039.25	5.28	0.36	46.95	44.51	50.68
87s	4	50.00	(21.00)	(5.25)	0.22	50.00	50.00	50.00
77	170	54.71	(942.75)	(5.55)	(0.04)	44.20	42.03	55.17
66	165	51.52	448.04	2.72	0.10	43.26	31.21	54.55
55	159	57.23	785.50	4.94	0.26	45.60	35.20	56.82
44	173	45.09	(2,417.68)	(13.98)	(0.34)	30.66	35.04	37.50
33	1	-	(4.00)	(4.00)	(4.00)	-	100.00	-
Total	7,854	60.15	81,199.79	10.34	0.42	51.04	44.04	54.24

Mid: 1 Off								
Hand	Trials	Win %	Amount ($)	Avg $/Hand	BB/ Hand	Win % WSF	Went to SD (%)	Won $ at SD (%)
AA	212	86.32	10,540.96	49.72	1.95	82.53	52.41	66.67
AKs	122	72.13	2,939.77	24.10	0.93	64.21	53.68	66.67
AKo	415	70.12	6,981.57	16.82	0.68	62.04	52.16	60.95
AQs	130	68.46	1,484.00	11.42	0.75	60.95	51.43	57.41
AQo	415	61.69	2,194.54	5.29	0.26	52.11	44.88	50.34
AJs	134	67.91	1,309.19	9.77	0.31	54.74	41.05	41.03
AJo	399	61.65	1,803.63	4.52	0.21	52.26	47.74	52.03
ATs	130	70.00	2,783.50	21.41	0.80	63.55	40.19	67.44
ATo	362	64.36	3,946.96	10.90	0.39	57.14	44.60	57.03
A9s	150	54.67	(779.50)	(5.20)	(0.20)	44.26	39.34	45.83
A9o	451	61.42	2,591.46	5.75	0.25	50.74	37.17	51.59
A8s	132	58.33	933.00	7.07	0.22	45.54	40.59	48.78
A8o	401	57.36	(45.74)	(0.11)	0.07	48.43	40.57	46.51
A7s	141	66.67	1,370.75	9.72	0.48	56.60	39.62	57.14
A7o	398	57.04	530.13	1.33	0.10	45.71	34.60	50.46
A6s	140	50.71	(422.25)	(3.02)	(0.23)	41.03	38.46	40.00
A6o	6	83.33	360.75	60.13	1.99	80.00	60.00	100.00
A5s	141	65.25	3,503.25	24.85	0.81	57.66	36.94	65.85
A4s	143	55.24	893.75	6.25	0.20	44.14	45.05	48.00
A3s	157	54.78	980.50	6.25	0.25	43.90	34.15	54.76
A2s	114	54.39	(39.71)	(0.35)	(0.26)	40.48	39.29	42.42
KK	201	85.57	7,752.13	38.57	1.72	81.29	62.58	71.13
KQs	129	63.57	1,220.00	9.46	0.56	56.07	39.25	52.38
KQo	410	64.63	6,031.00	14.71	0.50	54.11	38.92	56.91
KJs	125	64.00	629.07	5.03	0.42	57.69	31.73	60.61
KJo	400	61.25	3,459.25	8.65	0.35	51.32	34.21	52.88
KTs	137	59.85	960.00	7.01	0.11	47.52	36.63	45.95
KTo	397	59.70	1,753.87	4.42	0.33	49.84	36.74	60.00
K9s	138	57.25	479.62	3.48	0.24	46.23	43.40	52.17
K9o	3	100.00	64.00	21.33	0.72	-	-	-
K8s	122	58.20	2,170.75	17.79	0.31	48.98	22.45	63.64
K7s	121	61.16	1,215.25	10.04	0.28	49.44	20.22	55.56
K6s	132	63.64	1,922.50	14.56	0.50	53.06	33.67	54.55

Hand	Trials	Win %	Amount ($)	Avg $/Hand	BB/Hand	Win % WSF	Went to SD (%)	Won $ at SD (%)
K5s	8	75.00	47.50	5.94	0.35	60.00	-	-
QQ	181	78.45	6,773.65	37.42	1.39	71.74	57.25	63.29
QJs	110	57.27	442.47	4.02	0.21	48.31	42.70	42.11
QJo	382	57.33	(1,399.25)	(3.66)	(0.06)	46.62	33.78	39.00
QTs	134	65.67	1,335.90	9.97	0.36	56.19	41.90	50.00
QTo	437	58.35	1,472.62	3.37	0.20	48.84	36.71	58.27
Q9s	129	55.81	672.50	5.21	0.00	44.12	40.20	41.46
Q8s	148	60.81	1,801.37	12.17	0.42	52.50	35.83	65.12
JJ	207	73.43	3,842.95	18.57	0.78	65.63	58.75	53.19
JTs	143	64.34	901.50	6.30	0.41	54.87	37.17	52.38
JTo	429	60.84	2,295.35	5.35	0.23	49.69	37.81	48.76
J9s	144	64.58	2,037.25	14.15	0.64	54.13	32.11	68.57
J9o	3	33.33	(38.00)	(12.67)	0.41	33.33	33.33	100.00
J8s	129	58.91	80.77	0.63	0.23	50.49	40.78	57.14
TT	194	72.68	2,519.77	12.99	0.95	63.95	57.82	58.82
T9s	136	58.09	1,334.53	9.81	0.15	46.60	43.69	46.67
T8s	145	63.45	245.25	1.69	0.39	55.86	31.53	51.43
99	194	64.43	2,843.50	14.66	0.42	57.41	51.85	48.81
98s	143	54.55	(96.25)	(0.67)	(0.02)	40.19	39.25	50.00
97s	121	53.72	(742.00)	(6.13)	(0.09)	43.88	41.84	41.46
88	211	55.45	(1,167.25)	(5.53)	(0.06)	45.03	47.95	40.24
87s	110	50.91	(500.08)	(4.55)	(0.21)	40.91	31.82	39.29
77	204	66.67	3,089.02	15.14	0.62	55.26	48.68	58.11
76s	39	56.41	192.00	4.92	0.33	46.88	31.25	50.00
66	218	55.05	1,479.88	6.79	0.09	44.32	48.30	47.06
55	188	53.72	(578.06)	(3.07)	0.22	44.59	40.76	56.25
44	199	55.28	1,446.36	7.27	0.11	47.02	41.67	54.29
33	173	59.54	645.75	3.73	0.37	48.91	31.39	62.79
22	3	66.67	64.75	21.58	0.45	66.67	-	-
Total	11,872	62.18	102,561.70	8.64	0.37	52.59	41.38	53.77

Mid: Button								
Hand	Trials	Win %	Amount ($)	Avg $/Hand	BB/Hand	Win % WSF	Went to SD (%)	Won $ at SD (%)
AA	219	89.50	12,853.19	58.69	2.21	85.53	59.12	75.53
AKs	143	74.13	3,265.00	22.83	0.86	65.42	49.53	58.49
AKo	398	71.36	5,493.46	13.80	0.52	61.22	46.26	55.15
AQs	147	69.39	4,170.75	28.37	0.71	60.18	46.02	55.77
AQo	397	70.28	5,736.12	14.45	0.56	60.40	50.67	54.97
AJs	124	70.16	1,450.75	11.70	0.57	62.24	43.88	58.14
AJo	448	71.88	5,258.43	11.74	0.66	62.61	54.30	59.02
ATs	131	74.81	2,937.00	22.42	0.88	65.63	57.29	63.64
ATo	402	67.91	5,076.40	12.63	0.34	56.71	46.98	49.29
A9s	126	66.67	2,124.01	16.86	0.38	55.79	47.37	44.44
A9o	387	65.63	1,668.72	4.31	0.32	54.14	43.45	51.59

A8s	114	70.18	1,495.19	13.12	0.65	57.33	49.33	64.86
A8o	410	63.66	1,789.75	4.37	0.29	52.73	47.59	50.68
A7s	110	65.45	(159.75)	(1.45)	0.22	53.09	37.04	46.67
A7o	385	59.22	1,004.25	2.61	0.09	50.00	41.29	43.75
A6s	140	65.71	(601.63)	(4.30)	0.06	47.83	30.43	42.86
A6o	375	54.13	(379.63)	(1.01)	(0.09)	44.11	36.36	47.22
A5s	123	59.35	850.86	6.92	0.23	49.49	36.36	61.11
A5o	368	61.14	1,782.62	4.84	0.23	46.99	36.47	57.73
A4s	127	61.42	(193.03)	(1.52)	0.16	47.83	35.87	45.45
A4o	371	59.57	(553.06)	(1.49)	0.09	48.23	42.55	50.83
A3s	125	62.40	1,012.50	8.10	0.19	52.58	35.05	52.94
A3o	360	58.33	(373.08)	(1.04)	0.11	44.98	41.26	45.05
A2s	115	56.52	534.75	4.65	0.04	41.67	33.33	46.43
A2o	23	52.17	118.00	5.13	(0.17)	38.89	27.78	60.00
KK	172	81.40	6,673.57	38.80	1.65	75.94	63.16	63.10
KQs	112	60.71	755.37	6.74	0.19	47.62	35.71	43.33
KQo	373	65.15	2,175.63	5.83	0.38	54.23	40.49	53.91
KJs	122	63.11	1,486.94	12.19	0.53	53.19	42.55	57.50
KJo	406	63.30	(442.00)	(1.09)	0.08	50.00	32.55	44.33
KTs	101	67.33	1,148.25	11.37	0.44	57.89	36.84	60.71
KTo	397	66.25	5,270.04	13.27	0.43	56.62	34.77	56.19
K9s	140	61.43	117.47	0.84	0.13	52.21	38.94	47.73
K9o	340	62.65	2,365.74	6.96	0.26	52.29	35.11	52.17
K8s	125	59.20	(571.25)	(4.57)	0.04	43.96	25.27	43.48
K8o	364	62.36	2,199.50	6.04	0.20	48.06	29.85	57.14
K7s	120	58.33	(721.98)	(6.02)	0.11	44.94	39.33	57.14
K7o	328	58.54	2,095.29	6.39	0.14	45.08	27.87	54.41
K6s	140	67.86	1,946.00	13.90	0.51	54.64	31.96	58.06
K6o	9	66.67	148.50	16.50	0.51	50.00	16.67	100.00
K5s	114	53.51	55.25	0.48	(0.10)	44.21	28.42	51.85
K4s	116	68.10	1,963.62	16.93	0.55	58.89	27.78	56.00
K3s	118	56.78	256.09	2.17	(0.05)	40.48	41.67	40.00
K2s	112	59.82	(25.50)	(0.23)	0.07	41.56	23.38	61.11
QQ	175	80.57	5,269.50	30.11	1.40	75.56	62.22	66.67
QJs	143	67.13	1,377.25	9.63	0.45	56.88	33.95	54.05
QJo	372	64.25	1,364.07	3.67	0.30	55.24	29.02	50.60
QTs	109	67.89	2,704.50	24.81	0.86	58.33	39.29	78.79
QTo	370	62.97	1,550.55	4.19	0.16	51.99	36.46	51.49
Q9s	106	62.26	573.00	5.41	0.20	53.01	34.94	48.28
Q9o	336	60.71	659.25	1.96	0.27	49.22	28.52	49.32
Q8s	117	66.67	1,560.87	13.34	0.43	56.18	34.83	48.39
Q8o	2	100.00	30.00	15.00	0.67	-	-	-
Q7s	121	64.46	938.00	7.75	0.35	50.00	33.33	50.00
Q6s	106	55.66	234.75	2.21	0.13	41.25	32.50	46.15
Q5s	100	64.00	671.50	6.72	0.29	51.35	35.14	50.00
Q4s	115	50.43	(502.75)	(4.37)	(0.42)	40.22	30.43	21.43

Hand	Trials	Win %	Amount ($)	Avg $/Hand	BB/Hand	Win % WSF	Went to SD (%)	Won $ at SD (%)
JJ	184	81.52	4,375.00	23.78	0.98	73.85	48.46	60.32
JTs	113	61.95	(105.00)	(0.93)	0.13	52.22	37.78	41.18
JTo	346	61.85	948.65	2.74	0.20	50.38	36.84	51.02
J9s	120	61.67	1,799.25	14.99	0.58	53.19	36.17	70.59
J9o	346	60.12	1,668.03	4.82	0.09	47.66	37.50	44.79
J8s	112	61.61	(355.50)	(3.17)	0.13	46.91	38.27	51.61
J8o	2	100.00	9.00	4.50	0.75	-	-	-
J7s	95	57.89	9.50	0.10	0.04	43.48	28.99	45.00
TT	186	72.04	1,668.00	8.97	0.58	60.61	56.82	46.67
T9s	110	52.73	(698.50)	(6.35)	0.01	44.44	33.33	43.33
T9o	336	59.82	1,905.00	5.67	0.20	49.44	32.21	52.33
T8s	131	64.12	238.20	1.82	0.47	54.90	41.18	57.14
T8o	5	20.00	(94.00)	(18.80)	(1.07)	20.00	20.00	100.00
T7s	122	57.38	1,072.00	8.79	0.43	46.88	32.29	61.29
99	170	66.47	3,537.00	20.81	0.71	59.86	47.89	60.29
98s	99	67.68	668.75	6.76	0.57	58.90	35.62	65.38
98o	379	59.89	2,862.86	7.55	0.26	50.67	36.67	47.27
97s	129	51.94	(901.00)	(6.98)	(0.49)	41.51	32.08	32.35
88	188	65.43	2,298.00	12.22	0.48	56.67	52.00	50.00
87s	126	58.73	886.00	7.03	0.02	45.74	34.04	40.63
86s	127	59.06	8.50	0.07	0.11	47.92	31.25	56.67
77	172	62.79	908.81	5.28	0.19	52.24	47.01	46.03
76s	124	54.03	(941.34)	(7.59)	(0.07)	42.27	21.65	47.62
75s	118	55.08	(289.75)	(2.46)	(0.08)	39.53	31.40	37.04
66	198	60.61	(174.00)	(0.88)	(0.00)	46.58	43.15	42.86
65s	124	62.90	1,274.25	10.28	0.48	55.56	32.32	46.88
55	166	59.64	1,069.00	6.44	0.25	48.86	48.09	50.79
44	180	49.44	(1,356.50)	(7.54)	(0.29)	38.10	38.78	40.35
33	200	58.00	167.75	0.84	0.15	45.45	38.31	54.24
22	197	57.87	500.50	2.54	0.11	47.44	33.33	53.85
Total	16,854	63.61	122,647.05	7.28	0.32	52.60	39.39	52.40

Grinder: 3Off

Hand	Trials	Win %	Amount ($)	Avg $/Hand	BB/Hand	Win % WSF	Went to SD (%)	Won $ at SD (%)
AA	162	88.89	37,596.69	232.08	2.57	84.75	63.56	77.33
AKs	102	62.75	4,864.25	47.69	0.39	53.66	48.78	52.50
AKo	394	67.01	20,631.00	52.36	0.63	57.79	44.16	61.76
AQs	150	64.67	7,910.00	52.73	0.55	52.68	36.61	65.85
AQo	397	60.45	11,390.75	28.69	0.38	48.83	37.79	60.18
AJs	128	64.06	7,592.00	59.31	0.76	54.00	39.00	53.85
AJo	381	55.64	2,308.00	6.06	0.08	42.16	32.40	55.91
ATs	133	51.88	516.05	3.88	0.08	41.67	34.26	56.76
ATo	355	56.62	6,640.50	18.71	0.18	42.35	37.65	60.42
A9s	149	59.06	5,056.00	33.93	0.47	46.90	27.43	67.74

Hand	Trials	Win %	Amount ($)	Avg $/Hand	BB/Hand	Win % WSF	Went to SD (%)	Won $ at SD (%)
A9o	47	51.06	(1,324.02)	(28.17)	(0.04)	36.36	24.24	62.50
A8s	128	51.56	(2,021.00)	(15.79)	(0.29)	35.42	30.21	37.93
A8o	5	20.00	(1,000.00)	(200.00)	(1.65)	-	50.00	-
A7s	91	57.14	2,364.00	25.98	0.11	42.86	30.16	42.11
A6s	58	56.90	1,758.50	30.32	0.27	42.86	35.71	53.33
A5s	47	61.70	4,871.00	103.64	0.95	52.94	38.24	76.92
A4s	35	62.86	2,313.00	66.09	0.58	54.17	29.17	85.71
A3s	26	61.54	1,642.50	63.17	0.36	47.37	36.84	42.86
KK	202	75.25	20,469.50	101.33	1.32	68.15	56.05	61.36
KQs	115	49.57	413.50	3.60	(0.16)	36.96	27.17	40.00
KQo	401	58.35	15,367.25	38.32	0.42	43.99	32.30	61.70
KJs	131	58.02	6,475.00	49.43	0.48	44.44	48.48	58.33
KJo	245	47.76	(849.50)	(3.47)	0.00	38.54	30.73	57.14
KTs	121	40.50	(4,316.50)	(35.67)	(0.28)	30.00	31.00	38.71
KTo	9	55.56	(15.00)	(1.67)	(0.21)	50.00	50.00	66.67
QQ	159	76.73	21,080.50	132.58	1.49	70.87	52.76	62.69
QJs	126	61.90	1,949.00	15.47	0.40	50.53	34.74	51.52
QJo	12	50.00	74.00	6.17	0.11	37.50	25.00	50.00
QTs	120	53.33	(1,932.41)	(16.10)	0.17	37.78	31.11	53.57
JJ	201	73.63	19,512.67	97.08	1.19	64.90	52.98	62.50
JTs	123	60.16	5,776.50	46.96	0.88	51.49	38.61	66.67
J9s	20	50.00	231.50	11.58	(0.13)	47.37	26.32	40.00
TT	179	64.25	8,672.50	48.45	0.54	52.27	45.45	60.00
T9s	55	58.18	(149.00)	(2.71)	0.09	42.50	17.50	42.86
99	197	62.94	8,616.25	43.74	0.58	52.29	44.44	63.24
98s	38	36.84	(4,554.00)	(119.84)	(1.08)	20.00	40.00	25.00
88	166	55.42	1,556.50	9.38	0.14	40.32	39.52	46.94
87s	20	50.00	(1,538.00)	(76.90)	(0.66)	9.09	9.09	-
77	168	57.74	2,985.00	17.77	0.44	43.65	38.89	55.10
66	163	61.96	10,880.75	66.75	0.73	49.17	35.83	62.79
55	99	53.54	1,843.50	18.62	0.23	40.26	25.97	55.00
44	39	53.85	1,736.00	44.51	0.41	35.71	28.57	62.50
33	17	41.18	(1,389.00)	(81.71)	(0.42)	28.57	-	-
Total	5,914	60.23	226,005.73	38.22	0.47	48.52	38.37	58.76

Grinder: 2 Off								
Hand	Trials	Win %	Amount ($)	Avg $/Hand	BB/ Hand	Win % WSF	Went to SD (%)	Won $ at SD (%)
AA	176	88.07	32,637.50	185.44	2.27	84.89	54.68	76.32
AKs	115	73.04	7,898.00	68.68	0.83	63.53	45.88	61.54
AKo	383	72.06	25,766.98	67.28	0.73	62.32	48.94	61.15
AQs	124	62.90	5,467.97	44.10	0.72	56.19	40.00	61.90
AQo	326	60.12	10,369.84	31.81	0.42	50.00	35.77	61.29
AJs	116	68.97	1,835.50	15.82	0.49	53.85	35.90	53.57
AJo	318	64.15	15,117.50	47.54	0.68	55.23	33.05	60.76

ATs	122	63.11	6,099.50	50.00	0.61	55.00	38.00	60.53
ATo	334	55.69	(3,927.00)	(11.76)	0.04	43.53	33.73	52.33
A9s	106	65.09	2,960.00	27.92	0.37	51.35	36.49	59.26
A9o	231	57.14	(1,101.00)	(4.77)	(0.04)	37.84	31.76	44.68
A8s	91	62.64	1,425.25	15.66	0.36	52.86	32.86	43.48
A8o	102	54.90	1,485.00	14.56	0.06	39.47	31.58	50.00
A7s	107	54.21	906.50	8.47	0.02	38.75	28.75	52.17
A7o	32	65.63	28.50	0.89	0.32	54.17	29.17	42.86
A6s	111	54.96	1,435.00	12.93	0.24	39.24	26.58	61.90
A6o	9	66.67	(52.00)	(5.78)	0.02	50.00	16.67	-
A5s	82	56.10	(2,478.50)	(30.23)	(0.05)	43.55	20.97	23.08
A4s	94	56.38	2,749.00	29.24	0.24	49.37	31.65	64.00
A3s	71	57.75	139.00	1.96	0.15	46.30	25.93	57.14
A2s	59	52.54	1,492.75	25.30	0.22	44.00	26.00	46.15
KK	157	76.43	16,456.50	104.82	1.57	70.40	57.60	63.89
KQs	109	71.56	8,422.50	77.27	1.08	61.25	46.25	75.68
KQo	297	55.22	10,405.25	35.03	0.44	45.65	33.04	64.47
KJs	101	59.41	3,241.50	32.09	0.51	48.05	33.77	65.38
KJo	297	49.49	(5,948.00)	(20.03)	(0.10)	35.96	28.95	46.97
KTs	99	51.52	(2,737.00)	(27.65)	(0.03)	41.46	35.37	51.72
KTo	132	55.30	1,622.50	12.29	0.17	41.24	23.71	47.83
K9s	53	49.06	3,906.00	73.70	0.15	35.71	23.81	50.00
QQ	165	70.91	15,159.25	91.87	0.96	63.36	59.54	60.26
QJs	106	64.15	4,143.00	39.08	0.52	51.90	30.38	70.83
QJo	213	53.52	4,125.50	19.37	0.37	43.53	27.65	65.96
QTs	91	53.85	446.50	4.91	0.14	42.47	35.62	46.15
QTo	17	58.82	24.00	1.41	(0.09)	36.36	18.18	-
Q9s	40	80.00	6,269.00	156.73	1.44	70.37	40.74	72.73
JJ	170	74.71	16,236.48	95.51	1.21	65.87	55.56	61.43
JTs	102	51.96	1,212.00	11.88	(0.01)	40.96	31.33	53.85
JTo	7	42.86	(332.50)	(47.50)	(0.76)	33.33	16.67	-
J9s	61	59.02	5,141.50	84.29	0.87	51.92	34.62	66.67
TT	158	67.09	4,457.25	28.21	0.64	57.02	46.28	57.14
T9s	75	56.00	2,471.80	32.96	0.40	44.07	22.03	69.23
T8s	50	66.00	5,203.50	104.07	0.59	52.78	27.78	60.00
99	151	68.21	14,495.00	95.99	1.13	57.52	44.25	70.00
98s	62	45.16	2,698.00	43.52	(0.12)	35.85	35.85	47.37
97s	17	70.59	934.00	54.94	0.82	58.33	33.33	75.00
88	165	57.58	6,159.00	37.33	0.39	46.56	41.22	53.70
87s	75	49.33	2,195.50	29.27	0.08	35.59	28.81	52.94
86s	12	75.00	1,480.50	123.38	1.16	72.73	45.45	60.00
77	178	61.80	10,262.50	57.65	0.54	53.42	34.25	62.00
76s	36	55.56	853.00	23.69	0.10	44.83	37.93	63.64
66	148	56.08	5,313.02	35.90	0.36	44.92	31.36	54.05
65s	11	45.45	1,292.00	117.45	1.03	33.33	33.33	66.67
55	104	55.77	3,327.00	31.99	0.25	43.90	34.15	53.57

Hand	Trials	Win %	Amount ($)	Avg $/Hand	BB/ Hand	Win % WSF	Went to SD (%)	Won $ at SD (%)
44	78	62.82	5,856.88	75.09	0.75	51.67	18.33	81.82
33	45	48.89	366.75	8.15	0.04	37.84	29.73	36.36
22	17	47.06	(1,511.00)	(88.88)	(0.34)	25.00	25.00	-
Total	6,708	61.34	263,903.97	39.34	0.50	50.52	36.52	58.98
Grinder: 1 Off								
AA	140	95.00	26,487.00	189.19	2.35	92.47	47.31	86.36
AKs	84	70.24	2,113.50	25.16	0.52	62.12	39.39	50.00
AKo	282	74.47	20,945.50	74.27	0.81	64.53	34.98	59.15
AQs	97	81.44	9,152.00	94.35	1.14	72.73	45.45	66.67
AQo	268	62.31	(1,765.50)	(6.59)	0.07	47.62	45.50	48.84
AJs	90	75.56	5,681.75	63.13	0.90	64.52	48.39	70.00
AJo	281	70.82	18,224.90	64.86	0.91	60.78	42.65	73.56
ATs	89	65.17	2,485.00	27.92	0.37	53.73	47.76	53.13
ATo	270	63.70	3,136.25	11.62	0.17	50.26	33.85	48.48
A9s	80	66.25	2,173.50	27.17	0.30	51.79	30.36	64.71
A9o	270	58.89	9,548.00	35.36	0.25	48.08	33.17	55.07
A8s	98	57.14	551.50	5.63	0.05	44.00	33.33	44.00
A8o	222	60.36	6,595.50	29.71	0.40	48.47	33.74	60.00
A7s	73	52.05	(885.50)	(12.13)	(0.18)	37.04	31.48	29.41
A7o	141	60.28	6,067.00	43.03	0.25	46.08	33.33	52.94
A6s	94	60.64	1,388.00	14.77	0.05	46.38	31.88	40.91
A6o	97	58.76	(563.00)	(5.80)	0.01	42.65	20.59	57.14
A5s	85	50.59	147.00	1.73	(0.16)	39.71	33.82	56.52
A5o	56	62.50	(1,263.00)	(22.55)	(0.10)	44.44	16.67	50.00
A4s	78	56.41	(1,810.00)	(23.21)	(0.10)	44.26	36.07	45.45
A4o	52	65.38	1,266.50	24.36	0.19	51.35	37.84	78.57
A3s	84	58.33	1,911.50	22.76	0.05	42.37	28.81	47.06
A3o	31	51.61	(1,088.00)	(35.10)	(0.21)	28.57	33.33	57.14
A2s	88	54.55	(117.50)	(1.34)	0.26	42.65	25.00	52.94
A2o	14	71.43	701.50	50.11	0.38	60.00	20.00	50.00
KK	134	73.13	14,838.00	110.73	1.18	68.42	60.53	57.97
KQs	88	63.64	3,685.25	41.88	0.62	50.77	23.08	73.33
KQo	259	59.07	6,060.25	23.40	0.28	45.79	31.05	61.02
KJs	100	67.00	6,537.50	65.38	0.73	54.17	27.78	70.00
KJo	269	58.74	8,388.57	31.18	0.33	46.27	28.86	58.62
KTs	82	62.20	430.00	5.24	0.08	44.64	30.36	47.06
KTo	270	58.52	4,859.50	18.00	0.22	46.00	33.00	62.12
K9s	80	58.75	2,909.00	36.36	0.24	40.00	29.09	50.00
K9o	31	67.74	1,264.50	40.79	0.46	47.37	21.05	75.00
K8s	46	58.70	(939.00)	(20.41)	(0.11)	39.29	35.71	20.00
K7s	32	62.50	1,541.00	48.16	0.35	45.45	22.73	40.00
K6s	39	71.79	2,985.50	76.55	0.45	61.54	26.92	42.86

K5s	19	52.63	870.00	45.79	(0.08)	42.86	21.43	33.33
QQ	128	80.47	12,106.50	94.58	1.25	72.53	56.04	68.63
QJs	98	54.08	1,045.49	10.67	0.02	41.33	41.33	45.16
QJo	254	59.84	4,993.50	19.66	0.24	48.19	32.12	50.00
QTs	79	64.56	6,715.00	85.00	0.76	52.54	40.68	58.33
QTo	173	55.49	2,241.95	12.96	0.25	45.45	32.58	51.16
Q9s	74	55.41	333.00	4.50	(0.01)	43.10	24.14	42.86
Q9o	16	62.50	658.00	41.13	0.45	50.00	8.33	100.00
Q8s	50	56.00	180.50	3.61	(0.21)	39.39	36.36	33.33
JJ	130	76.92	9,836.00	75.66	0.98	68.42	48.42	60.87
JTs	100	59.00	4,210.50	42.11	0.21	48.10	29.11	65.22
JTo	137	51.09	(1,670.50)	(12.19)	(0.02)	38.89	36.11	58.97
J9s	84	55.95	3,026.23	36.03	0.12	42.19	37.50	54.17
J9o	19	21.05	(996.50)	(52.45)	(0.77)	16.67	22.22	25.00
J8s	26	50.00	(1,596.00)	(61.38)	(0.36)	31.58	31.58	33.33
J8o	8	50.00	374.50	46.81	0.60	40.00	20.00	100.00
TT	122	66.39	4,842.50	39.69	0.67	57.73	52.58	56.86
T9s	71	56.34	(360.00)	(5.07)	0.09	41.51	24.53	53.85
T9o	8	62.50	201.00	25.13	0.92	50.00	33.33	100.00
T8s	67	59.70	3,896.50	58.16	0.77	50.91	36.36	65.00
T7s	20	70.00	1,335.00	66.75	0.83	57.14	14.29	100.00
99	120	65.00	7,922.50	66.02	0.61	52.81	33.71	56.67
98s	65	47.69	(418.50)	(6.44)	(0.22)	32.00	40.00	45.00
98o	7	28.57	(1,632.00)	(233.14)	(1.85)	16.67	16.67	-
97s	50	62.00	672.50	13.45	0.37	51.28	41.03	50.00
96s	11	54.55	263.00	23.91	0.08	44.44	22.22	-
88	132	60.61	4,441.34	33.65	0.38	49.02	30.39	54.84
87s	72	58.33	1,304.50	18.12	0.26	43.14	37.25	52.63
87o	4	25.00	(165.00)	(41.25)	(1.44)	-	33.33	-
86s	39	53.85	652.00	16.72	0.45	43.33	20.00	66.67
77	130	62.31	7,522.00	57.86	0.47	47.31	36.56	55.88
76s	50	60.00	3,408.75	68.18	0.67	54.55	22.73	80.00
76o	5	80.00	520.00	104.00	1.86	75.00	50.00	100.00
75s	17	58.82	938.50	55.21	0.53	41.67	16.67	50.00
66	122	56.56	824.50	6.76	0.01	39.77	35.23	54.84
65s	38	47.37	(845.00)	(22.24)	(0.23)	33.33	33.33	30.00
64s	9	77.78	2,285.50	253.94	1.51	66.67	16.67	100.00
55	140	46.43	(951.12)	(6.79)	(0.21)	34.51	34.51	43.59
54s	23	73.91	2,090.50	90.89	0.88	57.14	14.29	50.00
44	103	60.19	3,776.75	36.67	0.46	48.75	40.00	56.25
43s	3	33.33	(1,115.00)	(371.67)	(3.08)	-	100.00	-
33	68	52.94	4,723.00	69.46	0.16	38.46	36.54	42.11
22	28	53.57	(137.50)	(4.91)	(0.13)	35.00	25.00	40.00
Total	7,513	62.23	251,967.86	33.54	0.38	49.87	35.33	56.41

Hand	Trials	Win %	Amount ($)	Avg $/Hand	BB/ Hand	Win % WSF	Went to SD (%)	Won $ at SD(%)
			Grinder: Button					
AA	101	91.09	15,065.50	149.16	1.85	87.32	47.89	76.47
AKs	69	78.26	7,055.50	102.25	1.13	65.91	50.00	54.55
AKo	173	73.99	7,071.00	40.87	0.71	62.81	51.24	59.68
AQs	61	81.97	7,745.50	126.98	1.75	77.08	52.08	80.00
AQo	188	69.15	7,841.00	41.71	0.54	58.27	51.08	66.20
AJs	84	80.95	5,817.00	69.25	0.80	67.35	51.02	64.00
AJo	207	67.63	4,428.00	21.39	0.35	56.49	37.01	49.12
ATs	71	71.83	2,433.50	34.27	0.10	58.33	50.00	41.67
ATo	237	64.56	6,003.00	25.33	0.24	52.54	50.85	45.56
A9s	71	70.42	4,742.00	66.79	0.83	62.50	44.64	76.00
A9o	217	69.12	10,390.00	47.88	0.49	57.42	39.35	59.02
A8s	68	60.29	(1,111.50)	(16.35)	(0.01)	46.00	28.00	50.00
A8o	210	63.81	5,293.50	25.21	0.29	50.00	36.18	56.36
A7s	77	68.83	1,704.50	22.14	0.49	53.85	38.46	50.00
A7o	162	64.20	6,922.00	42.73	0.31	54.10	36.07	59.09
A6s	72	55.56	(2,075.50)	(28.83)	(0.06)	44.83	37.93	31.82
A6o	138	55.80	(1,028.00)	(7.45)	(0.04)	39.39	42.42	45.24
A5s	54	64.81	1,797.00	33.28	0.40	55.81	39.53	47.06
A5o	122	59.02	775.00	6.35	0.08	42.86	35.71	43.33
A4s	63	68.25	3,095.33	49.13	0.38	59.18	34.69	58.82
A4o	127	55.12	(2,292.00)	(18.05)	(0.00)	41.05	30.53	44.83
A3s	66	66.67	1,771.00	26.83	0.23	54.17	25.00	41.67
A3o	94	67.02	7,706.00	81.98	0.73	55.88	35.29	79.17
A2s	63	69.84	1,494.50	23.72	0.60	56.82	31.82	85.71
A2o	54	59.26	464.50	8.60	0.14	38.24	41.18	50.00
KK	115	89.57	25,172.50	218.89	2.19	86.67	47.78	79.07
KQs	66	60.61	2,058.00	31.18	0.44	46.94	32.65	37.50
KQo	188	67.55	7,949.84	42.29	0.51	53.44	36.64	64.58
KJs	62	72.58	5,284.50	85.23	1.04	63.83	38.30	72.22
KJo	183	54.10	2,307.50	12.61	0.13	43.15	35.62	48.08
KTs	53	71.70	1,772.50	33.44	0.70	62.50	40.00	56.25
KTo	160	61.25	3,526.00	22.04	0.38	53.44	33.59	52.27
K9s	61	60.66	1,770.50	29.02	0.08	48.89	31.11	42.86
K9o	137	56.20	72.50	0.53	0.17	42.72	23.30	62.50
K8s	71	50.70	(1,610.00)	(22.68)	0.10	38.89	29.63	56.25
K8o	29	58.62	(109.00)	(3.76)	(0.17)	25.00	37.50	33.33
K7s	57	61.40	2,475.50	43.43	0.24	51.16	25.58	72.73
K7o	9	66.67	416.00	46.22	0.38	66.67	33.33	66.67
K6s	58	58.62	4,278.50	73.77	0.62	45.45	47.73	61.90
K5s	33	54.55	874.50	26.50	0.13	42.31	46.15	58.33
K4s	54	55.56	(385.50)	(7.14)	0.17	45.45	31.82	71.43
K3s	42	59.52	1,788.00	42.57	0.10	37.50	33.33	25.00
K2s	22	54.55	844.50	38.39	0.32	47.37	21.05	75.00

QQ	82	80.49	6,079.00	74.13	0.91	71.93	54.39	51.61
QJs	72	58.33	993.50	13.80	0.19	45.45	41.82	39.13
QJo	193	56.48	3,220.50	16.69	0.08	43.24	31.08	52.17
QTs	54	57.41	894.50	16.56	0.34	45.24	42.86	55.56
QTo	172	63.37	8,933.33	51.94	0.63	49.59	30.08	62.16
Q9s	52	55.77	(1,101.00)	(21.17)	0.29	43.90	34.15	64.29
Q9o	88	56.82	4,350.50	49.44	0.30	44.93	26.09	50.00
Q8s	46	60.87	2,424.50	52.71	0.41	43.75	18.75	100.00
Q8o	20	50.00	2,302.00	115.10	0.61	41.18	35.29	66.67
Q7s	32	31.25	(3,648.75)	(114.02)	(1.03)	12.00	16.00	-
Q6s	35	54.29	1,367.00	39.06	0.47	46.43	28.57	50.00
Q5s	22	40.91	(928.00)	(42.18)	(0.26)	33.33	33.33	50.00
Q4s	10	40.00	(552.00)	(55.20)	(1.00)	14.29	28.57	-
Q3s	7	57.14	26.00	3.71	0.17	50.00	50.00	33.33
JJ	98	70.41	5,681.00	57.97	0.47	58.57	51.43	44.44
JTs	60	68.33	2,840.00	47.33	0.54	52.50	40.00	56.25
JTo	166	56.63	(213.50)	(1.29)	0.16	40.98	38.52	51.06
J9s	72	66.67	3,935.50	54.66	0.42	50.00	33.33	68.75
J9o	90	56.67	1,253.50	13.93	0.15	46.38	28.99	55.00
J8s	51	56.86	1,643.00	32.22	0.18	45.00	27.50	63.64
J8o	1	100.00	25.00	25.00	0.83	-	-	-
J7s	21	52.38	(1,244.50)	(59.26)	(0.24)	37.50	43.75	42.86
TT	87	78.16	8,978.50	103.20	1.24	70.31	51.56	63.64
T9s	46	58.70	315.50	6.86	(0.07)	38.71	38.71	25.00
T9o	102	63.73	4,762.00	46.69	0.47	47.83	23.19	68.75
T8s	53	66.04	580.50	10.95	0.12	47.06	29.41	50.00
T8o	23	60.87	586.50	25.50	0.19	50.00	27.78	40.00
T7s	42	66.67	2,929.00	69.74	0.79	54.84	35.48	63.64
T6s	14	57.14	42.00	3.00	0.04	50.00	16.67	50.00
99	85	71.76	6,410.00	75.41	0.91	63.08	44.62	62.07
98s	51	50.98	782.00	15.33	(0.19)	41.86	48.84	47.62
98o	67	50.75	(2,163.00)	(32.28)	(0.12)	36.00	30.00	40.00
97s	47	57.45	892.00	18.98	0.29	51.22	19.51	37.50
97o	4	100.00	572.00	143.00	1.06	100.00	-	-
96s	24	58.33	792.00	33.00	0.18	41.18	17.65	33.33
95s	1	100.00	223.00	223.00	2.23	100.00	-	-
88	101	53.47	(2,880.50)	(28.52)	(0.07)	40.51	46.84	37.84
87s	60	75.00	5,730.50	95.51	0.86	60.53	34.21	69.23
87o	23	65.22	405.50	17.63	0.22	56.25	37.50	33.33
86s	39	64.10	419.50	10.76	0.25	51.72	24.14	42.86
85s	13	46.15	(836.00)	(64.31)	(1.05)	30.00	30.00	33.33
77	78	66.67	3,182.50	40.80	0.63	58.73	42.86	66.67
76s	53	67.92	1,691.50	31.92	0.41	51.43	37.14	61.54
76o	4	50.00	298.50	74.63	0.61	50.00	25.00	100.00
75s	32	59.38	(1,129.00)	(35.28)	0.14	43.48	39.13	66.67
66	70	61.43	3,320.45	47.44	0.68	50.91	36.36	55.00

65s	48	62.50	1,076.50	22.43	0.30	43.75	28.13	55.56
64s	12	50.00	(1,632.00)	(136.00)	(0.81)	33.33	44.44	25.00
55	77	62.34	3,571.50	46.38	0.87	52.46	34.43	61.90
54s	40	67.50	1,570.25	39.26	0.71	55.17	27.59	75.00
53s	4	-	(1,200.00)	(300.00)	(2.63)	-	50.00	-
44	90	57.78	(293.25)	(3.26)	(0.01)	47.22	26.39	36.84
43s	5	60.00	(177.50)	(35.50)	(0.21)	33.33	33.33	-
33	69	55.07	1,927.50	27.93	0.21	37.50	35.42	47.06
22	51	45.10	(3,204.50)	(62.83)	(0.43)	28.21	20.51	37.50
Total	7,208	63.75	237,419.20	32.94	0.40	51.39	37.31	55.42

Playing in a Steal Situation

A possible steal situation occurs when you are in the cutoff, on the button, or in the small blind and everyone has folded to you. The first decision you need to make is whether or not you are going to attempt to steal. This depends on how good your cards are and how your remaining opponents play. A good default steal percentage for higher limit games is just a bit under 30 percent in the cutoff and 40 percent on the button. This would break down approximately as follows:

From the cutoff: 22+, A2s+, A5o+, K7s+, K9o+, Q9s+, QTo+, J8s+, T8s+, 97s+, 87s, 76s
Total = 378 combinations out of 1,326, or 28.5 percent of hands.

From the button: 22+, A2s+, A3o+, K2s+, K9o+, Q5s+, Q9o+, J7s+, J9o+, T7s+, T8o+, 97s+, 98o, 86s+, 75s+, 65s.
This totals 40 percent of the hands.

These are good defaults for open-raising. They are based on millions of hands of actual play and tens of millions of hands of computer simulations. However, you certainly should not blindly adopt these standards and follow them roboticly. There are many instances where deviating from them will be more profitable. Specifically, if the blinds play very tight pre-flop, you can expand your stealing standards. This is because a large portion of the expected value you derive from opening with your weakest hands like

and

is from stealing the blinds outright. The number of hands you should add depends on the degree to which the blinds under defend. Conversely, if the blinds over defend (i.e. the big blind folds to a small blind steal less than 15 percent of the time), then you should tighten up your stealing requirements.

It should be noted that there is a counterbalancing force at work here. If you are expanding your stealing range because the blinds are tight, be very careful not to go too far. The reason for this is that tight blinds will have a stronger hand on average, and they have the option to three-bet. The fact that you may be three-bet more often when you do see flops (because a tight defender is more likely to play a hand he will three-bet) detracts from the extra value you get from stealing the blinds with a higher frequency. This is why you should often adjust your standards only slightly for tighter or looser blinds.

You should also consider how much of a post-flop edge you have versus your opponent. If they play poorly, you should play more hands. This is especially true when you are in the cutoff or on the button since you will be in position and be able to maximize the opportunities to exploit your post-flop edge.

Stealing from the Small Blind

Developing a set of guidelines for stealing from the small blind is far more difficult because it is much more dependent on how your opponent plays both pre-flop and post-flop. For example, if your opponent severely under defends his big blind, you should be willing to raise with any two cards. In the chapter, "Opening the Pot for a Raise," we examined empirical results for open-raising from the cutoff and button. Looking at similar empirical results for play from the small blind can provide a good starting point for developing a set of stealing guidelines. Below is a table showing the results for the high-limit and mid-limit players when they raised, called, or folded from the small blind.

			High-Limit Player Stats First in From the Small Blind					
Action	Trials	% of Trials	Amount	Avg/ Hand	BB/ Hand	Win % WSF	Went to SD	Win at SD
Raised	9,222	59	$233,771.28	$25.35	0.100	55.10	32.81%	55.70%
Called	707	5	$24,787.00	$35.06	0.110	54.65	32.62%	58.77%
Folded	5,620	36	$(323,888.00)	$(57.63)	(0.250)	-	-	-
Totals	15,549		$(65,329.72)	$(4.20)	(0.026)			

			Mid-Limit Player Stats First in From the Small Blind					
Raised	11,924	54	$43,400.50	$3.64	0.160	57.07	36.23%	49.57%
Called	1,120	5	$2,897.75	$2.59	0.090	52.87	30.43%	51.33%
Folded	8,908	41	$(50,608.25)	$(5.68)	(0.250)	-	-	-
Totals	21,952		$(4,310.00)	$(0.20)	(0.010)			

The mid-limit player performed better overall. Why is that? It could be party explained by sample size. After all, the databases used contain roughly 300,000 to 400,000 hands. Once we filter for the exact scenario (3 or more players at the table and folded to the small blind), we really reduce the number of trials. However, from the table above we can still make a few hypotheses. First, in a blind versus blind battle, going to showdown slightly more often seems better. Second, open-raising with 59 percent of your hands from the small blind is probably a bit too loose.

Another reason the mid-limit player performed better when open-raising might be that, on average, the players at those limits incorrectly under-defend their big blind. To test this hypothesis, we filtered out the number of times our candidate player won the pot without seeing a flop. As evidenced by the table below, there appears to be some truth to our hypothesis. In the mid-limit games, when our subjects open-raised from the small blind, there was no flop an astounding 30/31 percent of the time, compared to only 19 percent for our high-limit player.

No Flop when Raised	Trials	Amount	Avg/ Hand	BB/ Hand	% No Flop
High	1,708	$191,192.00	$111.94	0.50	19
Mid	3,572	$38,747.25	$10.99	0.50	30
Grd	1,670	$71,740.00	$42.96	0.50	31

It is also interesting to see how well each player fared when they went to showdown. The high-limit player won at showdowns much more often and did much better when there was a showdown. Generally, this will be a metric on the quality of a player's post-flop play, but overall, there are too many variables to isolate the explanation for this small number of cases.

Went to SD	Trials	Amount	Win at SD	Avg/ Hand	BB/ Hand
Mid	3,042	$2,891.00	49.57%	$0.95	(0.02)
High	2,465	$154,739.00	55.70%	$62.77	0.29
Grinder	1,332	$(134.93)	48.95%	$(0.10)	0.01

With the tables below, we are hoping to get a general idea of what may be good open-raising ranges from the small blind. This is difficult to do, however, because winning the blinds without a fight can comprise a huge portion of your expectation in this spot, and when this happens, your cards do not matter. However, if the big blind does not have the exploitable tendency to fold too much, the results from the tables are more useful.

High: Open-Raise From SB								
Hand	Trials	Win %	Amount ($)	Avg $/Hand	BB /Hand	Win % WSF	Went to SD (%)	Won $ at SD (%)
AA	30	96.67	12,892.00	429.73	1.73	95.45	40.91	88.89
AKs	52	82.69	7,967.00	153.21	0.72	76.32	63.16	66.67
AKo	185	74.59	14,874.00	80.40	0.40	66.43	47.14	57.58
AQs	38	76.32	1,214.00	31.95	0.26	66.67	29.63	50.00
AQo	146	74.66	16,359.00	112.05	0.52	68.64	34.75	53.66
AJs	47	74.47	9,237.50	196.54	0.66	67.57	35.14	69.23
AJo	159	72.96	13,051.74	82.09	0.51	69.06	44.60	62.90
ATs	56	60.71	(3,581.00)	(63.95)	(0.07)	55.10	46.94	43.48
ATo	159	67.30	11,056.50	69.54	0.23	60.90	33.83	53.33
A9s	45	64.44	3,007.50	66.83	0.20	52.94	35.29	66.67
A9o	156	63.46	(8,390.87)	(53.79)	(0.14)	53.66	43.09	45.28
A8s	40	72.50	8,265.00	206.63	0.87	69.44	52.78	73.68
A8o	170	67.65	8,157.00	47.98	0.26	61.27	33.80	50.00
A7s	50	72.00	3,935.00	78.70	0.57	61.11	52.78	57.89
A7o	165	69.70	8,606.00	52.16	0.22	60.63	33.86	60.47
A6s	47	65.96	5,225.50	111.18	0.19	57.89	21.05	75.00
A6o	134	67.16	10,578.00	78.94	0.38	61.40	32.46	72.97
A5s	47	63.83	3,225.13	68.62	0.47	59.52	38.10	75.00
A5o	150	58.00	(1,506.00)	(10.04)	(0.01)	51.16	29.46	55.26
A4s	35	48.57	(2,894.00)	(82.69)	(0.46)	40.00	16.67	40.00
A4o	136	61.76	(551.50)	(4.06)	(0.05)	53.15	35.14	56.41
A3s	47	65.96	(646.00)	(13.74)	0.18	57.89	28.95	63.64
A3o	129	53.49	(4,712.00)	(36.53)	(0.15)	45.45	28.18	54.84
A2s	51	56.86	(1,297.50)	(25.44)	(0.09)	51.11	42.22	52.63

A2o	149	63.09	(2,912.00)	(19.54)	(0.10)	54.17	42.50	54.90
KK	22	86.36	9,727.50	442.16	1.63	85.00	60.00	75.00
KQs	38	73.68	6,325.00	166.45	0.84	67.74	32.26	60.00
KQo	153	71.24	17,421.84	113.87	0.51	63.33	35.00	64.29
KJs	38	73.68	3,141.50	82.67	0.26	61.54	38.46	60.00
KJo	155	73.55	14,544.00	93.83	0.43	66.12	32.23	56.41
KTs	43	58.14	(1,398.00)	(32.51)	(0.06)	48.57	34.29	41.67
KTo	159	60.38	(2,752.50)	(17.31)	(0.13)	50.79	37.30	42.55
K9s	37	70.27	4,228.50	114.28	0.31	66.67	42.42	57.14
K9o	149	62.42	1,334.50	8.96	0.00	52.14	32.48	47.37
K8s	57	64.91	6,216.00	109.05	0.30	52.38	23.81	70.00
K8o	142	59.86	1,096.50	7.72	0.06	52.10	32.77	51.28
K7s	45	55.56	(2,045.26)	(45.45)	(0.15)	44.44	58.33	42.86
K7o	139	61.15	7,525.00	54.14	0.11	53.04	33.91	56.41
K6s	41	68.29	4,186.50	102.11	0.48	58.06	32.26	90.00
K6o	123	64.23	3,953.50	32.14	0.20	54.64	27.84	70.37
K5s	40	50.00	(2,729.50)	(68.24)	(0.18)	47.37	31.58	41.67
K5o	108	62.96	(1,561.00)	(14.45)	(0.07)	52.94	30.59	53.85
K4s	26	53.85	(4,105.00)	(157.88)	(0.58)	45.45	27.27	50.00
K4o	91	57.14	1,333.00	14.65	0.01	48.68	25.00	63.16
K3s	36	50.00	(2,717.00)	(75.47)	(0.42)	37.93	24.14	42.86
K3o	84	58.33	(2,987.00)	(35.56)	(0.13)	47.76	26.87	33.33
K2s	34	64.71	2,826.00	83.12	0.14	58.62	31.03	44.44
K2o	69	53.62	1,303.50	18.89	(0.09)	48.39	30.65	68.42
QQ	41	85.37	12,038.00	293.61	1.13	82.86	37.14	76.92
QJs	44	59.09	(4,326.00)	(98.32)	(0.20)	48.57	34.29	41.67
QJo	150	69.33	10,169.44	67.80	0.35	63.20	31.20	61.54
QTs	44	56.82	(6,722.50)	(152.78)	(0.69)	44.12	35.29	25.00
QTo	151	58.28	488.89	3.24	(0.02)	50.39	33.07	52.38
Q9s	45	73.33	7,870.50	174.90	0.43	65.71	40.00	50.00
Q9o	119	65.55	(1,430.00)	(12.02)	(0.11)	53.93	30.34	48.15
Q8s	42	61.90	130.50	3.11	(0.15)	50.00	31.25	40.00
Q8o	117	62.39	3,514.00	30.03	0.09	55.56	31.31	61.29
Q7s	43	55.81	(1,219.00)	(28.35)	(0.20)	44.12	23.53	50.00
Q7o	90	60.00	1,474.50	16.38	0.15	50.00	38.89	60.71
Q6s	31	58.06	1,706.00	55.03	(0.10)	45.83	29.17	28.57
Q6o	97	56.70	(3,408.50)	(35.14)	(0.12)	50.00	23.81	60.00
Q5s	35	62.86	(1,953.00)	(55.80)	(0.08)	50.00	15.38	50.00
Q5o	81	60.49	(2,251.00)	(27.79)	(0.01)	48.39	20.97	53.85
Q4s	30	56.67	(2,018.50)	(67.28)	(0.08)	51.85	14.81	75.00
Q4o	45	44.44	(6,536.00)	(145.24)	(0.80)	34.21	28.95	18.18
Q3s	14	85.71	6,026.00	430.43	1.56	80.00	50.00	80.00
Q3o	36	44.44	(5,792.00)	(160.89)	(0.63)	37.50	21.88	28.57
Q2s	28	75.00	2,333.00	83.32	0.46	68.18	18.18	75.00

Q2o	29	75.86	708.50	24.43	0.24	66.67	19.05	75.00
JJ	56	78.57	12,517.50	223.53	0.96	75.51	38.78	68.42
JTs	37	72.97	7,331.50	198.15	0.78	64.29	39.29	63.64
JTo	141	64.54	11,658.50	82.68	0.20	56.52	32.17	59.46
J9s	49	67.35	3,884.00	79.27	0.19	57.89	44.74	41.18
J9o	134	65.67	6,030.00	45.00	0.19	54.00	30.00	63.33
J8s	45	42.22	(5,324.00)	(118.31)	(0.65)	31.58	23.68	44.44
J8o	120	55.83	(8,224.50)	(68.54)	(0.29)	44.21	25.26	45.83
J7s	40	70.00	2,641.00	66.03	0.33	57.14	25.00	71.43
J7o	110	55.45	(1,395.50)	(12.69)	(0.16)	50.00	28.57	42.86
J6s	41	56.10	(1,564.00)	(38.15)	(0.02)	48.57	28.57	60.00
J6o	88	64.77	(1,337.00)	(15.19)	(0.02)	53.73	28.36	57.89
J5s	21	71.43	1,149.00	54.71	0.35	62.50	25.00	75.00
J5o	46	45.65	(6,229.50)	(135.42)	(0.80)	40.48	16.67	14.29
J4s	25	68.00	(1,023.00)	(40.92)	(0.16)	46.67	26.67	25.00
J4o	25	76.00	3,323.50	132.94	0.67	70.59	29.41	80.00
J3s	21	42.86	(3,281.50)	(156.26)	(0.58)	36.84	52.63	40.00
J3o	20	55.00	1,688.00	84.40	0.09	50.00	11.11	100.00
J2s	31	61.29	(725.50)	(23.40)	(0.22)	55.56	37.04	40.00
J2o	10	80.00	343.00	34.30	0.24	75.00	37.50	66.67
TT	58	81.03	11,113.00	191.60	0.73	75.56	40.00	61.11
T9s	54	59.26	(2,529.00)	(46.83)	(0.14)	51.11	24.44	54.55
T9o	127	73.23	13,894.49	109.41	0.46	63.44	34.41	62.50
T8s	50	60.00	2,447.00	48.94	0.15	47.37	26.32	60.00
T8o	134	62.69	(1,372.50)	(10.24)	0.03	54.55	30.00	48.48
T7s	41	56.10	487.50	11.89	(0.02)	41.94	54.84	70.59
T7o	86	59.30	(5,776.00)	(67.16)	(0.18)	52.70	25.68	52.63
T6s	40	62.50	(1,872.50)	(46.81)	(0.17)	54.55	30.30	50.00
T6o	54	48.15	(5,052.00)	(93.56)	(0.47)	40.43	25.53	50.00
T5s	12	58.33	276.00	23.00	0.08	50.00	40.00	75.00
T5o	8	62.50	(656.00)	(82.00)	(0.26)	50.00	50.00	66.67
T4s	12	66.67	(511.00)	(42.58)	(0.38)	50.00	37.50	33.33
T4o	9	66.67	434.00	48.22	0.33	62.50	12.50	100.00
T3s	8	75.00	1,288.00	161.00	0.62	75.00	25.00	100.00
T3o	7	28.57	(1,290.00)	(184.29)	(1.71)	16.67	33.33	-
T2s	13	46.15	(2,439.00)	(187.62)	(0.62)	30.00	10.00	-
T2o	6	33.33	(850.00)	(141.67)	(0.92)	33.33	-	-
99	70	75.71	13,182.00	188.31	0.70	71.19	50.85	63.33
98s	43	67.44	5,393.50	125.43	0.31	58.82	26.47	44.44
98o	132	53.79	(13,090.00)	(99.17)	(0.28)	45.54	30.36	50.00
97s	39	61.54	877.00	22.49	0.22	54.55	36.36	66.67
97o	106	59.43	(2,955.00)	(27.88)	(0.07)	47.56	32.93	59.26
96s	39	53.85	(7,372.50)	(189.04)	(0.81)	41.94	32.26	20.00
96o	51	58.82	46.50	0.91	(0.05)	47.50	35.00	71.43

95s	13	69.23	1,294.00	99.54	0.30	63.64	9.09	100.00
95o	5	60.00	747.00	149.40	0.30	33.33	33.33	100.00
94s	11	54.55	(300.00)	(27.27)	(0.06)	54.55	54.55	50.00
94o	6	50.00	869.00	144.83	0.66	40.00	40.00	100.00
93s	6	66.67	1,991.00	331.83	1.24	66.67	33.33	100.00
93o	5	80.00	491.00	98.20	0.44	75.00	25.00	100.00
92s	5	60.00	44.00	8.80	0.10	60.00	-	-
92o	4	25.00	(903.00)	(225.75)	(1.51)	25.00	-	-
88	65	72.31	6,367.00	97.95	0.53	66.67	48.15	65.38
87s	57	63.16	3,486.00	61.16	0.27	55.32	31.91	60.00
87o	104	56.73	249.00	2.39	0.02	49.44	33.71	53.33
86s	44	65.91	6,036.00	137.18	0.32	59.46	24.32	55.56
86o	91	62.64	3,960.38	43.52	0.21	53.42	23.29	52.94
85s	19	73.68	1,023.00	53.84	0.59	66.67	26.67	75.00
85o	13	30.77	(2,796.00)	(215.08)	(1.04)	25.00	25.00	33.33
84s	10	60.00	1,855.00	185.50	0.54	55.56	44.44	75.00
84o	7	71.43	815.00	116.43	0.91	71.43	42.86	100.00
83s	7	42.86	(956.00)	(136.57)	(0.29)	33.33	33.33	50.00
83o	7	28.57	(1,363.00)	(194.71)	(0.37)	16.67	33.33	50.00
82s	6	50.00	776.50	129.42	(0.08)	50.00	66.67	50.00
82o	2	50.00	(3.00)	(1.50)	(0.02)	50.00	-	-
77	68	67.65	4,307.50	63.35	(0.01)	60.00	34.55	52.63
76s	47	55.32	(2,351.50)	(50.03)	(0.09)	43.24	35.14	30.77
76o	64	68.75	3,885.00	60.70	0.25	60.78	33.33	58.82
75s	51	64.71	6,060.50	118.83	0.44	57.14	30.95	69.23
75o	15	60.00	(25.00)	(1.67)	0.19	53.85	38.46	60.00
74s	7	28.57	(3,198.00)	(456.86)	(1.95)	16.67	16.67	-
74o	6	33.33	(843.00)	(140.50)	(0.92)	20.00	-	-
73s	5	40.00	197.00	39.40	0.10	25.00	25.00	100.00
73o	7	42.86	(436.00)	(62.29)	(0.65)	42.86	14.29	-
72s	5	60.00	794.00	158.80	0.50	60.00	-	-
72o	4	25.00	(843.00)	(210.75)	(1.63)	25.00	-	-
66	69	71.01	10,408.50	150.85	0.43	64.91	31.58	72.22
65s	36	50.00	(4,120.00)	(114.44)	(0.48)	45.45	24.24	25.00
65o	28	57.14	678.00	24.21	0.03	50.00	16.67	25.00
64s	30	53.33	(1,365.00)	(45.50)	(0.26)	50.00	39.29	36.36
64o	4	50.00	(153.00)	(38.25)	(0.38)	33.33	-	-
63s	5	80.00	1,641.00	328.20	1.49	80.00	40.00	100.00
63o	9	55.56	(606.00)	(67.33)	(0.28)	42.86	14.29	100.00
62s	5	40.00	(653.00)	(130.60)	(1.70)	50.00	50.00	-
62o	5	40.00	(430.00)	(86.00)	(0.70)	40.00	-	-
55	73	69.86	3,344.00	45.81	0.37	63.33	33.33	65.00
54s	30	60.00	421.00	14.03	(0.06)	50.00	41.67	50.00
54o	22	59.09	(1,607.00)	(73.05)	(0.39)	50.00	22.22	75.00

53s	18	77.78	3,072.00	170.67	0.77	73.33	20.00	100.00
53o	6	50.00	(540.00)	(90.00)	(0.83)	25.00	50.00	50.00
52s	7	57.14	291.00	41.57	0.13	57.14	28.57	50.00
52o	8	50.00	422.00	52.75	(0.28)	40.00	40.00	50.00
44	73	63.01	(3,101.00)	(42.48)	(0.10)	51.79	23.21	38.46
43s	10	60.00	298.00	29.80	0.19	50.00	12.50	100.00
43o	6	50.00	144.00	24.00	(0.09)	40.00	20.00	100.00
42s	7	85.71	1,124.00	160.57	0.28	83.33	16.67	100.00
42o	12	50.00	(975.00)	(81.25)	(0.59)	50.00	41.67	60.00
33	75	44.00	(13,084.50)	(174.46)	(0.75)	35.38	26.15	29.41
32s	7	71.43	643.00	91.86	0.42	71.43	-	-
32o	8	75.00	(106.00)	(13.25)	0.18	71.43	14.29	100.00
22	80	51.25	(5,170.50)	(64.63)	(0.36)	42.65	35.29	41.67
Total	9,222	63.37	233,771.28	25.35	0.10	55.10	32.81	55.70

High: Open-Call From SB								
Hand	Trials	Win %	Amount ($)	Avg $/Hand	BB/ Hand	Win % WSF	Went to SD (%)	Won $ at SD (%)
AA	34	85.29	10,183.00	299.50	1.28	85.29	47.06	68.75
AKs	1	100.00	87.00	87.00	1.45	100.00	-	-
AKo	1	-	(3,000.00)	(3,000.00)	(10.00)	-	100.00	-
AQo	2	100.00	195.00	97.50	0.48	100.00	50.00	100.00
AJs	1	-	(100.00)	(100.00)	(1.00)	-	-	-
AJo	1	100.00	147.00	147.00	0.49	100.00	-	-
ATo	2	100.00	1,046.00	523.00	1.74	100.00	50.00	100.00
A8o	2	100.00	294.00	147.00	0.49	100.00	50.00	100.00
A7o	1	100.00	1,497.00	1,497.00	4.99	100.00	100.00	100.00
A6o	1	100.00	2,697.00	2,697.00	4.50	100.00	100.00	100.00
A2o	3	-	(2,250.00)	(750.00)	(2.50)	-	66.67	-
KK	46	76.09	4,476.50	97.32	0.63	76.09	50.00	60.87
K9o	2	50.00	58.00	29.00	0.48	50.00	-	-
K7s	2	50.00	(153.00)	(76.50)	(0.26)	50.00	-	-
K7o	21	57.14	312.00	14.86	0.16	57.14	14.29	66.67
K6s	2	50.00	(153.00)	(76.50)	(0.26)	50.00	-	-
K6o	18	38.89	(1,632.00)	(90.67)	(0.34)	38.89	27.78	20.00
K5s	9	66.67	1,457.00	161.89	0.71	66.67	55.56	80.00
K5o	1	100.00	345.00	345.00	3.45	100.00	-	-
K4s	6	66.67	39.00	6.50	(0.09)	66.67	16.67	100.00
K4o	4	50.00	(216.00)	(54.00)	0.61	50.00	25.00	100.00
K3s	3	-	(1,150.00)	(383.33)	(1.17)	-	33.33	-
K3o	6	16.67	(663.00)	(110.50)	(0.67)	16.67	-	-
K2s	6	83.33	1,411.00	235.17	0.90	83.33	16.67	100.00
K2o	4	50.00	(406.00)	(101.50)	(0.38)	66.67	66.67	50.00

QQ	32	75.00	6,781.50	211.92	0.72	75.00	34.38	54.55
QTo	2	50.00	(193.00)	(96.50)	(1.77)	50.00	100.00	50.00
Q9o	3	100.00	1,140.00	380.00	2.31	100.00	66.67	100.00
Q8o	4	25.00	(152.00)	(38.00)	(0.38)	25.00	25.00	100.00
Q7s	8	87.50	2,750.50	343.81	1.08	87.50	50.00	75.00
Q7o	5	60.00	195.00	39.00	0.10	60.00	20.00	100.00
Q6s	13	61.54	954.00	73.38	0.38	61.54	38.46	60.00
Q6o	2	100.00	1,144.00	572.00	3.23	100.00	100.00	100.00
Q5s	13	53.85	3,330.00	256.15	0.73	53.85	30.77	75.00
Q5o	3	33.33	499.00	166.33	0.67	50.00	50.00	100.00
Q4s	13	30.77	(2,190.50)	(168.50)	(0.47)	30.77	15.38	50.00
Q4o	2	50.00	(76.50)	(38.25)	(0.13)	50.00	50.00	100.00
Q3s	7	85.71	(392.50)	(56.07)	(0.08)	85.71	14.29	-
Q3o	2	50.00	77.00	38.50	0.98	50.00	50.00	100.00
Q2s	5	20.00	(1,203.00)	(240.60)	(0.80)	20.00	-	-
Q2o	4	75.00	321.00	80.25	0.48	75.00	-	-
JJ	16	75.00	2,416.00	151.00	0.21	75.00	50.00	62.50
JTs	1	-	(5.00)	(5.00)	(0.50)	-	-	-
JTo	4	75.00	421.00	105.25	0.36	75.00	25.00	100.00
J9s	2	-	(360.00)	(180.00)	(2.00)	-	50.00	-
J9o	10	50.00	611.50	61.15	0.29	50.00	10.00	100.00
J8o	7	14.29	(2,143.00)	(306.14)	(1.22)	14.29	14.29	-
J7s	2	100.00	944.00	472.00	1.99	100.00	50.00	100.00
J7o	6	83.33	1,837.00	306.17	0.83	83.33	16.67	100.00
J6s	5	40.00	(608.00)	(121.60)	(0.41)	40.00	-	-
J6o	8	37.50	(817.00)	(102.13)	(0.70)	37.50	12.50	100.00
J5s	5	60.00	(195.00)	(39.00)	(0.61)	60.00	20.00	-
J5o	1	100.00	47.00	47.00	0.47	100.00	-	-
J4s	6	50.00	1,017.00	169.50	0.33	50.00	16.67	100.00
J4o	1	-	(300.00)	(300.00)	(1.00)	-	-	-
J3s	7	42.86	(1,957.00)	(279.57)	(0.93)	42.86	14.29	-
J3o	1	100.00	47.00	47.00	0.47	100.00	100.00	100.00
J2s	2	100.00	296.00	148.00	0.49	100.00	-	-
J2o	2	50.00	27.00	13.50	(0.76)	50.00	50.00	100.00
TT	15	60.00	(2,802.50)	(186.83)	(0.68)	60.00	26.67	50.00
T9o	9	44.44	(1,012.00)	(112.44)	(0.34)	44.44	22.22	50.00
T8s	3	66.67	(156.00)	(52.00)	0.32	66.67	-	-
T8o	7	42.86	1,141.00	163.00	0.57	42.86	42.86	66.67
T7s	5	40.00	(314.00)	(62.80)	(0.21)	40.00	20.00	100.00
T7o	13	46.15	1,772.00	136.31	0.19	46.15	46.15	66.67
T6s	7	42.86	2,141.00	305.86	0.57	42.86	57.14	50.00
T6o	5	80.00	187.00	37.40	0.19	80.00	20.00	-
T5s	7	28.57	(1,641.00)	(234.43)	(1.22)	33.33	50.00	-
T5o	2	50.00	(473.00)	(236.50)	(1.03)	50.00	50.00	-

T4s	5	40.00	(3.00)	(0.60)	0.28	40.00	-	-
T4o	4	-	(750.00)	(187.50)	(0.75)	-	-	-
T3s	2	50.00	1,095.50	547.75	2.74	50.00	100.00	50.00
T3o	1	100.00	97.00	97.00	0.49	100.00	100.00	100.00
T2s	3	-	(500.00)	(166.67)	(1.00)	-	-	-
T2o	1	-	(300.00)	(300.00)	(1.00)	-	-	-
99	5	80.00	488.00	97.60	0.39	80.00	80.00	75.00
98s	4	25.00	(403.00)	(100.75)	(0.38)	25.00	-	-
98o	6	33.33	(707.50)	(117.92)	(0.51)	33.33	50.00	66.67
97s	6	33.33	165.00	27.50	0.24	33.33	16.67	100.00
97o	17	29.41	(2,883.00)	(169.59)	(0.74)	29.41	41.18	28.57
96s	7	42.86	248.00	35.43	0.08	42.86	14.29	-
96o	14	57.14	120.50	8.61	0.06	57.14	35.71	40.00
95s	3	66.67	1,294.00	431.33	1.33	66.67	66.67	100.00
95o	1	-	(300.00)	(300.00)	(1.00)	-	-	-
94s	3	66.67	243.00	81.00	(0.01)	66.67	66.67	50.00
93s	1	100.00	197.00	197.00	1.97	100.00	-	-
88	4	75.00	139.50	34.88	(0.39)	75.00	25.00	-
87s	1	100.00	598.00	598.00	1.00	100.00	-	-
87o	23	47.83	(2,483.00)	(107.96)	(0.38)	47.83	30.43	42.86
86s	9	44.44	(694.00)	(77.11)	(0.18)	44.44	33.33	66.67
86o	27	40.74	1,377.50	51.02	0.05	40.74	40.74	45.45
85s	6	33.33	(306.00)	(51.00)	(0.09)	40.00	20.00	100.00
85o	1	100.00	147.00	147.00	0.49	100.00	100.00	100.00
84o	1	100.00	147.00	147.00	0.49	100.00	100.00	100.00
83s	1	100.00	597.00	597.00	1.99	100.00	100.00	100.00
82s	1	-	(100.00)	(100.00)	(1.00)	-	-	-
76s	6	66.67	(62.00)	(10.33)	(0.34)	66.67	33.33	100.00
76o	20	50.00	861.50	43.08	0.04	52.63	10.53	100.00
75s	10	60.00	973.00	97.30	0.24	60.00	20.00	50.00
75o	6	50.00	772.50	128.75	0.16	50.00	33.33	100.00
74s	1	-	(100.00)	(100.00)	(1.00)	-	-	-
74o	1	100.00	14.00	14.00	0.47	100.00	-	-
73s	1	-	(300.00)	(300.00)	(1.00)	-	-	-
72s	1	100.00	47.00	47.00	0.47	100.00	-	-
65s	6	16.67	(903.00)	(150.50)	(0.92)	16.67	33.33	-
65o	9	44.44	163.00	18.11	0.22	50.00	50.00	50.00
64s	5	-	(1,601.50)	(320.30)	(1.10)	-	60.00	-
64o	2	50.00	567.00	283.50	0.75	50.00	-	-
63s	2	100.00	1,594.00	797.00	3.99	100.00	50.00	100.00
55	1	100.00	897.00	897.00	2.99	100.00	100.00	100.00
54s	3	33.33	597.00	199.00	0.50	33.33	-	-
54o	6	33.33	(1,029.50)	(171.58)	(0.59)	33.33	33.33	50.00
53s	8	25.00	(1,430.00)	(178.75)	(0.65)	25.00	25.00	50.00

Hand	Trials	Win %	Amount ($)	Avg $/Hand	BB/ Hand	Win % WSF	Went to SD (%)	Won $ at SD (%)
53o	1	-	(1.50)	(1.50)	(0.02)	-	100.00	-
52s	1	-	(1,050.00)	(1,050.00)	(3.50)	-	100.00	-
43s	1	-	(50.00)	(50.00)	(0.50)	-	-	-
43o	2	-	(350.00)	(175.00)	(0.75)	-	-	-
42s	1	100.00	27.00	27.00	0.45	100.00	-	-
Total	707	54.03	24,787.00	35.06	0.11	54.65	32.62	58.77
			High: Open-Fold From SB					
Hand	Trials	Win %	Amount ($)	Avg $/Hand	BB/ Hand	Win % WSF	Went to SD (%)	Won $ at SD (%)
AA	1	-	(75.00)	(75.00)	(0.25)	-	-	-
AJo	1	-	(50.00)	(50.00)	(0.25)	-	-	-
A5o	1	-	(37.00)	(37.00)	(0.25)	-	-	-
A4o	3	-	(125.00)	(41.67)	(0.25)	-	-	-
A3o	5	-	(115.00)	(23.00)	(0.25)	-	-	-
A2o	7	-	(326.00)	(46.57)	(0.24)	-	-	-
KJs	1	-	(75.00)	(75.00)	(0.25)	-	-	-
K8o	2	-	(75.00)	(37.50)	(0.25)	-	-	-
K7o	3	-	(150.00)	(50.00)	(0.25)	-	-	-
K6o	3	-	(137.00)	(45.67)	(0.25)	-	-	-
K5o	30	-	(1,782.00)	(59.40)	(0.25)	-	-	-
K4o	42	-	(2,429.00)	(57.83)	(0.25)	-	-	-
K3s	1	-	(75.00)	(75.00)	(0.25)	-	-	-
K3o	52	-	(3,114.00)	(59.88)	(0.25)	-	-	-
K2s	1	-	(75.00)	(75.00)	(0.25)	-	-	-
K2o	78	-	(4,442.00)	(56.95)	(0.25)	-	-	-
Q8o	3	-	(125.00)	(41.67)	(0.25)	-	-	-
Q7o	35	-	(1,804.00)	(51.54)	(0.25)	-	-	-
Q6o	25	-	(1,502.00)	(60.08)	(0.25)	-	-	-
Q5s	2	-	(125.00)	(62.50)	(0.25)	-	-	-
Q5o	57	-	(3,564.00)	(62.53)	(0.25)	-	-	-
Q4s	2	-	(51.00)	(25.50)	(0.21)	-	-	-
Q4o	93	-	(5,512.00)	(59.27)	(0.25)	-	-	-
Q3s	9	-	(487.00)	(54.11)	(0.25)	-	-	-
Q3o	98	-	(6,040.00)	(61.63)	(0.25)	-	-	-
Q2s	16	-	(850.00)	(53.13)	(0.24)	-	-	-
Q2o	121	-	(7,363.00)	(60.85)	(0.25)	-	-	-
J9o	2	-	(100.00)	(50.00)	(0.25)	-	-	-
J8o	2	-	(150.00)	(75.00)	(0.25)	-	-	-
J7o	25	-	(1,699.00)	(67.96)	(0.25)	-	-	-
J6s	1	-	(25.00)	(25.00)	(0.25)	-	-	-
J6o	46	-	(2,627.00)	(57.11)	(0.25)	-	-	-
J5s	4	-	(225.00)	(56.25)	(0.25)	-	-	-

J5o	101	-	(5,616.00)	(55.60)	(0.25)	-	-	-
J4s	10	-	(551.00)	(55.10)	(0.24)	-	-	-
J4o	98	-	(5,114.00)	(52.18)	(0.25)	-	-	-
J3s	21	-	(1,017.00)	(48.43)	(0.25)	-	-	-
J3o	95	-	(5,247.50)	(55.24)	(0.25)	-	-	-
J2s	25	-	(1,587.00)	(63.48)	(0.25)	-	-	-
J2o	137	-	(7,859.00)	(57.37)	(0.25)	-	-	-
TT	1	-	(75.00)	(75.00)	(0.25)	-	-	-
T8o	4	-	(100.00)	(25.00)	(0.27)	-	-	-
T7s	1	-	(25.00)	(25.00)	(0.25)	-	-	-
T7o	23	-	(1,145.00)	(49.78)	(0.25)	-	-	-
T6s	4	-	(250.00)	(62.50)	(0.25)	-	-	-
T6o	86	-	(5,160.00)	(60.00)	(0.25)	-	-	-
T5s	28	-	(1,851.00)	(66.11)	(0.26)	-	-	-
T5o	103	-	(6,340.00)	(61.55)	(0.25)	-	-	-
T4s	29	-	(1,332.00)	(45.93)	(0.25)	-	-	-
T4o	124	-	(7,507.00)	(60.54)	(0.25)	-	-	-
T3s	33	-	(2,088.00)	(63.27)	(0.25)	-	-	-
T3o	117	-	(6,333.00)	(54.13)	(0.25)	-	-	-
T2s	39	-	(2,286.00)	(58.62)	(0.25)	-	-	-
T2o	131	-	(7,625.00)	(58.21)	(0.25)	-	-	-
98o	7	-	(349.00)	(49.86)	(0.25)	-	-	-
97s	1	-	(50.00)	(50.00)	(0.25)	-	-	-
97o	3	-	(100.00)	(33.33)	(0.25)	-	-	-
96s	1	-	(75.00)	(75.00)	(0.25)	-	-	-
96o	72	-	(4,221.00)	(58.63)	(0.25)	-	-	-
95s	25	-	(1,426.00)	(57.04)	(0.25)	-	-	-
95o	133	-	(7,687.00)	(57.80)	(0.25)	-	-	-
94s	35	-	(2,215.50)	(63.30)	(0.25)	-	-	-
94o	143	-	(8,493.00)	(59.39)	(0.25)	-	-	-
93s	44	-	(2,501.00)	(56.84)	(0.25)	-	-	-
93o	134	-	(7,225.00)	(53.92)	(0.25)	-	-	-
92s	46	-	(2,796.00)	(60.78)	(0.25)	-	-	-
92o	175	-	(10,054.00)	(57.45)	(0.25)	-	-	-
87o	3	-	(75.00)	(25.00)	(0.25)	-	-	-
86o	36	-	(1,842.00)	(51.17)	(0.25)	-	-	-
85s	30	-	(1,880.00)	(62.67)	(0.26)	-	-	-
85o	116	-	(6,752.00)	(58.21)	(0.25)	-	-	-
84s	42	-	(2,414.00)	(57.48)	(0.25)	-	-	-
84o	138	-	(8,071.00)	(58.49)	(0.25)	-	-	-
83s	27	-	(1,612.00)	(59.70)	(0.25)	-	-	-
83o	126	-	(7,186.00)	(57.03)	(0.25)	-	-	-
82s	44	-	(2,451.00)	(55.70)	(0.25)	-	-	-
82o	139	-	(7,976.00)	(57.38)	(0.25)	-	-	-

76s	1	-	(50.00)	(50.00)	(0.25)	-	-	-
76o	62	-	(3,821.50)	(61.64)	(0.25)	-	-	-
75s	6	-	(275.00)	(45.83)	(0.25)	-	-	-
75o	131	-	(7,299.00)	(55.72)	(0.25)	-	-	-
74s	29	-	(1,671.00)	(57.62)	(0.25)	-	-	-
74o	128	-	(6,960.00)	(54.38)	(0.25)	-	-	-
73s	38	-	(2,134.00)	(56.16)	(0.25)	-	-	-
73o	121	-	(6,895.00)	(56.98)	(0.25)	-	-	-
72s	29	-	(1,829.00)	(63.07)	(0.25)	-	-	-
72o	111	-	(6,157.00)	(55.47)	(0.25)	-	-	-
65s	3	-	(53.00)	(17.67)	(0.21)	-	-	-
65o	112	-	(6,600.00)	(58.93)	(0.25)	-	-	-
64s	8	-	(465.00)	(58.13)	(0.25)	-	-	-
64o	100	-	(5,786.00)	(57.86)	(0.25)	-	-	-
63s	27	-	(1,517.00)	(56.19)	(0.25)	-	-	-
63o	132	-	(7,188.00)	(54.45)	(0.25)	-	-	-
62s	30	-	(1,620.50)	(54.02)	(0.25)	-	-	-
62o	109	-	(6,291.00)	(57.72)	(0.25)	-	-	-
54s	3	-	(90.00)	(30.00)	(0.25)	-	-	-
54o	98	-	(5,933.00)	(60.54)	(0.25)	-	-	-
53s	18	-	(1,112.00)	(61.78)	(0.25)	-	-	-
53o	134	-	(7,652.00)	(57.10)	(0.25)	-	-	-
52s	37	-	(2,330.00)	(62.97)	(0.25)	-	-	-
52o	124	-	(7,018.00)	(56.60)	(0.25)	-	-	-
43s	34	-	(2,274.00)	(66.88)	(0.25)	-	-	-
43o	127	-	(7,386.00)	(58.16)	(0.25)	-	-	-
42s	42	-	(2,262.00)	(53.86)	(0.25)	-	-	-
42o	130	-	(7,803.00)	(60.02)	(0.25)	-	-	-
32s	37	-	(2,237.00)	(60.46)	(0.25)	-	-	-
32o	157	-	(9,288.00)	(59.16)	(0.25)	-	-	-
Total	5,620	-	(323,888.00)	(57.63)	(0.25)	-	-	-

Mid: Open-Raise From SB								
Hand	Trials	Win %	Amount ($)	Avg $/Hand	BB/ Hand	Win % WSF	Went to SD (%)	Won $ at SD (%)
AA	90	92.22	3,784.50	42.05	1.67	88.33	51.67	77.42
AKs	68	76.47	527.50	7.76	0.42	67.35	48.98	45.83
AKo	225	76.00	614.39	2.73	0.24	66.04	43.40	44.93
AQs	75	82.67	752.50	10.03	0.43	71.74	45.65	47.62
AQo	229	79.04	3,799.88	16.59	0.55	69.03	47.10	54.79
AJs	59	71.19	157.75	2.67	0.16	59.52	50.00	38.10
AJo	213	76.53	3,277.50	15.39	0.46	67.11	57.24	54.02
ATs	81	77.78	499.75	6.17	0.31	67.86	44.64	56.00

ATo	210	71.90	419.37	2.00	0.24	60.93	54.97	40.96
A9s	67	79.10	111.25	1.66	0.42	68.89	42.22	52.63
A9o	216	76.85	1,679.50	7.78	0.33	65.99	44.90	54.55
A8s	79	63.29	115.14	1.46	(0.41)	51.67	46.67	28.57
A8o	195	75.90	316.50	1.62	0.28	62.70	51.59	52.31
A7s	67	68.66	447.25	6.68	(0.04)	54.35	47.83	31.82
A7o	183	73.22	968.50	5.29	0.42	61.11	47.62	63.33
A6s	69	72.46	195.25	2.83	0.10	55.81	39.53	29.41
A6o	169	69.82	346.75	2.05	0.27	62.69	38.06	58.82
A5s	64	68.75	9.25	0.14	0.21	57.45	46.81	54.55
A5o	201	64.68	(1,188.00)	(5.91)	(0.19)	49.65	45.39	35.94
A4s	71	70.42	(172.00)	(2.42)	(0.06)	52.27	36.36	43.75
A4o	184	64.13	514.25	2.79	(0.03)	51.11	40.00	42.59
A3s	68	66.18	273.25	4.02	(0.08)	53.06	51.02	40.00
A3o	187	66.84	(322.59)	(1.73)	(0.01)	56.43	45.71	43.75
A2s	53	75.47	1,009.00	19.04	0.72	60.61	57.58	63.16
A2o	158	65.82	1,247.00	7.89	0.12	52.21	42.48	50.00
KK	74	89.19	2,438.25	32.95	1.53	86.44	47.46	71.43
KQs	79	77.22	1,181.00	14.95	0.53	68.97	32.76	57.89
KQo	182	71.98	574.45	3.16	0.16	63.31	27.34	47.37
KJs	59	72.88	559.50	9.48	0.31	62.79	34.88	60.00
KJo	209	67.46	1,348.75	6.45	0.20	55.84	28.57	59.09
KTs	62	69.35	858.00	13.84	0.48	60.42	50.00	54.17
KTo	189	73.55	1,645.00	8.70	0.16	61.24	25.58	48.48
K9s	67	77.61	440.75	6.58	0.32	61.54	30.77	33.33
K9o	189	68.25	755.75	4.00	0.09	55.56	32.59	54.55
K8s	80	61.25	(54.50)	(0.68)	(0.08)	49.18	36.07	45.45
K8o	188	63.83	(369.30)	(1.96)	0.04	52.45	27.27	56.41
K7s	63	73.02	850.25	13.50	0.45	60.47	30.23	69.23
K7o	204	61.76	(494.30)	(2.42)	(0.15)	43.88	32.37	44.44
K6s	51	72.55	805.00	15.78	0.56	61.11	41.67	60.00
K6o	158	70.89	(176.50)	(1.12)	0.15	58.56	18.92	47.62
K5s	83	68.67	147.25	1.77	0.24	53.57	26.79	46.67
K5o	185	62.70	(220.25)	(1.19)	(0.16)	42.50	20.00	41.67
K4s	64	70.31	600.75	9.39	0.38	57.78	33.33	66.67
K4o	158	60.76	(1,054.50)	(6.67)	(0.14)	43.12	31.19	44.12
K3s	51	50.98	(901.00)	(17.67)	(0.71)	30.56	25.00	22.22
K3o	125	60.00	(918.00)	(7.34)	(0.24)	41.18	30.59	46.15
K2s	59	66.10	(77.25)	(1.31)	(0.10)	53.49	32.56	50.00
K2o	52	67.31	(153.50)	(2.95)	0.14	54.05	16.22	50.00
QQ	82	90.24	2,096.50	25.57	1.29	86.89	42.62	73.08
QJs	69	73.91	316.00	4.58	0.08	59.09	36.36	43.75
QJo	241	67.22	236.02	0.98	(0.00)	58.20	31.22	47.46
QTs	78	76.92	342.00	4.38	0.32	66.67	51.85	53.57

QTo	218	65.60	1,253.00	5.75	0.06	52.23	30.57	58.33
Q9s	51	74.51	626.00	12.27	0.46	62.86	40.00	57.14
Q9o	193	68.91	1,324.00	6.86	0.25	56.20	27.74	60.53
Q8s	69	78.26	804.75	11.66	0.36	60.53	39.47	46.67
Q8o	196	61.73	(1,641.74)	(8.38)	(0.20)	46.04	31.65	45.45
Q7s	65	61.54	(517.25)	(7.96)	0.02	47.92	22.92	45.45
Q7o	117	64.10	(666.25)	(5.69)	(0.27)	45.45	27.27	28.57
Q6s	65	60.00	(410.30)	(6.31)	(0.31)	42.22	42.22	36.84
Q6o	80	66.25	(458.50)	(5.73)	(0.16)	51.79	23.21	38.46
Q5s	54	64.81	191.00	3.54	0.01	53.66	31.71	46.15
Q5o	85	67.06	(223.13)	(2.63)	(0.01)	49.09	21.82	50.00
Q4s	45	64.44	(187.00)	(4.16)	0.05	46.67	23.33	71.43
Q4o	45	62.22	614.50	13.66	0.29	51.43	31.43	72.73
Q3s	41	63.41	275.94	6.73	(0.09)	42.31	30.77	37.50
Q3o	16	75.00	575.00	35.94	1.01	50.00	50.00	100.00
Q2s	26	73.08	613.00	23.58	0.55	56.25	37.50	50.00
Q2o	9	44.44	(184.00)	(20.44)	(0.41)	37.50	25.00	50.00
JJ	85	80.00	789.25	9.29	0.53	68.52	46.30	52.00
JTs	55	74.55	1,097.50	19.95	0.57	66.67	45.24	57.89
JTo	192	72.92	1,781.76	9.28	0.20	59.38	35.16	55.56
J9s	69	66.67	793.50	11.50	0.62	57.41	31.48	58.82
J9o	175	68.00	(153.50)	(0.88)	(0.02)	53.72	34.71	42.86
J8s	70	62.86	(542.75)	(7.75)	(0.27)	52.73	32.73	33.33
J8o	181	66.85	366.50	2.02	0.04	52.00	36.00	51.11
J7s	65	70.77	(358.50)	(5.52)	(0.15)	52.50	27.50	27.27
J7o	98	69.39	1,080.50	11.03	0.28	55.88	26.47	50.00
J6s	55	74.55	(48.75)	(0.89)	0.21	60.00	28.57	60.00
J6o	38	65.79	(25.50)	(0.67)	0.02	45.83	25.00	50.00
J5s	46	76.09	47.50	1.03	0.16	60.71	28.57	50.00
J5o	36	47.22	(952.50)	(26.46)	(0.66)	29.63	18.52	20.00
J4s	37	72.97	109.11	2.95	0.30	62.96	25.93	57.14
J4o	14	64.29	136.00	9.71	0.09	50.00	20.00	100.00
J3s	18	66.67	(84.50)	(4.69)	(0.19)	50.00	16.67	-
J3o	3	33.33	(83.00)	(27.67)	(0.69)	33.33	33.33	-
J2s	8	87.50	173.00	21.63	0.78	75.00	25.00	100.00
J2o	1	100.00	30.00	30.00	0.50	-	-	-
TT	112	75.00	665.00	5.94	0.47	67.82	51.72	44.44
T9s	64	70.31	(7.00)	(0.11)	0.08	57.78	37.78	41.18
T9o	186	69.35	1,438.75	7.74	0.20	58.09	32.35	43.18
T8s	71	73.24	705.50	9.94	0.20	62.75	31.37	50.00
T8o	164	64.02	(578.25)	(3.53)	0.03	50.83	34.17	53.66
T7s	53	79.25	457.50	8.63	0.60	72.50	22.50	55.56
T7o	64	73.44	540.00	8.44	0.41	61.36	29.55	46.15
T6s	58	68.97	783.95	13.52	0.36	62.50	29.17	64.29

T6o	44	63.64	(6.50)	(0.15)	0.03	48.39	35.48	54.55
T5s	34	82.35	(154.75)	(4.55)	0.27	70.00	20.00	50.00
T5o	18	66.67	41.00	2.28	0.29	50.00	33.33	75.00
T4s	21	57.14	(105.00)	(5.00)	(0.66)	30.77	38.46	40.00
T4o	6	50.00	(202.00)	(33.67)	(0.84)	25.00	25.00	-
T3s	9	55.56	(297.00)	(33.00)	(0.68)	33.33	-	-
T3o	1	-	(210.00)	(210.00)	(3.50)	-	100.00	-
T2s	3	66.67	37.00	12.33	(0.03)	50.00	-	-
T2o	1	100.00	30.00	30.00	0.50	-	-	-
99	88	79.55	1,758.75	19.99	0.76	71.43	52.38	60.61
98s	69	72.46	(99.50)	(1.44)	0.24	63.46	30.77	43.75
98o	174	64.37	176.91	1.02	(0.07)	51.56	36.72	42.55
97s	58	63.79	(102.25)	(1.76)	(0.07)	56.25	20.83	50.00
97o	95	70.53	203.25	2.14	0.05	47.17	33.96	33.33
96s	33	72.73	(335.25)	(10.16)	(0.15)	55.00	25.00	20.00
96o	14	42.86	(442.00)	(31.57)	(1.05)	33.33	25.00	-
95s	27	62.96	(357.50)	(13.24)	(0.19)	44.44	38.89	28.57
95o	8	87.50	204.00	25.50	0.54	66.67	66.67	100.00
94s	7	85.71	118.00	16.86	0.87	75.00	50.00	50.00
94o	2	50.00	(170.50)	(85.25)	(1.78)	50.00	100.00	50.00
93s	1	100.00	48.00	48.00	4.80	100.00	100.00	100.00
93o	1	100.00	30.00	30.00	0.50	-	-	-
92s	2	50.00	67.00	33.50	0.46	50.00	-	-
92o	1	100.00	10.00	10.00	0.50	-	-	-
88	88	81.82	1,622.50	18.44	0.62	72.88	45.76	66.67
87s	57	68.42	275.75	4.84	0.37	59.09	34.09	46.67
87o	128	69.53	140.68	1.10	(0.01)	55.68	29.55	46.15
86s	46	65.22	(312.50)	(6.79)	(0.21)	55.56	19.44	28.57
86o	42	71.43	137.25	3.27	0.31	61.29	29.03	66.67
85s	21	80.95	329.00	15.67	0.62	63.64	27.27	100.00
85o	14	57.14	(52.75)	(3.77)	(0.34)	33.33	22.22	100.00
84s	7	57.14	24.00	3.43	(0.80)	40.00	20.00	100.00
84o	2	50.00	(269.00)	(134.50)	(2.00)	-	100.00	-
83s	1	100.00	57.00	57.00	2.85	100.00	100.00	100.00
83o	1	-	(210.00)	(210.00)	(3.50)	-	100.00	-
82s	2	100.00	32.00	16.00	0.75	100.00	-	-
77	128	69.53	581.00	4.54	0.07	56.67	50.00	48.89
76s	52	65.38	274.00	5.27	(0.22)	59.09	43.18	36.84
76o	83	78.31	647.83	7.81	0.51	60.87	30.43	57.14
75s	42	57.14	229.18	5.46	(0.02)	45.45	27.27	55.56
75o	29	58.62	23.00	0.79	(0.22)	40.00	25.00	40.00
74s	9	77.78	187.00	20.78	0.35	66.67	-	-
74o	3	33.33	(85.00)	(28.33)	(1.83)	-	-	-
73s	4	75.00	103.00	25.75	0.24	50.00	50.00	-

52 Part One: Pre-Flop Play

73o	2	100.00	23.50	11.75	0.93	100.00	-	-
72s	1	-	(60.00)	(60.00)	(1.50)	-	-	-
66	90	66.67	(586.25)	(6.51)	(0.16)	54.55	48.48	46.88
65s	52	71.15	146.25	2.81	0.28	58.33	27.78	50.00
65o	31	51.61	(410.00)	(13.23)	(0.52)	28.57	28.57	16.67
64s	33	63.64	68.00	2.06	(0.08)	52.00	24.00	50.00
64o	2	50.00	(10.00)	(5.00)	(0.50)	-	-	-
63s	7	57.14	(77.00)	(11.00)	(0.72)	25.00	-	-
63o	2	50.00	(50.00)	(25.00)	(0.50)	-	-	-
62o	1	-	(90.00)	(90.00)	(1.50)	-	-	-
55	104	67.31	(64.75)	(0.62)	0.03	58.54	42.68	48.57
54s	48	66.67	(60.75)	(1.27)	(0.06)	51.52	30.30	30.00
54o	6	50.00	(108.00)	(18.00)	(0.34)	40.00	20.00	-
53s	16	75.00	695.50	43.47	0.80	66.67	16.67	100.00
52s	2	100.00	25.00	12.50	0.50	-	-	-
52o	1	-	(2.00)	(2.00)	(1.00)	-	-	-
44	84	70.24	(87.50)	(1.04)	0.04	59.02	29.51	44.44
43s	4	75.00	(75.00)	(18.75)	0.35	66.67	-	-
43o	1	100.00	27.00	27.00	0.90	100.00	-	-
42s	3	66.67	(8.50)	(2.83)	(0.18)	50.00	-	-
33	91	74.73	477.50	5.25	0.39	62.30	34.43	57.14
32s	2	100.00	8.50	4.25	0.71	100.00	-	-
32o	1	100.00	15.00	15.00	0.50	-	-	-
22	89	64.04	(681.25)	(7.65)	(0.26)	45.76	30.51	27.78
Total	11,924	69.75	43,400.50	3.64	0.16	57.07	36.23	49.57

Mid: Open-Call From SB								
Hand	Trials	Win %	Amount ($)	Avg $/Hand	BB/Hand	Win % WSF	Went to SD (%)	Won $ at SD (%)
AA	22	81.82	958.50	43.57	1.37	81.82	54.55	66.67
AKs	1	100.00	19.00	19.00	0.48	100.00	-	-
AKo	4	75.00	112.00	28.00	0.73	75.00	50.00	50.00
AQo	1	100.00	28.50	28.50	0.48	100.00	-	-
AJo	3	66.67	31.75	10.58	0.75	66.67	66.67	100.00
ATo	2	50.00	70.00	35.00	0.36	50.00	-	-
A9o	4	25.00	72.00	18.00	0.11	25.00	25.00	100.00
A8s	2	50.00	(5.25)	(2.63)	0.99	50.00	50.00	100.00
A8o	8	75.00	177.75	22.22	0.62	75.00	37.50	66.67
A7o	7	71.43	209.00	29.86	1.16	71.43	57.14	50.00
A6s	3	66.67	(40.00)	(13.33)	0.31	66.67	-	-
A6o	15	60.00	(41.25)	(2.75)	0.20	60.00	26.67	75.00
A5s	7	28.57	21.00	3.00	(0.58)	28.57	57.14	50.00
A5o	19	57.89	285.00	15.00	(0.11)	57.89	31.58	33.33

A4s	4	75.00	96.00	24.00	0.34	75.00	25.00	-
A4o	33	69.70	445.75	13.51	0.45	71.88	31.25	50.00
A3s	2	50.00	122.00	61.00	0.59	50.00	100.00	50.00
A3o	28	46.43	(330.50)	(11.80)	(0.48)	46.43	42.86	33.33
A2s	8	25.00	(94.50)	(11.81)	(0.51)	25.00	25.00	50.00
A2o	34	61.76	(102.50)	(3.01)	(0.14)	61.76	55.88	47.37
KK	23	91.30	497.50	21.63	0.90	91.30	34.78	75.00
KQo	6	50.00	(130.75)	(21.79)	0.28	50.00	33.33	100.00
KJo	1	100.00	28.00	28.00	0.93	100.00	-	-
KTo	5	60.00	(108.25)	(21.65)	0.21	60.00	40.00	50.00
K9s	2	-	(31.00)	(15.50)	(1.75)	-	50.00	-
K9o	1	-	(3.00)	(3.00)	(0.50)	-	100.00	-
K8o	2	-	(45.00)	(22.50)	(1.75)	-	50.00	-
K7o	4	50.00	26.50	6.63	0.05	50.00	50.00	50.00
K6s	3	33.33	(90.50)	(30.17)	0.25	33.33	33.33	100.00
K6o	9	33.33	(374.00)	(41.56)	(1.29)	33.33	33.33	-
K5s	2	-	(255.00)	(127.50)	(2.25)	-	50.00	-
K5o	8	62.50	267.52	33.44	1.09	62.50	62.50	80.00
K4s	3	33.33	244.00	81.33	0.15	33.33	33.33	-
K4o	14	50.00	(78.00)	(5.57)	(0.07)	50.00	14.29	50.00
K3s	5	40.00	128.00	25.60	(0.02)	40.00	20.00	-
K3o	18	44.44	117.00	6.50	0.10	47.06	47.06	50.00
K2s	3	66.67	(101.00)	(33.67)	0.13	66.67	66.67	50.00
K2o	3	66.67	(1.00)	(0.33)	0.38	66.67	33.33	100.00
QQ	5	100.00	60.50	12.10	1.63	100.00	40.00	100.00
QJo	3	66.67	178.00	59.33	1.15	66.67	33.33	100.00
QTo	5	60.00	76.75	15.35	1.14	60.00	40.00	100.00
Q9s	2	50.00	11.00	5.50	2.08	50.00	50.00	100.00
Q9o	9	33.33	(154.50)	(17.17)	(0.35)	33.33	11.11	-
Q8s	6	50.00	15.00	2.50	0.15	50.00	16.67	100.00
Q8o	9	66.67	(35.00)	(3.89)	0.54	66.67	22.22	100.00
Q7s	4	50.00	(130.87)	(32.72)	(1.34)	50.00	50.00	50.00
Q7o	17	47.06	(53.00)	(3.12)	(0.16)	47.06	17.65	33.33
Q6s	9	44.44	(148.25)	(16.47)	(0.24)	44.44	33.33	33.33
Q6o	11	36.36	(132.00)	(12.00)	(0.16)	36.36	18.18	50.00
Q5s	13	46.15	(111.75)	(8.60)	(0.30)	46.15	15.38	-
Q5o	11	63.64	(1.00)	(0.09)	0.36	63.64	18.18	100.00
Q4s	8	37.50	(130.00)	(16.25)	(0.46)	37.50	-	-
Q4o	6	16.67	(90.00)	(15.00)	(0.50)	16.67	-	-
Q3s	7	42.86	58.00	8.29	0.24	42.86	71.43	60.00
Q3o	1	-	(15.00)	(15.00)	(0.50)	-	-	-
Q2s	14	64.29	39.25	2.80	0.61	64.29	42.86	66.67
Q2o	1	100.00	1.50	1.50	1.50	100.00	-	-
JJ	1	100.00	18.00	18.00	0.45	100.00	-	-

JTs	4	25.00	(69.75)	(17.44)	0.14	25.00	75.00	33.33
JTo	1	-	(15.00)	(15.00)	(1.50)	-	100.00	-
J9s	3	33.33	1.00	0.33	(0.52)	33.33	33.33	-
J9o	5	80.00	317.00	63.40	1.70	80.00	40.00	100.00
J8s	1	-	(7.00)	(7.00)	(3.50)	-	100.00	-
J8o	13	53.85	(26.25)	(2.02)	0.18	53.85	30.77	75.00
J7s	5	60.00	(18.25)	(3.65)	0.07	60.00	-	-
J7o	10	40.00	(157.50)	(15.75)	(0.38)	40.00	10.00	-
J6s	14	42.86	98.50	7.04	0.18	42.86	35.71	60.00
J6o	7	28.57	(371.00)	(53.00)	(1.29)	28.57	-	-
J5s	7	71.43	169.00	24.14	0.94	71.43	42.86	66.67
J5o	7	42.86	(79.50)	(11.36)	(0.61)	50.00	33.33	-
J4s	22	68.18	112.50	5.11	0.17	68.18	27.27	50.00
J4o	1	-	(15.00)	(15.00)	(0.50)	-	-	-
J3s	6	66.67	40.50	6.75	0.06	66.67	33.33	50.00
J3o	1	-	(15.00)	(15.00)	(0.50)	-	-	-
J2s	3	-	(16.00)	(5.33)	(0.84)	-	33.33	-
J2o	1	100.00	132.00	132.00	4.40	100.00	100.00	100.00
TT	2	50.00	(17.00)	(8.50)	0.08	50.00	100.00	50.00
T9o	23	73.91	364.75	15.86	0.80	73.91	30.43	85.71
T8s	6	33.33	(144.00)	(24.00)	(0.94)	33.33	33.33	-
T8o	16	31.25	(17.50)	(1.09)	(0.27)	31.25	25.00	50.00
T7s	10	50.00	199.00	19.90	0.98	50.00	40.00	75.00
T7o	11	54.55	50.20	4.56	(0.12)	54.55	27.27	66.67
T6s	17	52.94	(343.50)	(20.21)	(0.35)	52.94	29.41	20.00
T6o	9	44.44	93.00	10.33	0.30	44.44	22.22	100.00
T5s	10	50.00	313.50	31.35	0.37	50.00	50.00	40.00
T5o	6	16.67	(29.00)	(4.83)	(0.34)	16.67	-	-
T4s	5	40.00	1.00	0.20	(0.53)	40.00	20.00	-
T4o	1	100.00	58.00	58.00	1.93	100.00	-	-
T3s	3	33.33	3.00	1.00	0.77	33.33	33.33	100.00
T2s	3	66.67	2.25	0.75	0.14	66.67	-	-
T2o	1	-	(60.00)	(60.00)	(2.00)	-	100.00	-
99	1	100.00	53.00	53.00	1.77	100.00	-	-
98s	8	37.50	214.00	26.75	0.12	37.50	25.00	50.00
98o	33	66.67	355.50	10.77	0.31	66.67	24.24	62.50
97s	9	66.67	116.00	12.89	0.52	66.67	11.11	100.00
97o	17	52.94	(296.25)	(17.43)	(0.49)	52.94	17.65	-
96s	19	57.89	(29.00)	(1.53)	(0.16)	57.89	21.05	25.00
96o	6	16.67	(301.00)	(50.17)	(1.59)	16.67	33.33	-
95s	7	57.14	(59.25)	(8.46)	0.19	57.14	14.29	100.00
95o	4	50.00	(141.00)	(35.25)	(1.01)	50.00	50.00	-
94s	3	66.67	51.50	17.17	0.46	66.67	-	-
93s	7	42.86	(25.50)	(3.64)	0.02	42.86	57.14	25.00

92s	1	-	(3.00)	(3.00)	(0.50)	-	-	-
92o	1	-	(30.00)	(30.00)	(1.00)	-	-	-
88	1	-	(60.00)	(60.00)	(1.00)	-	-	-
87s	4	75.00	59.50	14.88	0.80	75.00	25.00	100.00
87o	37	56.76	150.25	4.06	0.14	56.76	43.24	56.25
86s	11	45.45	(304.25)	(27.66)	(0.65)	45.45	36.36	25.00
86o	10	50.00	550.00	55.00	1.14	50.00	30.00	100.00
85s	21	38.10	324.25	15.44	0.27	38.10	28.57	50.00
85o	2	-	(90.00)	(45.00)	(1.00)	-	-	-
84s	11	45.45	48.88	4.44	0.38	45.45	36.36	75.00
84o	2	100.00	11.75	5.88	0.45	100.00	-	-
83s	1	-	(3.00)	(3.00)	(0.50)	-	-	-
83o	1	-	(15.00)	(15.00)	(0.50)	-	-	-
82s	2	50.00	(1.00)	(0.50)	(0.02)	100.00	-	-
77	2	50.00	66.00	33.00	(1.03)	50.00	-	-
76s	10	40.00	39.25	3.93	(0.08)	40.00	30.00	33.33
76o	21	42.86	(296.50)	(14.12)	(0.35)	42.86	23.81	60.00
75s	14	57.14	89.82	6.42	0.32	57.14	42.86	33.33
75o	13	46.15	150.00	11.54	0.13	46.15	23.08	66.67
74s	17	35.29	(74.00)	(4.35)	(0.04)	35.29	11.76	100.00
74o	1	-	(15.00)	(15.00)	(1.50)	-	-	-
73s	5	40.00	(51.50)	(10.30)	(0.22)	40.00	20.00	-
73o	1	-	(15.00)	(15.00)	(0.50)	-	-	-
72s	1	-	(10.00)	(10.00)	(0.50)	-	-	-
65s	14	64.29	49.75	3.55	(0.09)	64.29	50.00	42.86
65o	10	90.00	211.75	21.18	1.38	90.00	30.00	100.00
64s	19	36.84	(491.00)	(25.84)	(0.94)	36.84	31.58	-
64o	1	-	(12.00)	(12.00)	(2.00)	-	-	-
63s	6	50.00	125.00	20.83	(0.27)	50.00	33.33	50.00
63o	2	-	(30.00)	(15.00)	(0.50)	-	-	-
62s	1	-	(0.50)	(0.50)	(0.50)	-	-	-
55	1	-	(10.00)	(10.00)	(0.50)	-	-	-
54s	15	53.33	(3.00)	(0.20)	0.13	53.33	13.33	50.00
54o	6	66.67	(147.25)	(24.54)	(0.72)	66.67	16.67	-
53s	9	55.56	(23.30)	(2.59)	0.21	55.56	11.11	-
53o	1	100.00	9.00	9.00	0.90	100.00	-	-
52s	5	40.00	(37.75)	(7.55)	(0.28)	40.00	-	-
52o	2	100.00	92.50	46.25	1.69	100.00	-	-
44	3	33.33	27.00	9.00	0.31	33.33	-	-
43s	10	80.00	705.00	70.50	1.83	80.00	20.00	100.00
43o	1	100.00	15.00	15.00	0.50	100.00	-	-
42s	5	20.00	(145.25)	(29.05)	(0.91)	20.00	-	-
33	4	25.00	(14.00)	(3.50)	(0.13)	25.00	-	-
32s	4	25.00	(17.50)	(4.38)	(0.89)	25.00	25.00	-

56 Part One: Pre-Flop Play

Hand	Trials	Win %	Amount ($)	Avg $/Hand	BB/ Hand	Win % WSF	Went to SD (%)	Won $ at SD (%)
32o	1	-	(0.50)	(0.50)	(0.50)	-	100.00	-
22	1	-	(0.50)	(0.50)	(0.50)	-	-	-
Total	1,120	52.59	2,897.75	2.59	0.09	52.87	30.43	51.33
Mid: Open-Fold From SB								
AKo	1	-	(2.50)	(2.50)	(0.25)	-	-	-
ATo	2	-	(7.50)	(3.75)	(0.25)	-	-	-
A7s	1	-	(2.50)	(2.50)	(0.25)	-	-	-
A5o	6	-	(34.00)	(5.67)	(0.24)	-	-	-
A4s	1	-	(2.50)	(2.50)	(0.25)	-	-	-
A4o	1	-	(20.00)	(20.00)	(0.50)	-	-	-
A3o	3	-	(6.75)	(2.25)	(0.25)	-	-	-
A2s	1	-	(15.00)	(15.00)	(0.25)	-	-	-
A2o	2	-	(25.00)	(12.50)	(0.25)	-	-	-
K9o	1	-	(1.50)	(1.50)	(0.25)	-	-	-
K8o	9	-	(43.50)	(4.83)	(0.22)	-	-	-
K7o	4	-	(22.25)	(5.56)	(0.24)	-	-	-
K6o	8	-	(60.25)	(7.53)	(0.27)	-	-	-
K5o	4	-	(27.50)	(6.88)	(0.25)	-	-	-
K4o	28	-	(112.50)	(4.02)	(0.24)	-	-	-
K3s	1	-	(2.00)	(2.00)	(0.20)	-	-	-
K3o	54	-	(229.00)	(4.24)	(0.25)	-	-	-
K2o	148	-	(748.00)	(5.05)	(0.25)	-	-	-
QJo	1	-	(1.50)	(1.50)	(0.25)	-	-	-
Q9o	2	-	(12.00)	(6.00)	(0.23)	-	-	-
Q8o	12	-	(42.50)	(3.54)	(0.23)	-	-	-
Q7o	59	-	(230.75)	(3.91)	(0.24)	-	-	-
Q6o	88	-	(352.00)	(4.00)	(0.25)	-	-	-
Q5o	90	-	(374.00)	(4.16)	(0.25)	-	-	-
Q4s	1	-	(2.50)	(2.50)	(0.25)	-	-	-
Q4o	136	-	(707.00)	(5.20)	(0.25)	-	-	-
Q3s	12	-	(49.50)	(4.13)	(0.25)	-	-	-
Q3o	167	-	(906.00)	(5.43)	(0.26)	-	-	-
Q2s	24	-	(67.50)	(2.81)	(0.24)	-	-	-
Q2o	199	-	(1,183.00)	(5.94)	(0.25)	-	-	-
JTo	2	-	(2.25)	(1.13)	(0.23)	-	-	-
J9o	3	-	(14.00)	(4.67)	(0.22)	-	-	-
J8o	17	-	(73.00)	(4.29)	(0.24)	-	-	-
J7o	84	-	(353.50)	(4.21)	(0.25)	-	-	-
J6s	8	-	(15.50)	(1.94)	(0.21)	-	-	-
J6o	151	-	(855.00)	(5.66)	(0.25)	-	-	-

J5s	6	-	(24.50)	(4.08)	(0.23)	-	-	-
J5o	179	-	(943.50)	(5.27)	(0.25)	-	-	-
J4s	25	-	(129.50)	(5.18)	(0.25)	-	-	-
J4o	166	-	(945.50)	(5.70)	(0.25)	-	-	-
J3s	39	-	(180.00)	(4.62)	(0.25)	-	-	-
J3o	199	-	(1,056.00)	(5.31)	(0.25)	-	-	-
J2s	41	-	(223.50)	(5.45)	(0.25)	-	-	-
J2o	177	-	(1,038.50)	(5.87)	(0.26)	-	-	-
T8o	22	-	(97.50)	(4.43)	(0.24)	-	-	-
T7o	104	-	(556.00)	(5.35)	(0.25)	-	-	-
T6s	4	-	(8.50)	(2.13)	(0.24)	-	-	-
T6o	143	-	(792.00)	(5.54)	(0.25)	-	-	-
T5s	14	-	(67.50)	(4.82)	(0.25)	-	-	-
T5o	161	-	(1,006.00)	(6.25)	(0.26)	-	-	-
T4s	44	-	(246.00)	(5.59)	(0.25)	-	-	-
T4o	209	-	(1,247.00)	(5.97)	(0.26)	-	-	-
T3s	70	-	(372.00)	(5.31)	(0.25)	-	-	-
T3o	189	-	(1,218.50)	(6.45)	(0.26)	-	-	-
T2s	52	-	(306.00)	(5.88)	(0.25)	-	-	-
T2o	186	-	(1,119.00)	(6.02)	(0.25)	-	-	-
98o	1	-	(2.00)	(2.00)	(0.20)	-	-	-
97o	98	-	(486.50)	(4.96)	(0.25)	-	-	-
96s	13	-	(54.50)	(4.19)	(0.24)	-	-	-
96o	166	-	(960.00)	(5.78)	(0.25)	-	-	-
95s	27	-	(129.00)	(4.78)	(0.25)	-	-	-
95o	198	-	(1,210.25)	(6.11)	(0.25)	-	-	-
94s	46	-	(276.50)	(6.01)	(0.26)	-	-	-
94o	193	-	(1,192.50)	(6.18)	(0.25)	-	-	-
93s	62	-	(369.50)	(5.96)	(0.26)	-	-	-
93o	212	-	(1,301.00)	(6.14)	(0.25)	-	-	-
92s	60	-	(357.50)	(5.96)	(0.26)	-	-	-
92o	188	-	(1,219.50)	(6.49)	(0.26)	-	-	-
87o	35	-	(176.00)	(5.03)	(0.25)	-	-	-
86s	1	-	(2.00)	(2.00)	(0.20)	-	-	-
86o	163	-	(875.75)	(5.37)	(0.25)	-	-	-
85s	21	-	(93.00)	(4.43)	(0.24)	-	-	-
85o	186	-	(1,075.50)	(5.78)	(0.25)	-	-	-
84s	43	-	(259.00)	(6.02)	(0.26)	-	-	-
84o	193	-	(1,081.50)	(5.60)	(0.26)	-	-	-
83s	73	-	(440.00)	(6.03)	(0.26)	-	-	-
83o	211	-	(1,236.25)	(5.86)	(0.25)	-	-	-
82s	76	-	(464.25)	(6.11)	(0.26)	-	-	-
82o	186	-	(1,130.00)	(6.08)	(0.26)	-	-	-
76o	81	-	(418.00)	(5.16)	(0.25)	-	-	-

Hand	Trials	Win %	Amount ($)	Avg $/Hand	BB/Hand	Win % WSF	Went to SD (%)	Won $ at SD (%)
75o	164	-	(985.50)	(6.01)	(0.25)	-	-	-
74s	29	-	(129.00)	(4.45)	(0.24)	-	-	-
74o	188	-	(1,202.00)	(6.39)	(0.26)	-	-	-
73s	56	-	(310.00)	(5.54)	(0.26)	-	-	-
73o	166	-	(934.25)	(5.63)	(0.25)	-	-	-
72s	56	-	(332.50)	(5.94)	(0.25)	-	-	-
72o	209	-	(1,243.50)	(5.95)	(0.25)	-	-	-
65o	147	-	(792.50)	(5.39)	(0.25)	-	-	-
64s	5	-	(27.00)	(5.40)	(0.25)	-	-	-
64o	170	-	(1,061.75)	(6.25)	(0.26)	-	-	-
63s	52	-	(283.00)	(5.44)	(0.26)	-	-	-
63o	193	-	(1,213.00)	(6.29)	(0.26)	-	-	-
62s	50	-	(259.00)	(5.18)	(0.25)	-	-	-
62o	204	-	(1,129.50)	(5.54)	(0.25)	-	-	-
54s	3	-	(9.00)	(3.00)	(0.25)	-	-	-
54o	161	-	(885.50)	(5.50)	(0.25)	-	-	-
53s	41	-	(261.50)	(6.38)	(0.25)	-	-	-
53o	171	-	(1,031.25)	(6.03)	(0.26)	-	-	-
52s	41	-	(223.00)	(5.44)	(0.25)	-	-	-
52o	190	-	(1,115.50)	(5.87)	(0.25)	-	-	-
43s	48	-	(278.00)	(5.79)	(0.26)	-	-	-
43o	187	-	(1,049.50)	(5.61)	(0.26)	-	-	-
42s	55	-	(335.00)	(6.09)	(0.25)	-	-	-
42o	182	-	(1,114.75)	(6.13)	(0.26)	-	-	-
32s	59	-	(288.50)	(4.89)	(0.25)	-	-	-
32o	187	-	(1,123.50)	(6.01)	(0.25)	-	-	-
Total	8,908	-	(50,608.25)	(5.68)	(0.25)	-	-	-

Grinder: Open-Raise From SB								
Hand	Trials	Win %	Amount ($)	Avg $/Hand	BB/Hand	Win % WSF	Went to SD (%)	Won $ at SD (%)
AA	18	94.4444	2,981.50	165.64	2.31	93.3333	53.3333	87.5
AKs	38	84.2105	3,185.00	83.82	0.95	78.5714	32.1429	66.6667
AKo	121	77.686	4,569.00	37.76	0.33	64.4737	52.6316	52.5
AQs	33	66.6667	(1,086.54)	(32.93)	(0.13)	54.1667	66.6667	37.5
AQo	127	77.1654	1,205.00	9.49	0.29	65.4762	36.9048	61.2903
AJs	43	88.3721	4,306.50	100.15	1.16	82.7586	55.1724	75
AJo	119	75.6303	3,443.00	28.93	0.39	66.6667	42.5287	51.3514
ATs	53	71.6981	966.00	18.23	0.20	63.4146	41.4634	47.0588
ATo	127	74.0157	2,094.00	16.49	0.30	60.7143	50	38.0952
A9s	37	75.6757	1,094.00	29.57	0.29	62.5	58.3333	64.2857
A9o	116	57.7586	(4,779.50)	(41.20)	(0.28)	43.0233	54.6512	36.1702
A8s	48	70.8333	(108.75)	(2.27)	0.20	57.5758	45.4545	66.6667

A8o	100	70	455.00	4.55	0.21	55.8824	51.4706	54.2857
A7s	32	81.25	1,568.50	49.02	0.64	70	50	70
A7o	107	75.7009	267.00	2.50	0.42	64.3836	47.9452	57.1429
A6s	25	76	2,475.00	99.00	0.86	73.913	43.4783	70
A6o	101	70.297	481.00	4.76	0.10	53.125	42.1875	40.7407
A5s	37	56.7568	(1,965.00)	(53.11)	(0.33)	38.4615	34.6154	33.3333
A5o	91	63.7363	679.50	7.47	0.16	45.9016	40.9836	36
A4s	28	82.1429	2,626.50	93.80	0.73	73.6842	31.5789	50
A4o	104	64.4231	(2,206.00)	(21.21)	(0.34)	47.1429	38.5714	22.2222
A3s	37	64.8649	(269.00)	(7.27)	(0.02)	51.8519	29.6296	25
A3o	102	72.549	3,595.00	35.25	0.37	60	41.4286	58.6207
A2s	44	70.4545	154.00	3.50	0.18	53.5714	50	50
A2o	93	67.7419	1,239.25	13.33	0.17	52.381	41.2698	50
KK	38	86.8421	2,811.00	73.97	0.97	79.1667	58.3333	64.2857
KQs	41	75.6098	4,421.00	107.83	0.69	62.963	40.7407	45.4545
KQo	104	71.1538	5,005.00	48.13	0.34	56.5217	44.9275	58.0645
KJs	33	75.7576	1,915.27	58.04	0.59	68	24	83.3333
KJo	102	70.5882	1,403.00	13.75	0.21	56.5217	24.6377	64.7059
KTs	38	78.9474	1,799.84	47.36	0.60	65.2174	30.4348	71.4286
KTo	90	68.8889	140.00	1.56	0.09	48.1481	29.6296	56.25
K9s	37	59.4595	(907.00)	(24.51)	(0.30)	42.3077	38.4615	30
K9o	98	68.3673	322.50	3.29	0.13	53.0303	25.7576	52.9412
K8s	31	61.2903	(1,223.50)	(39.47)	(0.30)	42.8571	33.3333	28.5714
K8o	96	67.7083	2,540.00	26.46	0.11	53.7313	31.3433	52.381
K7s	28	57.1429	650.50	23.23	0.32	47.8261	17.3913	75
K7o	98	69.3878	2,650.50	27.05	0.28	55.2239	35.8209	54.1667
K6s	26	57.6923	(960.00)	(36.92)	0.05	42.1053	31.5789	83.3333
K6o	94	56.383	(2,733.50)	(29.08)	(0.31)	39.7059	26.4706	33.3333
K5s	37	75.6757	1,765.00	47.70	0.22	62.5	20.8333	60
K5o	69	65.2174	(1,553.00)	(22.51)	(0.20)	50	22.9167	18.1818
K4s	28	60.7143	(742.00)	(26.50)	(0.23)	38.8889	11.1111	50
K4o	68	61.7647	(38.50)	(0.57)	0.14	48	36	55.5556
K3s	30	70	(366.50)	(12.22)	(0.03)	47.0588	5.8824	0
K3o	56	62.5	(738.00)	(13.18)	0.05	43.2432	27.027	50
K2s	34	67.6471	1,067.00	31.38	0.02	47.619	9.5238	50
K2o	29	58.6207	(145.00)	(5.00)	(0.31)	36.8421	36.8421	42.8571
QQ	49	81.6327	4,592.00	93.71	0.99	75.6757	51.3514	57.8947
QJs	38	50	(1,621.00)	(42.66)	(0.94)	32.1429	25	14.2857
QJo	108	72.2222	2,149.50	19.90	0.24	55.2239	28.3582	68.4211
QTs	26	65.3846	(820.00)	(31.54)	(0.21)	55	25	20
QTo	97	68.0412	1,473.50	15.19	0.18	58.1081	25.6757	57.8947
Q9s	34	64.7059	651.50	19.16	0.10	53.8462	46.1538	50
Q9o	90	56.6667	(2,890.00)	(32.11)	(0.27)	39.0625	25	31.25
Q8s	27	77.7778	1,027.00	38.04	0.33	64.7059	41.1765	42.8571

Q8o	85	63.5294	1,430.00	16.82	(0.01)	48.3333	20	50
Q7s	31	58.0645	(1,016.00)	(32.77)	(0.12)	31.5789	15.7895	33.3333
Q7o	26	38.4615	(1,220.00)	(46.92)	(0.78)	23.8095	28.5714	33.3333
Q6s	29	62.069	432.00	14.90	(0.20)	47.619	28.5714	33.3333
Q6o	22	59.0909	(35.00)	(1.59)	0.14	50	27.7778	80
Q5s	41	56.0976	(396.00)	(9.66)	0.02	37.931	24.1379	42.8571
Q5o	17	52.9412	605.50	35.62	(0.23)	46.6667	20	0
Q4s	21	57.1429	(838.00)	(39.90)	(0.06)	43.75	25	50
Q4o	8	62.5	(139.50)	(17.44)	(0.58)	40	20	0
Q3s	24	58.3333	357.50	14.90	0.21	44.4444	27.7778	40
Q3o	11	81.8182	244.50	22.23	0.65	71.4286	14.2857	100
Q2s	16	62.5	(178.00)	(11.13)	(0.23)	33.3333	11.1111	0
Q2o	4	50	(105.00)	(26.25)	(0.50)	0	0	0
JJ	55	76.3636	2,365.00	43.00	0.48	63.8889	55.5556	60
JTs	33	69.697	(206.00)	(6.24)	(0.06)	44.4444	16.6667	33.3333
JTo	103	61.165	(1,911.00)	(18.55)	(0.18)	44.4444	30.5556	40.9091
J9s	34	67.6471	1,460.00	42.94	(0.07)	47.619	38.0952	62.5
J9o	86	65.1163	(1,665.50)	(19.37)	(0.03)	47.3684	28.0702	43.75
J8s	25	76	12.50	0.50	0.29	57.1429	28.5714	25
J8o	42	61.9048	99.50	2.37	(0.21)	44.8276	41.3793	33.3333
J7s	26	50	(2,156.00)	(82.92)	(0.51)	18.75	50	12.5
J7o	12	75	550.00	45.83	0.77	62.5	37.5	66.6667
J6s	19	42.1053	(1,446.00)	(76.11)	(0.89)	42.1053	21.0526	25
J6o	6	83.3333	127.00	21.17	0.57	66.6667	0	0
J5s	18	66.6667	983.00	54.61	0.29	50	33.3333	50
J5o	2	50	(105.00)	(52.50)	(0.75)	0	0	0
J4s	5	80	115.50	23.10	0.68	66.6667	33.3333	100
J4o	1	0	(1.50)	(1.50)	(0.05)	0	100	0
J3s	8	62.5	136.50	17.06	0.56	57.1429	28.5714	100
J3o	1	100	15.00	15.00	0.50	0	0	0
J2s	3	33.3333	(375.00)	(125.00)	(1.33)	0	50	0
TT	42	90.4762	4,236.00	100.86	1.25	86.2069	44.8276	76.9231
T9s	24	75	3,081.50	128.40	0.83	71.4286	23.8095	60
T9o	56	62.5	(1,918.50)	(34.26)	(0.12)	46.1538	28.2051	36.3636
T8s	22	63.6364	(1,404.50)	(63.84)	(0.47)	42.8571	14.2857	0
T8o	35	54.2857	(1,039.50)	(29.70)	(0.34)	33.3333	12.5	33.3333
T7s	23	78.2609	263.50	11.46	0.18	61.5385	7.6923	100
T7o	10	70	769.00	76.90	0.49	50	16.6667	100
T6s	22	81.8182	1,303.50	59.25	0.66	69.2308	30.7692	75
T6o	3	66.6667	277.00	92.33	1.45	66.6667	66.6667	100
T5s	12	66.6667	538.00	44.83	0.24	55.5556	44.4444	50
T5o	2	100	273.50	136.75	1.70	100	0	0
T4s	11	54.5455	(246.00)	(22.36)	0.04	28.5714	28.5714	50
T4o	2	50	(123.00)	(61.50)	(1.03)	50	0	0

T3s	3	33.3333	(93.00)	(31.00)	(0.51)	33.3333	0	0
T2s	5	80	(42.50)	(8.50)	1.36	75	25	100
99	56	75	3,742.50	66.83	0.81	68.1818	52.2727	65.2174
98s	23	60.8696	(1,031.00)	(44.83)	(0.62)	40	40	33.3333
98o	53	60.3774	(1,015.00)	(19.15)	(0.25)	46.1538	33.3333	30.7692
97s	21	61.9048	306.00	14.57	0.02	52.9412	23.5294	25
97o	20	65	379.50	18.98	(0.16)	41.6667	25	0
96s	22	77.2727	3,806.50	173.02	1.14	71.4286	35.7143	100
96o	6	33.3333	(960.50)	(160.08)	(1.58)	0	50	0
95s	14	42.8571	(765.00)	(54.64)	(0.58)	33.3333	16.6667	50
95o	3	100	45.00	15.00	0.50	0	0	0
94s	6	50	(225.00)	(37.50)	(0.84)	25	25	0
94o	2	100	30.00	15.00	0.50	0	0	0
93s	5	60	(270.00)	(54.00)	(0.90)	0	0	0
92s	1	100	495.00	495.00	4.95	100	0	0
88	44	75	2,895.50	65.81	0.57	68.5714	51.4286	55.5556
87s	38	71.0526	1,773.00	46.66	0.18	52.1739	26.087	50
87o	22	40.9091	(2,523.50)	(114.70)	(0.94)	23.5294	23.5294	25
86s	29	65.5172	1,312.50	45.26	0.33	52.381	33.3333	57.1429
86o	11	54.5455	(575.00)	(52.27)	(0.73)	28.5714	14.2857	0
85s	9	66.6667	398.00	44.22	0.16	50	16.6667	100
84s	5	60	(523.00)	(104.60)	0.67	50	75	66.6667
83s	1	100	30.00	30.00	0.50	0	0	0
82o	1	100	87.00	87.00	2.90	100	100	100
77	40	70	(614.00)	(15.35)	(0.05)	55.5556	33.3333	55.5556
76s	17	52.9412	(1,155.00)	(67.94)	(0.86)	42.8571	42.8571	16.6667
76o	10	90	465.00	46.50	0.28	80	20	0
75s	9	55.5556	(676.00)	(75.11)	(0.29)	50	37.5	33.3333
75o	2	0	(345.00)	(172.50)	(2.25)	0	100	0
74s	11	72.7273	380.00	34.55	(0.24)	62.5	50	50
73s	4	75	217.00	54.25	0.74	50	100	50
73o	1	100	15.00	15.00	0.50	0	0	0
72o	1	0	(60.00)	(60.00)	(2.00)	0	0	0
66	47	61.7021	(1,955.00)	(41.60)	(0.27)	45.4545	54.5455	33.3333
65s	14	71.4286	808.50	57.75	0.59	55.5556	55.5556	60
65o	1	0	(45.00)	(45.00)	(1.50)	0	0	0
64s	18	77.7778	1,037.00	57.61	0.54	60	20	50
64o	2	50	(121.50)	(60.75)	(0.28)	50	0	0
63s	1	100	147.00	147.00	4.90	100	100	100
55	44	50	(445.00)	(10.11)	(0.14)	45	37.5	40
54s	11	54.5455	(740.00)	(67.27)	(1.05)	44.4444	22.2222	0
53s	2	100	310.00	155.00	0.99	100	0	0
53o	1	100	15.00	15.00	0.50	0	0	0
52o	1	100	15.00	15.00	0.50	0	0	0

44	40	65	(87.00)	(2.18)	(0.25)	44	44	36.3636
43s	2	50	(402.00)	(201.00)	0.73	50	100	50
42o	1	100	57.00	57.00	0.95	100	0	0
33	48	62.5	2,988.00	62.25	0.23	50	22.2222	50
22	34	50	(611.00)	(17.97)	(0.52)	29.1667	29.1667	28.5714
Total	5,395	67.73	58,241.57	10.80	0.13	53.29	35.76	48.95

			Grinder: Open-Call From SB					
Hand	**Trials**	**Win %**	**Amount ($)**	**Avg $/Hand**	**BB/ Hand**	**Win % WSF**	**Went to SD (%)**	**Won $ at SD (%)**
AA	53	84.9057	4,903.00	92.51	1.19	85	47	68
AKs	1	100	237.00	237.00	3.95	100	100	100
AKo	1	100	207.00	207.00	3.45	100	100	100
ATs	1	0	(15.00)	(15.00)	(0.50)	-	-	-
ATo	3	33.3333	(16.00)	(5.33)	(0.18)	33	-	-
A9s	1	0	(15.00)	(15.00)	(0.50)	-	-	-
A9o	7	14.2857	(303.00)	(43.29)	(0.83)	17	17	-
A8o	2	50	83.00	41.50	0.24	50	50	100
A7s	1	0	(15.00)	(15.00)	(0.50)	-	-	-
A7o	4	0	(145.00)	(36.25)	(0.50)	-	-	-
A6s	1	0	(210.00)	(210.00)	(3.50)	-	100	-
A6o	4	75	160.00	40.00	1.33	75	25	100
A5s	1	0	(60.00)	(60.00)	(1.00)	-	100	-
A5o	8	25	(0.50)	(0.06)	(0.11)	25	13	100
A4o	11	9.0909	(503.00)	(45.73)	(0.87)	13	-	-
A3s	2	50	117.00	58.50	0.98	50	100	50
A3o	4	0	(455.00)	(113.75)	(1.75)	-	33	-
A2o	4	25	32.00	8.00	0.61	25	25	100
KK	24	75	33.00	1.38	0.23	75	38	44
KQo	3	33.3333	(7.50)	(2.50)	(0.01)	33	-	-
KJs	2	0	(130.00)	(65.00)	(0.75)	-	-	-
KJo	5	40	322.50	64.50	0.38	40	20	100
KTs	1	100	98.50	98.50	0.99	100	-	-
KTo	6	16.6667	(128.00)	(21.33)	(0.76)	17	-	-
K9o	5	20	(306.50)	(61.30)	(1.05)	20	20	-
K8s	2	0	(60.00)	(30.00)	(0.50)	-	-	-
K8o	10	30	(378.50)	(37.85)	(0.51)	30	10	-
K7s	3	0	(360.00)	(120.00)	(2.17)	-	33	-
K7o	13	7.6923	(367.50)	(28.27)	(0.54)	10	10	-
K6s	4	50	82.50	20.63	0.24	67	33	100
K6o	14	28.5714	(277.50)	(19.82)	(0.47)	29	36	40
K5s	2	50	57.00	28.50	0.48	50	-	-
K5o	12	16.6667	(656.00)	(54.67)	(0.96)	17	-	-

K4s	4	50	99.00	24.75	0.95	67	-	-
K4o	10	70	248.50	24.85	0.39	70	40	75
K3s	2	50	(21.50)	(10.75)	(0.51)	50	-	-
K3o	13	61.5385	195.00	15.00	0.25	62	23	33
K2s	5	0	(315.00)	(63.00)	(1.40)	-	20	-
K2o	8	37.5	(434.00)	(54.25)	(0.95)	43	29	-
QQ	9	88.8889	1,018.50	113.17	1.52	89	56	80
QJo	8	25	(239.50)	(29.94)	(0.45)	29	29	50
QTs	1	0	(180.00)	(180.00)	(3.00)	-	100	-
QTo	4	0	(135.00)	(33.75)	(0.88)	-	25	-
Q9s	3	66.6667	204.00	68.00	1.45	67	-	-
Q9o	12	66.6667	110.00	9.17	0.40	80	10	100
Q8s	1	0	(15.00)	(15.00)	(0.50)	-	100	-
Q8o	9	55.5556	(229.00)	(25.44)	0.14	63	13	-
Q7s	3	0	(380.00)	(126.67)	(1.33)	-	-	-
Q7o	16	50	(40.50)	(2.53)	(0.10)	53	7	-
Q6s	1	100	207.00	207.00	3.45	100	100	100
Q6o	14	35.7143	(289.00)	(20.64)	(0.30)	36	14	50
Q5s	2	50	(75.00)	(37.50)	(0.50)	50	50	-
Q5o	8	50	303.00	37.88	0.65	57	71	60
Q4s	5	60	(43.00)	(8.60)	(0.01)	60	-	-
Q4o	12	66.6667	(23.00)	(1.92)	0.15	73	9	100
Q3s	5	20	(171.50)	(34.30)	(0.41)	20	-	-
Q3o	13	53.8462	(62.50)	(4.81)	0.06	50	8	100
Q2s	7	71.4286	176.50	25.21	0.54	71	29	100
Q2o	6	66.6667	99.00	16.50	0.72	67	33	100
JJ	1	100	147.00	147.00	1.47	100	-	-
JTs	1	0	(30.00)	(30.00)	(0.50)	-	-	-
JTo	15	33.3333	112.50	7.50	0.11	33	13	50
J9s	2	50	(57.00)	(28.50)	0.22	50	-	-
J9o	15	33.3333	(236.00)	(15.73)	(0.24)	36	7	-
J8s	3	0	(330.00)	(110.00)	(2.00)	-	33	-
J8o	25	48	(712.50)	(28.50)	(0.04)	46	25	50
J7s	11	45.4545	(305.00)	(27.73)	(0.42)	45	9	-
J7o	11	54.5455	114.50	10.41	0.34	55	27	67
J6s	6	16.6667	(23.00)	(3.83)	(0.26)	17	17	100
J6o	12	41.6667	(234.33)	(19.53)	(0.22)	42	25	33
J5s	9	55.5556	(244.00)	(27.11)	(0.29)	56	11	-
J5o	10	50	19.00	1.90	0.24	56	11	100
J4s	12	66.6667	(274.00)	(22.83)	(0.10)	67	17	50
J4o	9	11.1111	(301.50)	(33.50)	(0.73)	13	-	-
J3s	7	71.4286	63.00	9.00	0.83	71	14	100
J3o	10	30	11.00	1.10	(0.36)	30	50	20
J2s	8	25	(119.00)	(14.88)	(0.63)	25	38	33

J2o	11	54.5455	(63.50)	(5.77)	(0.15)	55	9	-
T9s	2	50	(235.00)	(117.50)	(1.00)	-	100	-
T9o	32	59.375	33.50	1.05	0.01	59	22	57
T8s	10	40	(139.50)	(13.95)	(0.01)	44	22	50
T8o	26	50	(633.50)	(24.37)	(0.26)	48	12	100
T7s	7	71.4286	33.00	4.71	0.45	71	57	50
T7o	23	47.8261	(116.00)	(5.04)	(0.25)	48	13	67
T6s	3	66.6667	0.00	0.00	-	67	33	100
T6o	14	57.1429	(6.50)	(0.46)	0.04	57	14	50
T5s	8	62.5	(316.00)	(39.50)	(0.10)	63	50	50
T5o	14	21.4286	(400.00)	(28.57)	(0.71)	21	7	-
T4s	8	50	292.50	36.56	0.58	50	38	100
T4o	18	44.4444	(256.00)	(14.22)	(0.28)	50	-	-
T3s	6	33.3333	(478.00)	(79.67)	(0.93)	33	50	-
T3o	15	33.3333	(83.00)	(5.53)	(0.18)	33	20	33
T2s	8	50	(776.00)	(97.00)	0.17	50	25	50
T2o	7	57.1429	8.00	1.14	(0.03)	57	-	-
98s	5	60	104.00	20.80	0.48	60	-	-
98o	27	37.037	39.50	1.46	(0.09)	38	23	33
97s	7	57.1429	489.50	69.93	1.61	57	29	100
97o	26	50	(581.50)	(22.37)	(0.21)	52	20	40
96s	10	70	739.50	73.95	1.23	70	40	100
96o	23	52.1739	(456.00)	(19.83)	(0.58)	57	33	43
95s	16	56.25	(59.50)	(3.72)	0.07	60	20	67
95o	14	35.7143	(378.00)	(27.00)	(0.86)	42	33	25
94s	8	62.5	180.50	22.56	0.07	63	25	50
94o	14	50	(304.50)	(21.75)	(0.47)	54	15	50
93s	9	33.3333	(343.00)	(38.11)	(0.67)	33	11	-
93o	7	57.1429	42.00	6.00	0.20	57	-	-
92s	8	62.5	8.00	1.00	(0.09)	63	25	50
92o	12	41.6667	(276.00)	(23.00)	(0.38)	50	20	-
87s	7	28.5714	(96.50)	(13.79)	(0.65)	29	14	-
87o	27	55.5556	791.50	29.31	0.36	56	15	75
86s	10	50	(180.50)	(18.05)	(0.46)	50	20	-
86o	21	42.8571	(720.50)	(34.31)	(0.63)	43	19	25
85s	22	54.5455	73.50	3.34	(0.06)	55	14	33
85o	11	54.5455	(33.00)	(3.00)	(0.14)	55	9	-
84s	7	28.5714	(304.50)	(43.50)	(1.01)	29	29	50
84o	7	28.5714	(150.00)	(21.43)	(0.71)	29	29	-
83s	9	22.2222	(19.00)	(2.11)	(0.12)	22	22	50
83o	12	66.6667	85.00	7.08	0.32	73	9	100
82s	4	0	(480.00)	(120.00)	(2.13)	-	50	-
82o	11	45.4545	(136.50)	(12.41)	(0.41)	56	11	100
76s	6	50	21.50	3.58	0.24	50	17	100

Hand	Trials	Win %	Amount ($)	Avg $/Hand	BB/Hand	Win % WSF	Went to SD (%)	Won $ at SD (%)
76o	16	43.75	29.00	1.81	0.26	44	19	67
75s	15	40	(586.00)	(39.07)	(0.28)	40	-	-
75o	9	33.3333	(530.00)	(58.89)	(0.73)	33	44	25
74s	10	50	(430.00)	(43.00)	(0.31)	50	30	33
74o	13	38.4615	(329.00)	(25.31)	(0.42)	45	27	33
73s	10	40	(341.00)	(34.10)	(0.36)	40	10	100
73o	8	50	160.00	20.00	0.55	50	25	50
72s	1	0	(15.00)	(15.00)	(0.50)	-	-	-
72o	5	60	13.50	2.70	0.09	60	20	100
65s	5	20	(122.00)	(24.40)	(1.10)	20	-	-
65o	21	57.1429	723.00	34.43	0.36	57	14	100
64s	16	43.75	(550.00)	(34.38)	(0.36)	44	31	40
64o	8	25	(353.00)	(44.13)	(0.89)	25	38	33
63s	14	35.7143	(1,344.50)	(96.04)	(1.01)	36	21	-
63o	13	61.5385	115.00	8.85	0.29	62	8	100
62s	6	66.6667	(136.50)	(22.75)	(0.34)	67	-	-
62o	9	22.2222	(211.50)	(23.50)	(0.67)	25	13	100
55	1	100	87.00	87.00	2.90	100	100	100
54s	16	31.25	(518.50)	(32.41)	(0.63)	31	25	25
54o	19	26.3158	(322.00)	(16.95)	(0.48)	28	6	-
53s	12	50	(161.00)	(13.42)	(0.54)	50	25	67
53o	7	14.2857	(105.75)	(15.11)	(0.50)	20	20	-
52s	9	33.3333	(239.00)	(26.56)	(0.01)	33	22	-
52o	7	57.1429	115.50	16.50	0.55	57	14	100
43s	14	42.8571	(271.50)	(19.39)	(0.09)	43	43	33
43o	6	50	42.00	7.00	0.23	75	-	-
42s	5	60	341.00	68.20	0.57	60	20	100
42o	12	41.6667	(243.00)	(20.25)	(0.68)	42	17	-
33	3	33.3333	(153.00)	(51.00)	(0.85)	33	-	-
32s	8	25	(1,006.75)	(125.84)	(1.35)	25	63	20
32o	9	11.1111	(300.00)	(33.33)	(1.11)	13	25	-
22	3	66.6667	42.50	14.17	0.47	67	33	100
Total	1,425	45.68	(12,149.83)	(8.53)	(0.13)	47	21	48

Grinder: Open-Fold From SB								
Hand	Trials	Win %	Amount ($)	Avg $/Hand	BB/Hand	Win % WSF	Went to SD (%)	Won $ at SD (%)
AQo	1	0	(20.00)	(20.00)	(0.20)	0	0	0
A9o	1	0	(15.00)	(15.00)	(0.50)	0	0	0
A7o	1	0	(50.00)	(50.00)	(0.50)	0	0	0
A6o	1	0	(25.00)	(25.00)	(0.25)	0	0	0
A4o	4	0	(85.00)	(21.25)	(0.44)	0	0	0
A3o	1	0	(15.00)	(15.00)	(0.50)	0	0	0

A2o	6	0	(155.00)	(25.83)	(0.25)	0	0	0
K9o	1	0	(25.00)	(25.00)	(0.25)	0	0	0
K8o	1	0	(15.00)	(15.00)	(0.25)	0	0	0
K7o	13	0	(265.00)	(20.38)	(0.31)	0	0	0
K6s	1	0	(30.00)	(30.00)	(0.50)	0	0	0
K6o	7	0	(115.00)	(16.43)	(0.25)	0	0	0
K5o	32	0	(630.00)	(19.69)	(0.25)	0	0	0
K4s	1	0	(30.00)	(30.00)	(0.50)	0	0	0
K4o	25	0	(592.00)	(23.68)	(0.25)	0	0	0
K3o	51	0	(1,142.00)	(22.39)	(0.25)	0	0	0
K2s	1	0	(10.00)	(10.00)	(0.25)	0	0	0
K2o	76	0	(1,904.00)	(25.05)	(0.25)	0	0	0
QJo	1	0	(50.00)	(50.00)	(0.50)	0	0	0
Q9o	6	0	(105.00)	(17.50)	(0.33)	0	0	0
Q8o	20	0	(565.00)	(28.25)	(0.27)	0	0	0
Q7s	1	0	(10.00)	(10.00)	(0.33)	0	0	0
Q7o	64	0	(1,485.00)	(23.20)	(0.26)	0	0	0
Q6o	73	0	(1,710.00)	(23.42)	(0.25)	0	0	0
Q5o	82	0	(1,715.00)	(20.91)	(0.26)	0	0	0
Q4s	4	0	(40.00)	(10.00)	(0.27)	0	0	0
Q4o	79	0	(1,845.00)	(23.35)	(0.26)	0	0	0
Q3o	72	0	(1,760.00)	(24.44)	(0.25)	0	0	0
Q2s	7	0	(160.00)	(22.86)	(0.26)	0	0	0
Q2o	81	0	(1,830.00)	(22.59)	(0.25)	0	0	0
JTo	1	0	(15.00)	(15.00)	(0.25)	0	0	0
J9o	9	0	(165.00)	(18.33)	(0.28)	0	0	0
J8o	40	0	(990.00)	(24.75)	(0.26)	0	0	0
J7s	3	0	(55.00)	(18.33)	(0.25)	0	0	0
J7o	60	0	(1,490.00)	(24.83)	(0.25)	0	0	0
J6s	2	0	(50.00)	(25.00)	(0.25)	0	0	0
J6o	88	0	(2,040.00)	(23.18)	(0.25)	0	0	0
J5s	15	0	(335.00)	(22.33)	(0.26)	0	0	0
J5o	75	0	(1,920.00)	(25.60)	(0.26)	0	0	0
J4s	13	0	(265.00)	(20.38)	(0.25)	0	0	0
J4o	90	0	(2,112.00)	(23.47)	(0.26)	0	0	0
J3s	8	0	(215.00)	(26.88)	(0.26)	0	0	0
J3o	67	0	(1,490.00)	(22.24)	(0.25)	0	0	0
J2s	15	0	(395.00)	(26.33)	(0.25)	0	0	0
J2o	101	0	(2,162.00)	(21.41)	(0.26)	0	0	0
T9o	21	0	(395.00)	(18.81)	(0.26)	0	0	0
T8s	1	0	(15.00)	(15.00)	(0.50)	0	0	0
T8o	29	0	(575.00)	(19.83)	(0.26)	0	0	0
T7o	74	0	(1,800.00)	(24.32)	(0.26)	0	0	0
T6s	2	0	(30.00)	(15.00)	(0.25)	0	0	0

T6o	69	0	(1,715.00)	(24.86)	(0.25)	0	0	0
T5s	12	0	(245.00)	(20.42)	(0.26)	0	0	0
T5o	75	0	(1,665.00)	(22.20)	(0.25)	0	0	0
T4s	17	0	(330.00)	(19.41)	(0.25)	0	0	0
T4o	88	0	(2,082.00)	(23.66)	(0.26)	0	0	0
T3s	16	0	(342.00)	(21.38)	(0.25)	0	0	0
T3o	82	0	(1,855.00)	(22.62)	(0.25)	0	0	0
T2s	18	0	(400.00)	(22.22)	(0.25)	0	0	0
T2o	96	0	(2,040.00)	(21.25)	(0.26)	0	0	0
98s	1	0	(10.00)	(10.00)	(0.33)	0	0	0
98o	33	0	(630.00)	(19.09)	(0.26)	0	0	0
97o	67	0	(1,415.00)	(21.12)	(0.26)	0	0	0
96s	2	0	(50.00)	(25.00)	(0.25)	0	0	0
96o	85	0	(1,940.00)	(22.82)	(0.26)	0	0	0
95s	12	0	(242.00)	(20.17)	(0.27)	0	0	0
95o	90	0	(2,145.00)	(23.83)	(0.26)	0	0	0
94s	15	0	(285.00)	(19.00)	(0.26)	0	0	0
94o	93	0	(2,170.00)	(23.33)	(0.26)	0	0	0
93s	20	0	(370.00)	(18.50)	(0.26)	0	0	0
93o	65	0	(1,535.00)	(23.62)	(0.26)	0	0	0
92s	25	0	(575.00)	(23.00)	(0.25)	0	0	0
92o	100	0	(2,290.00)	(22.90)	(0.26)	0	0	0
87o	41	0	(875.00)	(21.34)	(0.26)	0	0	0
86o	76	0	(1,700.00)	(22.37)	(0.26)	0	0	0
85s	6	0	(145.00)	(24.17)	(0.28)	0	0	0
85o	91	0	(1,987.00)	(21.84)	(0.25)	0	0	0
84s	10	0	(200.00)	(20.00)	(0.25)	0	0	0
84o	72	0	(1,687.00)	(23.43)	(0.25)	0	0	0
83s	18	0	(400.00)	(22.22)	(0.25)	0	0	0
83o	100	0	(2,175.00)	(21.75)	(0.26)	0	0	0
82s	30	0	(575.00)	(19.17)	(0.25)	0	0	0
82o	80	0	(1,700.00)	(21.25)	(0.26)	0	0	0
76o	53	0	(1,212.00)	(22.87)	(0.25)	0	0	0
75s	3	0	(50.00)	(16.67)	(0.25)	0	0	0
75o	74	0	(1,815.00)	(24.53)	(0.26)	0	0	0
74s	15	0	(255.00)	(17.00)	(0.27)	0	0	0
74o	70	0	(1,532.00)	(21.89)	(0.26)	0	0	0
73s	23	0	(600.00)	(26.09)	(0.26)	0	0	0
73o	84	0	(1,845.00)	(21.96)	(0.26)	0	0	0
72s	34	0	(785.00)	(23.09)	(0.26)	0	0	0
72o	70	0	(1,590.00)	(22.71)	(0.25)	0	0	0
65o	82	0	(1,860.00)	(22.68)	(0.26)	0	0	0
64s	5	0	(70.00)	(14.00)	(0.27)	0	0	0
64o	87	0	(2,150.00)	(24.71)	(0.25)	0	0	0

63s	17	0	(360.00)	(21.18)	(0.26)	0	0	0
63o	81	0	(1,810.00)	(22.35)	(0.25)	0	0	0
62s	27	0	(620.00)	(22.96)	(0.26)	0	0	0
62o	96	0	(2,305.00)	(24.01)	(0.26)	0	0	0
54s	3	0	(75.00)	(25.00)	(0.25)	0	0	0
54o	88	0	(2,010.00)	(22.84)	(0.26)	0	0	0
53s	14	0	(295.00)	(21.07)	(0.25)	0	0	0
53o	94	0	(1,965.00)	(20.90)	(0.26)	0	0	0
52s	24	0	(460.00)	(19.17)	(0.25)	0	0	0
52o	82	0	(1,880.00)	(22.93)	(0.26)	0	0	0
43s	14	0	(350.00)	(25.00)	(0.26)	0	0	0
43o	80	0	(1,697.00)	(21.21)	(0.26)	0	0	0
42s	26	0	(515.00)	(19.81)	(0.25)	0	0	0
42o	82	0	(1,750.00)	(21.34)	(0.26)	0	0	0
32s	22	0	(480.00)	(21.82)	(0.25)	0	0	0
32o	81	0	(1,705.00)	(21.05)	(0.26)	0	0	0
22	8	0	(125.00)	(15.63)	(0.26)	0	0	0
Total	4,472	0	(100,853.00)	(22.55)	(0.26)	0	0	0

The results in the individual hand charts above suggest that we should open-raise with an even wider range than both the high-limit and mid-limit player used (High = 59 percent and Mid = 54 percent). However, the analysis is difficult, and there are going to be some contradictions in the data because we have no information about the big blind which is essential in deciding whether to raise or fold the marginal holdings. Using an empirical approach to determine an open-raising range from the small blind, we would arrive at the following for each player:

High: 33+, A2s+, A2o+, K2s+, K2o+, Q2s+, Q5o+, J4s+, J5o+, T5s+, T7o+, 96s+, 96o+, 85s+, and 86o+.

Mid: 33+, A2s+, A2o+, K2s+, K2o+, Q2s+, Q3o+, J2s+, J6o+, T5s+, T6o+, 96s+, 97o+, 85s+, and 86o+.

Grinder: 33+, A2s+, A2o+, K2s+, K2o+, Q2s+, Q5o+, J5s+, J6o+, T4s+, T5o+, 96s+, 97o+, 85s+, and 86o+.

We can combine these to produce the following "default" opening range to be used against an unknown opponent: 33+, A2s+, A2o+, K2s+, K2o+, Q2s+, Q5o+, J4s+, J6o+, T5s+, T7o+, 96s+, 97o+, 85s+, 86o+, 75s+, 75o+, and 65s.

Notes About the Ranges

Surprisingly, a pair of deuces was a loser for all of these players when they open-raised from the small blind. The high-limit player lost 0.36 big bets per trial, the mid-limit player lost 0.26 big bets per trial, and the full-ring grinder lost 0.52 big bets per trial. Additionally, the high-limit player lost 0.75 big bets per trial with a pair of treys, which makes deuces appear even weaker. This is certainly contrary to the popular thought that any pair is worth a raise in a heads-up blind battle.

We also initially hypothesized that the high-limit player was open-raising too often at 59 percent of his hands. However, using the individual hand data, we came up with a default open-raising range even wider than that at almost 63 percent. This range is likely skewed towards the loose side since the weakest open-raising hands were favored by players in spots where the big blind played sub-optimally — either because he folded too often pre-flop, or played poorly post-flop. This would cause us to overstate the average expectation of weaker hands in this situation.

It should also be noted that this open-raising chart cannot determine whether raising is better than calling, only that raising is better than folding. However, we have seen that a large part of the value derived from playing these hands comes from stealing the big blind, so we can assume that open-raising is generally better than open-calling.

Isolating a Loose Player

When a loose player has limped ahead of you, you should raise with a lot more hands than you would if the limper was a good player. The reason for this is there is extra value in being in a pot with a player that will call post-flop bets to chase draws to a single overcard, inside straights, or backdoor flushes.

However, you should not take this concept too far because you still must consider that the players yet to act might wake up with a big hand. We recommend that you relax what would be your opening standards by one position. For example, if you are 3 seats off the button with

and a loose player limps in front of you, you should raise to isolate (we normally recommend that you open-raise with this hand 2 seats off the button). However, ace-six offsuit or worse is probably too weak from this position and should be folded.

Also, you should not raise to isolate with hands that have little showdown value and play better multi-way. An example is ten-eight suited. With these hands, you should just overlimp and hope to hit a favorable flop.

Besides being more inclined to isolate a loose player with a hand that has showdown value, such as an ace or pocket pair, you should also be more inclined to isolate an opponent who plays passively post-flop because he will be easier to play against. Again though, if a loose-aggressive player limps in front of you, you should still relax your opening requirements — particularly, with hands that have showdown value. This is because a loose-aggressive player would likely raise with his stronger hands, so your hand should have a large edge when he only limps.

Re-Stealing

When aggressive players open the pot from the hijack (2 seats off the button), or cutoff, they may be trying to steal with a marginal holding. When you are in the cutoff or button and are faced with such a situation, you can profit by three-betting with hands that figure to be a favorite, or even a slight underdog, against your opponents' range of hands. It may be surprising that you should three-bet as a slight underdog. However, you have an excellent chance of getting heads up which will create dead money from the blinds; plus, you will have positional advantage on your opponent for the rest of the hand.

It should be noted that you can apply this concept only up to a point. If the original raiser's range is very wide, you actually do need to be a favorite because the bottom part of your range will be so weak that it suffers terribly when a third player enters the pot.

In other words, there is a lower bound on the hands with which you should be willing to re-steal because of the chance that one of the players yet to act behind you might hold a big hand. For example, if you are in the cutoff with

and the player in the hijack (who is raising 100 percent of his hands) open-raises, your hand is a favorite against his range. However, you should fold because it is not strong enough when you consider there are players yet to act.

Many players prefer to cold-call in this situation with their strong, but not premium, hands. This is usually a mistake because you give up the opportunity to force out the blinds and create dead money in the pot. Cold calling should rarely be used if you are first or even second in after the original raiser and should be reserved for situations where there is a multi-way pot brewing — you are playing for implied odds. (Possible exceptions are hands like ace-jack suited and king-queen suited with three or more players still to act behind you.) For example, it might be correct to cold call a raise with A♠8♠ against a steal-raise from the cutoff depending on the stealers' tendencies. However, a hand like

should definitely be three-bet. Occasionally, you should cold call with aces and kings, but only against a thinking player where the deception it creates has the most value. This should provide a return that offsets the equity advantage you have foregone by not putting extra money into the pot pre-flop.

In general, when deciding whether to three-bet, the most important factor is, as usual, your own cards. However, the pre-flop raising range of your opponent and his position are important as well. Basically, you should try to determine what his hand range is and how your hand rates against it. Many players will open the pot too liberally from any seat at the table. These players will have a high pre-flop raise and attempt to steal percentages. Other players will only open the pot too liberally from the hijack, cutoff, or button. These players will have a normal pre-flop raise percentage, but a high attempt to steal percentage.

The following chart outlines what hands you should three-bet based on your opponent's attempt to steal percentage (the vertical axis) and your opponent's position (horizontal axis). This chart was derived by determining which hands will have 50 percent equity or greater versus your opponent's range. However, you should be cautious with weak aces and small pairs because of the reverse implied odds these hands have. Furthermore, if your opponent has a very wide stealing range, it may be better to just call pre-flop since he will be likely to play too loose and aggressive post-flop. There is value in keeping him in the "betting lead."

Also, there is a difference between three-betting from the small blind versus three-betting from the button. In the small blind it is cheaper to three-bet (costing you only 2.5 small bets), and there is only one player left to act (who may wake up with a big hand). However, these are balanced by the fact that you will be out of position post-flop. The differences largely offset each other and you can still use a 50 percent equity requirement as a baseline against the original raiser's range.

We have used our opponents' attempt to steal percentage to determine their hand ranges. Roughly speaking, steal ranges in the cutoff tend to be two-thirds of the button range, and the button range is usually very close to the overall attempt to steal percentage because of the weighted balance between the ranges from the cutoff, button, and small blind. These are certainly only estimates and will vary from player to player.

Looking at the chart below, someone who steal raises 20 percent of the time — so low that you will almost never see this, but necessary for outer bounds of the exercise — will have approximately a 15 percent range from the cutoff. This would be equal to a range of 77+, A7s+, ATo+, K9s+, KTo+, Q9s+, QJo, and JTs.[3] Against that range, hands that have 50 percent equity or more are 99+, AJs+, and AJo+.

For tighter opponents, premium hands make up a good portion of their raising range. So you may want to tighten up slightly from this 50 percent equity benchmark because of the risk

---

[3] Of course, his range doesn't have to be exactly this combination, but for our purposes this is a reasonable assumption.

of getting four-bet, and to avoid the higher chance of a negative implied odds situation post-flop. Conversely, with looser opponents, their open-raising range is so wide that some pretty trashy hands will have 50 percent equity against them — be careful in such a situation because those hands suffer greatly if a third player enters the pot.

For example, if your opponent's steal range is 45 percent: 22+, A2s+, A2o+, K2s+, K6o+, Q5s+, Q8o+, J7s+, J8o+, T7s+, T8o+, 96s+, 98o, 86s+, and 76s, which is much more common at mid and high limits, and he is on the button, you can resteal from the small blind (or big blind) with 44+, A2s+, A5o+, K9s+, KTo+, QTs+, and QJo.

Opp Att To Steal %	Opponent's Position		
	CO	Button	SB
20	99+, AJs+, AJo+	77+, A9s+, ATo+, KQs	55+, A7s+, A8o+, KJs+, KQo
25	77+, ATs+, AJo+	66+, A8s+, A9o+, KJs+, KQo	44+, A6s+, A8o+, KTs+, KJo+, QJs
30	77+, A9s+, ATo+, KQs	55+, A7s+, A8o+, KJs+, KQo	33+, A2s+, A4o+, K8s+, KTo+, QTs+, QJo
35	77+, A9s+, ATo+, KQs	44+, A6s+, A8o+, KTs+, KJo+, QJs	33+, A2s+, A4o+, K7s+, K9o+, QTs+, QJo
40	66+, A8s+, A9o+, KJs+, KQo	44+, A4s+, A7o+, KTs+, KJo+, QJs	33+, A2s+, A2o+, K6s, K8o+, Q9s+, QTo+, JTs
45	55+, A7s+, A8o+, KJs+, KQo	44+, A2s+, A5o+, K9s+, KTo+, QTs+, QJo	33+, A2s+, A2o+, K5s+, K7o+, Q8s, Q9o+, JTs, JTo
50	55+, A7s+, A8o+, KJs+, KQo	44+, A2s+, A4o+, K8s+, K9o+, Q9s+, QJo, JTs	33+, A2s, A2o+, K4s+, K6o+, Q7s, Q8s, Q9o, J9s+, JTo
55	44+, A6s+, A8o+, KTs+, KJo+, QJs	44+, A2s+, A3o+, K7s+, K9o+, Q9s+, QJo, JTs	Use same as 50
60	44+, A4s+, A7o+, KTs+, KJo+, QJs	33+, A2s+, A2o+, K6s+, K8o+, Q9s+, QTo+, JTs	Use same as 50

It is worth noting that in selecting these hands we have shown a slight preference for hands that play better heads-up post-flop as opposed to multi-way. For example, ace-eight offsuit may have slightly less equity than ten-nine suited against your opponent's range, but we may recommend three-betting with ace-eight offsuit and mucking ten-nine suited. The reason for this should be clear since one of the major goals of three-betting is to get the pot heads up. (Of course, this does not apply when the open-raise comes from the small blind and the pot is already heads up.)

Adjusting to Your Opponent's Post-Flop Tendencies

When faced with a close decision (based on hand equity) regarding whether or not you should re-steal, it is important to consider how your opponent plays post-flop. Against a looser opponent who goes to the showdown more often (roughly greater than 40 percent), you should be more inclined to three-bet with hands that have showdown value but may suffer from reverse implied odds, such as

However, you should be more inclined to fold hands that rely on implied odds, such as

The reason is that, on one hand, you will have less bluffing equity since your opponent is less likely to fold to a flop or turn continuation bet. On the other hand, your implied odds will be lower since your opponent is, on average, entering the pot with a weaker hand.

Conversely, against a tighter opponent who does not go to showdown that often (roughly less than 37 percent), you should be more inclined to three-bet with the hands that rely on implied odds. This is because you will have more bluffing equity against a tighter player and will win more small pots. Also, when you do hit a big hand, your implied odds will be greater since your opponent is, on average, entering the pot with a stronger hand, and your hand will be disguised since you three-bet pre-flop.

Stating that bluffing equity and implied odds both increase at the same time is somewhat counterintuitive. However, when you three-bet pre-flop against a tighter player and then bet any flop, you will win on the flop fairly often since he will generally play "fit or fold" (on the flop) versus a pre-flop three-bettor. If you do get past the flop, you have greater implied odds because you can figure that your opponent has at least a decent hand and will pay you off to the river. Moreover, he may give you a lot of action if you hit two pair or better since your hand is disguised and has the potential to make a very big final hand.

A Note on Post-Flop Play

When your three-bet succeeds in getting the pot heads up, you should see the vast majority of showdowns. If your opponent checks to you on the flop, which he most often will, making a flop continuation bet is almost always correct since the pot is offering 7.5-to-1 immediate odds (assuming you got heads up for 3 small bets pre-flop) and you have shown strength pre-flop.

If your opponent check raises the flop, you have four options:

1. **Fold.** Since the pot is now offering you 10-to-1, this should be done rarely. You should call with any 4 or more outs hand.

2. **Call with the intention of calling down.** You should do this with good, but not great, made hands.

3. **Call with the intention of raising the turn.** You should do this with a strong made hand against an aggressive opponent since he is more likely to lead the turn when weak. You should also occasionally raise the turn as a semi-bluff, but this play should only be used against very tight opponents.

4. **Three-bet the flop.** You should do this with a strong hand against a passive opponent because it will get the most money into the pot. You should also three-bet with strong over-cards in an attempt to gain a free card on the turn. And with a very strong draw, such as two over-cards and a flush or straight draw since you have an equity edge — plus you may increase your bluffing equity with a turn bet or may be able to take a free card.

If your opponent just calls your flop bet and checks the turn, it may be correct to check behind even if you think your hand may still be the best hand on the turn. For more on this see the chapter entitled "The Turn Value Check" in Part Two of this book.

Limping

Terminology

Limp: To enter the pot pre-flop by just calling the big blind.

Over-limp: To enter the pot pre-flop by just calling the big blind when one or more other players have already limped.

Discussion

When first to enter the pot in a position that is 3 or fewer seats from the button, you should always raise and never limp. This is because the potential to steal the blinds and the value of being the pre-flop aggressor is large, especially in tighter games. In fact, in the tightest and most aggressive games, you should almost always follow this raise or fold strategy from any position. In short-handed games (6 or fewer players), you should always raise or fold when first to enter the pot, since you will never be more than 3 seats off the button.

If you successfully steal the blinds, you profit 0.75 big bets, which exceeds the expected value of all but the very best hands. The following graph shows the historical value of various pre-flop hands from a database of 313,000 hands from a 1.5BB/100 hand winning player at mid and high stakes games — there are some variations from expectation due to a small sample size. For instance, queen-seven suited performs better than queen-eight suited in this database, and that is, of course, an anomaly produced by empirical data. Suited hands in particular will suffer most from empirical analysis because they are the least frequent of the starting hand groups and contain the most variance.

Hand Profitability

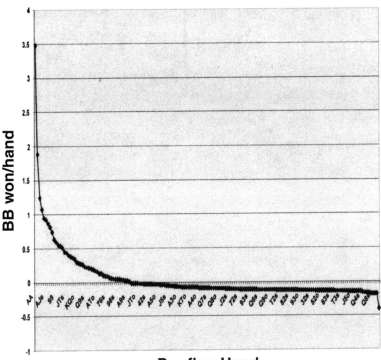

Pre-flop Hand

With your premium hands (aces and kings) at a 10-handed table, it may be more profitable to limp in an early position, hoping to re-raise later. However, if you are 5 or fewer seats from the button, you should raise because there are not enough players left to act. (That is, it is less likely someone will raise meaning you will not be able to re-raise.)

Since you are going to limp and re-raise in early position with aces and kings, you should also limp (and sometimes re-raise) with other hands for the sake of balance. You should limp with hands that tend to play well in multi-way or two- or three-handed pots. These hands include medium pairs like 77 and 88 and the smaller, suited broadway cards such as JTs, QTs, QJs. and KTs-KQs. Limping with these hands in a vacuum (i.e. for only one hand and with no history with the other players at the table), is probably slightly worse in expectation than open-raising with them.

In order to balance the times you reraise with aces or kings however, you should also limp with these hands just mentioned in games in which you have previously played (assuming they have seen you limp with aces or kings). This can work both ways as well because if you limp with the

and then reraise, your hand will certainly be well disguised and you gain deception value. Simply be aware of when and why to balance — in a game in which the players have no knowledge of you, it's an error to give up immediate expectation for the sake of balancing or deception.

Whether or not you should re-raise with these weaker hands depends on how many people have entered the pot behind you. When the pot is going to be 2- or 3-handed, you should re-raise with sevens or eights, because they will be more likely to win unimproved. When the pot will have four or more players, you should reraise with the smaller, suited broadway cards, because they will have an equity advantage against a large field.

You should over-limp with hands that play well in multi-way pots, but are not strong enough for a raise (such as small to medium pairs and small, suited, connecting cards). You should also be more inclined to over-limp if a bad player has already entered the pot. The following is a good set of guidelines for hands that you should over-limp with if you are in middle position and one other player has already entered the pot: 55-88, A5s-A9s, 76s-JTs, 86s-QTs, and J9s-KTs.

If more than one other player has entered the pot, you can play even more hands, adding: 22-44, A2s-A4s, 65s, 75s, T7s, J8s, and Q8s.

As usual, our starting hand recommendations are only a guide and should be adjusted according to specific game and playing situations. It is hard to define the precise situation where one play becomes less profitable than another. For instance, you have a close decision if you hold the

in a full-ring game with one limper in the pot before you. The following factors determine whether you should fold, call, or raise in this spot:

1. The style and quality of the limper's play.

2. The overall game conditions.

3. Your exact position. And,

4. The play of the two blinds, especially the big blind.

If the limper is UTG and is a tight, solid player, you should muck ace-four suited regardless of your position because a solid limper in this spot may often be trying to limp-re-raise with a big hand, and his range has a good equity advantage versus this holding. The fact that your hand is suited somewhat offsets this, but the better and tighter the player already in the pot is, the more likely you should be to just fold. However, if the rest of the criteria suggest that a different play is better, you must judge which of the factors are most important, which will depend on the degree to which the factors favor one action over another.

To take an extreme example, if you are playing in a "no fold 'em" game in which there are four or more players to every flop, you would definitely want to over-limp in this spot with any suited ace regardless of how solid the UTG limper plays. If you are playing in a tighter game, you would give more consideration to the quality of the existing player in the pot.

In regard to your exact position, it may counter-intuitively be better to over-limp in a worse position (i.e. further from the button) since there will be more players to act behind you, increasing the likelihood that you will get a multi-way pot. The chances of playing a multi-way pot increase even more when you over limp yourself, thus "pulling" other players into the hand by improving their odds.

For example, if you have a weak, suited ace on the button facing a single early-position limper, you have the best position (which certainly has value), but you have a marginal hand which is not really strong enough to go head-to-head against an early-position limper (even with your positional advantage). You would not be in a terrible situation if the pot ended up 4-handed, which is likely since the small blind will probably play for half a bet and the big blind will definitely play. But when this is the best possibility, it's not worth the risk of paying two bets to see the flop.

On the other hand, if you over-limp from an earlier position, the chance of having a 5- or 6-handed flop increases, in which case the cost of paying two bets to see the flop is less because the offsetting potential payoff (i.e. implied odds) will be larger. In other words, the advantage from pulling more people into a "family pot" with an over-limping type of hand is probably worth more than having good position in a pot with fewer players to the flop.

When the blinds play looser and more passively, you should be more inclined to over-limp since this increases the chance more people will play and decreases the chance there will be a pre-flop raise. Conversely, if the blinds play tighter and more aggressively, you should be inclined to over-limp with fewer hands.

Playing When Someone Has Three-Bet Before You Act

Obviously, when someone has three-bet pre-flop before the action reaches you, you should tighten up considerably. If the raise and three-bet both come from a solid player (i.e. they are legitimate raises), you should only play a few hands: JJ+, AKs, and AKo, and you should probably four-bet with all of these. Your decision will, of course, depend on the players who raised and three-bet, and their positions. If the raises come from early positions, you should play ever tighter.

If we assume the raisers are in middle and/or late positions, and have the following ranges:

First raiser: 55+, A7s+, ATo+, K9s+, KQo, QTs+, J9s+, and T9s

Three-bettor: 77+, A8s+, AJo+, and KQs

your equity with various hands will be as follows:[4]

TT = 37.09%	AKs = 38.78%
JJ = 42.03%	AKo = 35.66%
AQs = 33.19%	KQs = 28.82%

Even though a pair of tens has a slight equity advantage against your opponents' ranges, we recommend that you fold it because it will be difficult to play post-flop, particularly when overcards come.

---

[4] Note: your fair share of equity is 33.3 percent, which means that you will profit in the long run by splitting up the blind money with your opponents.

On the other hand, a hand like ace-king offsuit has a slight equity disadvantage pre-flop. But it should be played because it is much easier to play post-flop. If an ace or king flops, you will likely have the best hand and can bet and raise with confidence to protect it.

If the player who three-bets is a maniac, you can play more liberally, and you should usually four-bet to try to get heads up against him. In this situation, we would play 88+, AQs+, and AKo, and we would four-bet with all of these hands.

If we assume the raisers have the following ranges:

First raiser: 55+, A7s+, ATo+, K9s+, KQo, QTs+, J9s+, and T9s

Three-bettor: 22+, A2s+, A2o+, KTs+, and KJo+

your equity with various hands will be as follows:

66 = 32.22%	AQs = 38.29%
77 = 34.10%	AQo = 35.02%
88 = 36.39%	AKo = 39.10%
AJs = 34.60%	KQs = 32.50%

If you think there is a good chance you can force out the original raiser by four-betting, you can play a few more hands: 44-77, AJs, and AQo since they will be favored against the three-bettor's range.

Playing From the
Big Blind in Multi-Way Pots

Many players play too tight from the big blind pre-flop when the pot is raised and multi-way. In fact, with 6 (and sometimes 5) other players in the pot, you should call a raise in the big blind holding almost any two cards.

When holding any two cards, the probability of flopping two pair or better is 3.7 percent.[5] If you were to only play a trash hand like 7♠4♥ beyond the flop when you flop two pair or better, you will be folding 96.3 percent of the flops. Thus, you will need to win 27 small bets on average when you do flop a strong hand.

When six other players have entered a pot that was raised pre-flop and you are in the big blind, you are getting 13.5-to-1 odds to call one small bet. Thus, to justify a call with any two cards, you would only need to make 13.5 more small bets from 6 opponents when you flop a strong hand. You will flop two pair or better and win at showdown enough that calling with any two cards in this situation will be profitable. These favorable odds should create enough of an overlay to offset the times you flop a strong hand and lose.

For similar reasons, you should call against five other players with any two suited cards.

---

[5] Probability of flopping:

four of a kind =   0.0001
full house =   0.00092
three of a kind =   0.01571
two pair =   0.0202
0.037 = 0.0001 + 0.00092 + 0.01571 + 0.0202

Blind Versus Blind

Playing in the Small Blind

When the entire table folds to you in the small blind, you should play a majority of your hands because of the money that is already in the pot. Although the biggest factor in deciding when you should fold, call, or raise is your cards, it also depends largely on how your opponent plays.

You should consider the advice in this chapter along with the previous empirical analysis on stealing from the small blind presented earlier. Some of the conclusions will be contradictory, at which point you need to decide which factors are more relevant to the current situation, or which factor is more exploitable, and therefore, actionable.

In a game with a typical blind structure — big blind is twice the size of the small bind — against a big blind who folds more than 50 percent of his hands in this situation, raising any two cards becomes immediately profitable. You are risking 0.75 big bets to win 0.75 big bets, so if it is successful over 50 percent of the time, you should raise every time.

Tracking software can actually give you this specific statistic about a particular opponent (in PokerTracker it is in the more detail section of the general tab — labeled "folds BB to steal HU" and does not include steal raises from the cuttof or button). A word of warning: It is rare to find a good player at higher limits who commits this mistake.

This play can be profitable even if your opponent folds less than 50 percent of the time for two reasons:

1. There is a good chance that your opponent will not flop anything and fold to a flop continuation bet.

2. Even if you raise pre-flop with a hand as poor as

there is some chance that you will flop two pair or better and it will be best at the showdown. However, with premium hands like AA, KK, and QQ against a player who folds his big blind too often you should usually call because your post-flop expected value is large. (That is it is worth much more than the blinds that are already in the pot.)

When playing against an aggressive opponent that over defends his big blind — folds to an open raise from the small blind less than 10 percent of the time — it's our opinion you can fold approximately 20 percent of your hands: 32s, 43s-, 53s-, 63s-, 32o, 43o, 53o-, 63o-, 74o-, 84o-, 95o-, T5o-, and J3o-. Since your stealing equity is reduced in this situation, you should raise only with approximately 30 percent of your hands: 22+, A7o+, K8o+, Q9o+, J9o+, A3s+, K9s+, Q8s+, and J9s+, and call with the rest. You should also frequently limp/re-raise with a pair of nines or better. However, it is probably best to simply raise with aces and kings, as you want as much money as possible going in the pot pre-flop to tie him on to his hand, and this allows for the possibility of a three- and four-bet.

Another important factor to consider when deciding to enter the pot from the small blind is how well your opponent plays post-flop. Obviously, you should be willing to play more hands if your opponent plays poorly after that point. Against a passive opponent, you should be willing to play more hands because if you flop a marginal hand, such as bottom pair, it will be easier to determine whether you hand is good. Conversely, against an aggressive opponent, you should play fewer hands because you will be forced to make some tough call-downs.[6] Now you will win fewer pots, but they will be bigger. Against a passive opponent, you will win more pots, but they will be smaller.

When in the small blind, the blind structure also plays a large factor in determining how to play when folded to you. When it is two-thirds the big blind, you should play and raise with more hands, since there is additional money in the pot initially, which makes raising less expensive. Conversely, when the small blind is one-third or two-fifths the big blind, you should play and raise with fewer hands.

Playing Against an Opponent Who Three-Bets Frequently Pre-Flop

Many good players will three-bet a wide range of hands (correctly) when they are in the big blind and you open-raise from the small blind. This allows them to maximize their positional advantage and your folding equity later in the hand. (Folding equity is your equity in the pot resulting from the chance your opponent will fold to a bet or raise.) Playing against this type of player can be frustrating because you constantly feel like you may be folding the best hand with king-high or queen-high when you miss the flop.

When faced with such an opponent, it is often better to just limp with many of your marginal hands, especially against an opponent who rarely folds his big blind in a blind battle. This allows you to play a smaller pot when out of position, and you are not foregoing too much pre-flop folding equity against a tenacious defender. Against this type of player your implied odds/equity value rises and your fold equity decreases, so playing a small pot

---

[6] Against a super aggressive maniac you can play more hands because of implied odds.

pre-flop makes more sense. We recommend that you do still raise for value with your stronger hands: 22+, A5s+, A7o+, KTs+, and KJo+. However, with your marginal hands like

or

that figure to be a favorite over his range (which is two random cards at this point) we recommend that you only call. This allows you to play more of a "fit-or-fold" strategy post-flop because it will be easier to fold king-high even though it may be the best hand but in a smaller pot.

Also, when your opponent three-bets liberally, you should be more willing to four-bet. We recommend that you almost always four-bet 99-QQ, A9s+, and AJo+. Against someone who plays tight post-flop, you may in addition want to four-bet with KTs+ and KJo+ because you are still likely to be a favorite, and you increase your bluffing equity later in the hand — especially when an ace flops and your opponent does not hold one. Against someone who plays loose-aggressive post-flop you may also want to four-bet with your hands that have showdown value, such as 55-88, A6s-A8s, and A8o-ATo, since they are likely to be a favorite and you can comfortably get to the showdown with them. With the smaller pairs and smaller aces, you should be less inclined to four-bet because they figure to be either a slight favorite or a big underdog if your opponent does happen to have a legitimate three-betting hand. With aces and kings, we recommend that you usually just call a pre-flop three-bet and check raise most flops. The reason for this is that you will disguise your hand against thinking opponents who are trying to put you on a range since they will almost always eliminate aces or kings if you do not four-bet pre-flop. Also, as a metagame consideration, waiting to check raise the flop with aces and kings will add balance by giving more strength to your other check-raises. However, it is difficult to misplay aces or kings in this situation since four-betting pre-flop and leading the flop is certainly a good alternative.

A Note on Post-Flop Play

When you have raised from the small blind pre-flop, you should make a continuation bet on the flop nearly 100 percent of the time. The reason for this is the pot is offering you 4-to-1 immediate odds and the chance your opponent has flopped a pair or draw is less than 50 percent.

Many players will check their strong hands in this situation. However, this play looks suspicious and you sacrifice the chance to win a big pot when your opponent flops a good, second-best hand. With a strong hand against a hyper-aggressive player, you should be even more inclined to bet because he might raise with a marginal hand or as a bluff/semi-bluff allowing you to three-bet or go for a check-raise on the turn.

Playing in the Big Blind

Against a raise from the small blind, you should play the majority of your hands to avoid giving your opponent an opportunity for an immediate profit by raising with any two cards.

Again, while the single most important factor in deciding whether to fold, call, or re-raise is your cards, how often your opponent steals is also important. Against an aggressive stealer (i.e. raises in the small blind greater than 50 percent of the time), it's our opinion you should play approximately 70 percent of your hands, folding only: 32s, 43s-, 53s-, 63s-, 32o, 43o, 53o-, 64o-, 74o-, 85o-, 93o-, T2o. You should re-raise with the best 30 percent of your hands: 22+, A7o+, K8o+, Q9o+, J9o+, A3s+, K9s+, Q8s+, and J9s+. These are guidelines only and err on the side of "game theoretically optimal" while sacrificing deception value because an observant opponent may be able to narrow your range to some degree. We believe this is better than three-betting with hands like

in order to "switch it up" or "change gears" because, while you do get some deception value, you are certainly deviating from optimal play in doing so. Additionally, the range of hands you are raising with already have a decent amount of variation. Even if your opponent knew specifically that you re-raised with only your top 30 percent, it would still be difficult for him to put you on a specific hand because that range includes pairs, connectors, suited cards, and high card hands.

Against an opponent who rarely open-raises from the small blind, you can defend with fewer hands when he raises, but never less than 40 percent, and rarely less than 55 percent. Also, you should be aware that if you fold more than 50 percent of your hands against an observant opponent you may encourage him to "take shots at you" with any two cards.

Because you have position in this situation, how your opponent plays post-flop is less important since you will be better able to control how many bets go in on the later streets. However, against a passive opponent, you should be more inclined to play smaller suited and/or connected cards because you will be more likely to get free cards post-flop.

In this situation, the blind structure may seem to have no effect on how you should play pre-flop, as it will have no effect on the number of bets in the pot when you have to make a decision. There will always be 3 small bets if your opponent has raised, and 2 small bets if he has just called. However, you may be able to adjust your opponents range of hands using the blind structure as a consideration — better players will correctly loosen up in the 2/3 structure and correctly tighten up in the 1/3 structure. So although the odds you are getting will be the same, your opponent's hand range may be different.

Part Two

Blind Defense

Blind Defense

Introduction

In tough hold 'em games, since your opponents will frequently be aggressive and try to steal your blinds, you must defend tenaciously to avoid being run over. Many players go too far and believe you should defend with almost any two cards from the big blind against a steal position raise since they are getting 3.5-to-1 odds, and very few hands are that big of an underdog pre-flop. However, many of the marginal hands will lose more than 0.5 big bets, the amount you lose from folding, because they play poorly post-flop.

Learning when to defend is an integral part of playing short-handed and high-stakes hold 'em. Your profit from playing will be a function of the frequency and magnitude of the mistakes you and your opponents make, and playing in the blinds is significant in both areas. Whether or not you should defend depends on your opponent's range and your own two cards. We give specific guidelines to help you determine which hands are worth playing against which opponents in addition to the empirical results from over 85,000 blind defense hands of mid/high-stakes play.

We also go more in depth with chapters on playing when the small blind calls or three-bets, defending with pocket pairs, and defending from the small blind. Finally, the chapter on defending with queen-seven offsuit versus king-deuce illustrates the importance of the post-flop value of your hand when deciding whether to defend. Many players are uncomfortable when defending with marginal hands, and rightfully so since playing them out of position against aggressive opponents is difficult. Hopefully, the concepts presented in this section will help you build a solid foundation to make these scenarios somewhat easier.

Defending
From the Big Blind

When you are in the big blind and someone has opened the pot for a raise from late position (cutoff or button), you should be defending with the majority of your hands, roughly 60 percent depending on how aggressive the raiser is, and his position. A decent rule of thumb is that you should defend with hands that have 35 percent equity against the pre-flop raiser's range. However, you should be more willing to play a hand with good implied odds (e.g., suited connectors) and less willing to play hands that are likely to be dominated, especially against opponents with tighter hand ranges.

When defending from the big blind, you should often three-bet hands that figure to be best. Alternately, you can call and check raise a lot of flops with hands that benefit from getting folds, specifically smaller pairs and ace-high hands.

The following is a good set of guidelines for hands that you should defend with from the big blind against a typical steal raise: 22+, A2s+, A2o+, K2s+, K3o+, Q3s+, Q7o+, J4s+, J7o+, T5s+, T8o+, 96s+, 98o, 85s+, 86o+, 75s+, 75o+, 64s+, 65o, 53s+, and 43s.

These ranges are only rough estimates and are based on the empirical analysis presented later in this chapter. Although this is a good baseline, you should make adjustments as you get comfortable with the situations — particularly when deciding whether to three-bet, as this affects post-flop play. You should also alter your pre-flop range for the position and tightness of the stealer, adding hands against wider ranges and cutting hands against tighter ranges.

The table below shows the overall results from the big blind for our three players. The first three rows show overall results when a steal is attempted, and the last three rows show the results when our players defended against an attempted steal. (A steal attempt is defined as an open-raise from either the cutoff, button, or small blind.) You will notice that the high-limit player put money in the pot (other than his blind) less often at 51 percent versus the mid-limit player at 57 percent.

$$0.5112 = \frac{17,136}{33,524} \text{ and } 0.5732 = \frac{19,168}{33,444}$$

This is partly a function of the mid-limit player defending with a slightly wider range, but mostly a function of more of the high-limit pots being raised and three-bet before they get to the big blind.

Player	Trials	Win %	Amt $	Avg $ Per Hand	BB/Hand	Put $ in Pot	Win % WSF	Raised	Went to SD	Won at SD
High	33,524	21.08	-1,654,673.07	-52.48	-0.2	51.12%	38.77	11.15%	33.12%	56.78%
Mid	33,444	22.1	-201,648.47	-5.84	-0.3	57.32%	39.82	9.97%	38.22%	51.93%
Grd	19,490	16.32	-460,126.87	-23.61	-0.3	42.34%	38.53	7.60%	34.33%	57.03%
High Def.	17,136	38.78	19,423.93	1.13	0	100.00%	38.77	20.52%	33.10%	56.80%
Mid Def.	19,168	39.83	-7,113.47	-0.37	0	100.00%	39.82	17.97%	38.22%	51.93%
Grd Def.	8,252	38.55	163.13	0.02	0	100.00%	38.53	17.95%	34.33%	57.03%

The tables below show individual hand results when a steal is attempted and individual hand results when a steal was attempted and our players chose to put money into the pot.

Hand	Trials	Win%	Amount ($)	Avg $/Hand	BB/ Hand	Win % WSF	Went to SD (%)	Won at SD (%)
						High		
AA	153	84.97	101,869	665.81	2.86	84.87	54.61	73.49
AKs	99	65.66	32,047	323.70	1.53	65.66	60.61	63.33
AKo	299	62.88	75,306	251.86	1.02	62.88	61.87	63.78
AQs	103	64.08	18,769	182.22	0.93	64.08	48.54	64.00
AQo	299	56.52	20,947	70.06	0.39	56.52	49.5	58.11
AJs	93	60.22	17,266	185.66	0.72	60.22	52.69	61.22
AJo	294	53.06	16,767	57.03	0.35	53.24	39.25	60.00
ATs	108	61.11	28,404	263.00	1.26	61.68	53.27	75.44
ATo	267	44.19	10,185	38.14	0.11	49.79	43.04	60.78
A9s	95	45.26	796	8.38	0.19	46.24	38.71	55.56
A9o	249	39.76	15,976	64.16	0.16	51.30	43.01	59.04
A8s	79	40.51	3,060	38.73	(0.08)	44.44	44.44	50.00
A8o	331	33.53	(21,527)	(65.04)	(0.34)	41.26	39.03	45.71
A7s	96	33.33	(8,325)	(86.71)	(0.34)	38.10	36.9	45.16
A7o	318	30.19	(23,889)	(75.12)	(0.25)	38.40	33.2	59.04
A6s	96	36.46	2,434	25.35	0.32	42.17	42.17	60.00
A6o	296	32.77	(657)	(2.22)	(0.07)	43.30	35.27	62.03
A5s	87	45.98	5,853	67.27	0.46	54.79	39.73	65.52
A5o	291	30.24	(10,448)	(35.90)	(0.16)	42.11	35.89	62.67
A4s	95	37.89	9,336	98.27	0.42	48.00	34.67	69.23
A4o	286	26.92	(13,887)	(48.55)	(0.21)	39.69	32.99	59.38
A3s	85	24.71	(10,718)	(126.09)	(0.49)	30.00	44.29	48.39
A3o	295	23.73	(27,609)	(93.59)	(0.42)	34.15	32.68	49.25
A2s	87	39.08	(3,147)	(36.17)	(0.01)	47.89	36.62	57.69
A2o	272	23.9	(13,159)	(48.38)	(0.26)	39.63	35.98	59.32
KK	134	70.9	55,791	416.35	2.00	70.90	61.94	67.47
KQs	95	53.68	6,454	67.94	0.38	53.68	41.05	51.28
KQo	280	41.79	(1,526)	(5.45)	(0.10)	42.55	37.82	52.88
KJs	89	52.81	7,782	87.44	0.46	52.81	23.6	52.38
KJo	280	34.29	(13,368)	(47.74)	(0.24)	39.34	38.11	52.69
KTs	90	51.11	19,847	220.52	0.69	56.10	45.12	67.57
KTo	275	32	(11,222)	(40.81)	(0.29)	38.43	36.68	51.19
K9s	74	43.24	5,469	73.91	0.34	48.48	34.85	65.22
K9o	281	25.27	(15,374)	(54.71)	(0.36)	33.02	30.7	51.52
K8s	102	27.45	(19,559)	(191.75)	(0.89)	29.35	28.26	30.77
K8o	252	26.98	(16,363)	(64.93)	(0.28)	35.23	31.09	56.67

K7s	98	24.49	(9,601)	(97.97)	(0.35)	29.27	31.71	50.00
K7o	295	17.97	(28,045)	(95.07)	(0.49)	25.73	22.82	42.55
K6s	98	23.47	(11,668)	(119.06)	(0.54)	27.38	34.52	44.83
K6o	299	22.07	(23,007)	(76.95)	(0.27)	32.20	27.8	59.65
K5s	103	16.5	(17,478)	(169.68)	(0.73)	21.79	24.36	47.37
K5o	289	13.84	(32,117)	(111.13)	(0.52)	24.24	27.27	51.11
K4s	85	20	(6,913)	(81.32)	(0.30)	23.29	19.18	64.29
K4o	277	15.52	(21,878)	(78.98)	(0.36)	30.71	25	60.00
K3s	88	27.27	(3,516)	(39.95)	0.01	34.78	15.94	72.73
K3o	306	13.07	(19,322)	(63.14)	(0.33)	28.57	25.71	66.67
K2s	115	26.09	4,669	40.60	(0.05)	37.04	29.63	66.67
K2o	278	9.71	(33,980)	(122.23)	(0.48)	25.96	20.19	61.90
QQ	160	70	55,152	344.70	1.64	70.00	58.75	65.96
QJs	106	46.23	6,460	60.94	0.19	47.57	30.1	58.06
QJo	295	34.24	(16,276)	(55.17)	(0.19)	43.72	37.66	47.13
QTs	94	34.04	(11,342)	(120.66)	(0.44)	38.55	38.55	40.63
QTo	286	33.22	(4,521)	(15.81)	(0.03)	41.30	31.3	54.17
Q9s	90	34.44	6,520	72.44	0.14	41.33	33.33	64.00
Q9o	267	30.34	(4,459)	(16.70)	(0.16)	37.50	30.56	54.55
Q8s	77	15.58	(8,531)	(110.79)	(0.60)	20.00	21.67	38.46
Q8o	276	22.46	(19,618)	(71.08)	(0.36)	29.11	27.7	54.24
Q7s	104	25	(8,044)	(77.35)	(0.32)	32.10	24.69	55.00
Q7o	308	18.83	(39,211)	(127.31)	(0.47)	28.71	25.74	46.15
Q6s	99	24.24	(1,564)	(15.79)	(0.25)	31.17	35.06	51.85
Q6o	280	13.57	(34,685)	(123.87)	(0.55)	23.75	20	37.50
Q5s	94	24.47	(3,610)	(38.40)	(0.41)	32.86	22.86	50.00
Q5o	299	5.69	(43,056)	(144.00)	(0.64)	15.32	18.92	42.86
Q4s	84	17.86	(9,763)	(116.23)	(0.58)	25.42	20.34	58.33
Q4o	271	8.12	(28,451)	(104.99)	(0.48)	23.16	23.16	50.00
Q3s	98	18.37	(4,882)	(49.82)	(0.11)	29.03	20.97	76.92
Q3o	286	7.69	(30,639)	(107.13)	(0.47)	25.88	24.71	52.38
Q2s	92	14.13	(13,335)	(144.94)	(0.52)	26.00	24	50.00
Q2o	296	5.07	(28,543)	(96.43)	(0.41)	32.61	30.43	64.29
JJ	132	70.45	44,987	340.81	1.51	70.23	52.67	69.57
JTs	79	34.18	(7,210)	(91.27)	(0.63)	36.49	40.54	33.33
JTo	284	33.45	(5,862)	(20.64)	(0.08)	40.60	34.62	58.02
J9s	98	27.55	(11,201)	(114.29)	(0.41)	31.40	31.4	40.74
J9o	283	33.57	18,291	64.63	0.18	41.30	32.17	74.32
J8s	100	29	1,956	19.56	0.04	37.18	30.77	62.50
J8o	298	25.17	(25,087)	(84.18)	(0.43)	33.19	26.99	50.82
J7s	81	32.1	2,629	32.46	0.11	38.24	35.29	66.67
J7o	266	24.81	(10,924)	(41.07)	(0.21)	34.56	26.7	62.75
J6s	87	26.44	(2,279)	(26.19)	0.03	33.33	28.99	60.00
J6o	285	12.98	(31,044)	(108.92)	(0.49)	25.34	18.49	44.44

J5s	101	17.82	(10,410)	(103.07)	(0.28)	27.69	26.15	64.71
J5o	294	6.8	(36,906)	(125.53)	(0.51)	24.10	25.3	38.10
J4s	107	14.95	(8,899)	(83.17)	(0.42)	28.57	21.43	50.00
J4o	277	9.03	(26,773)	(96.65)	(0.41)	32.89	25	52.63
J3s	107	16.82	(5,960)	(55.70)	(0.19)	37.50	25	75.00
J3o	325	3.38	(42,496)	(130.76)	(0.58)	15.71	12.86	44.44
J2s	82	8.54	(9,466)	(115.44)	(0.45)	21.21	27.27	66.67
J2o	297	5.05	(32,613)	(109.81)	(0.50)	26.32	28.07	43.75
TT	124	57.26	27,764	223.90	0.79	57.26	52.42	55.38
T9s	99	39.39	(224)	(2.26)	0.12	42.86	34.07	54.84
T9o	275	29.82	(8,760)	(31.85)	(0.19)	37.27	30.91	58.82
T8s	89	28.09	(12,072)	(135.64)	(0.36)	32.89	31.58	54.17
T8o	290	30.34	754	2.60	(0.05)	38.77	31.72	61.11
T7s	99	28.28	(15,484)	(156.40)	(0.64)	33.73	20.48	41.18
T7o	288	20.49	(32,958)	(114.44)	(0.52)	29.06	26.11	47.17
T6s	91	21.98	(11,054)	(121.47)	(0.38)	28.57	18.57	61.54
T6o	295	13.56	(28,986)	(98.26)	(0.49)	26.14	24.84	36.84
T5s	107	12.15	(10,563)	(98.72)	(0.38)	28.85	28	57.14
T5o	294	5.1	(32,964)	(112.12)	(0.46)	28.85	13.46	57.14
T4s	96	4.17	(15,244)	(158.79)	(0.75)	12.90	19.35	33.33
T4o	280	2.5	(31,277)	(111.70)	(0.48)	25.00	14.29	50.00
T3s	104	3.85	(14,617)	(140.55)	(0.54)	19.05	19.05	50.00
T3o	293	0.68	(32,789)	(111.91)	(0.49)	28.57	14.29	100.00
T2s	84	8.33	(6,196)	(73.76)	(0.29)	38.89	11.11	100.00
T2o	284	0.35	(33,126)	(116.64)	(0.49)	20.00	20	100.00
99	147	55.1	24,565	167.11	0.53	55.10	47.62	67.14
98s	90	32.22	(2,478)	(27.53)	(0.11)	35.37	39.02	50.00
98o	283	24.38	(23,701)	(83.75)	(0.32)	30.94	25.56	47.37
97s	102	27.45	(7,607)	(74.58)	(0.31)	37.33	36	62.96
97o	273	16.85	(32,892)	(120.48)	(0.57)	23.12	23.62	48.94
96s	97	14.43	(16,863)	(173.84)	(0.78)	18.42	22.37	29.41
96o	286	16.78	(25,840)	(90.35)	(0.37)	31.37	26.8	63.41
95s	96	7.29	(11,367)	(118.41)	(0.48)	20.59	11.76	75.00
95o	278	3.24	(28,351)	(101.98)	(0.44)	39.13	30.43	57.14
94s	103	5.83	(10,602)	(102.93)	(0.42)	50.00	25	66.67
94o	281	-	(34,325)	(122.15)	(0.52)	-	-	-
93s	104	2.88	(13,554)	(130.33)	(0.59)	21.43	35.71	20.00
93o	263	1.14	(29,147)	(110.83)	(0.48)	42.86	28.57	100.00
92s	90	2.22	(10,641)	(118.23)	(0.51)	16.67	8.33	100.00
92o	301	0.33	(33,308)	(110.66)	(0.48)	33.33	33.33	100.00
88	144	47.92	10,652	73.97	0.18	48.25	42.66	59.02
87s	95	36.84	2,285	24.05	0.10	43.75	33.75	55.56
87o	290	29.66	(8,476)	(29.23)	(0.16)	36.13	34.87	49.40
86s	90	34.44	2,104	23.37	0.10	41.33	28	66.67

86o	300	21.33	(26,824)	(89.41)	(0.40)	28.32	22.57	50.98
85s	103	18.45	(11,642)	(113.03)	(0.42)	42.22	40	61.11
85o	270	3.7	(32,287)	(119.58)	(0.48)	37.04	25.93	28.57
84s	96	7.29	(12,326)	(128.40)	(0.53)	30.43	13.04	33.33
84o	262	1.15	(30,399)	(116.03)	(0.52)	25.00	25	-
83s	110	3.64	(12,482)	(113.47)	(0.39)	30.77	23.08	66.67
83o	266	-	(31,480)	(118.35)	(0.50)	-	-	-
82s	85	2.35	(8,326)	(97.95)	(0.49)	20.00	20	50.00
82o	287	-	(31,458)	(109.61)	(0.50)	-	-	-
77	120	45	(2,817)	(23.48)	(0.07)	45.38	38.66	43.48
76s	89	24.72	(11,072)	(124.40)	(0.54)	33.33	34.85	43.48
76o	299	19.73	(26,162)	(87.50)	(0.39)	28.37	23.56	55.10
75s	93	26.88	(2,951)	(31.73)	(0.08)	36.76	27.94	63.16
75o	264	6.06	(33,402)	(126.52)	(0.47)	27.12	18.64	72.73
74s	101	10.89	(10,953)	(108.44)	(0.46)	28.95	23.68	55.56
74o	290	0.34	(37,619)	(129.72)	(0.55)	10.00	30	33.33
73s	96	1.04	(11,564)	(120.46)	(0.53)	11.11	11.11	100.00
73o	274	-	(31,285)	(114.18)	(0.50)	-	-	-
72s	84	2.38	(9,842)	(117.17)	(0.51)	20.00	10	100.00
72o	244	-	(27,972)	(114.64)	(0.50)	-	100	-
66	130	50.77	11,575	89.03	0.40	50.77	36.92	66.67
65s	92	26.09	(9,454)	(102.76)	(0.40)	32.43	31.08	60.87
65o	280	16.79	(25,633)	(91.54)	(0.38)	30.52	31.17	58.33
64s	98	21.43	(1,600)	(16.33)	(0.21)	30.43	27.54	63.16
64o	291	2.06	(38,193)	(131.25)	(0.58)	13.64	27.27	33.33
63s	90	7.78	(13,868)	(154.09)	(0.55)	26.92	30.77	37.50
63o	261	0.77	(28,924)	(110.82)	(0.49)	50.00	50	50.00
62s	108	1.85	(13,006)	(120.43)	(0.51)	22.22	33.33	66.67
62o	290	-	(33,930)	(117.00)	(0.50)	-	-	-
55	160	50	25,913	161.95	0.59	50.00	40	65.63
54s	117	31.62	(3,548)	(30.32)	0.04	38.54	23.96	65.22
54o	284	10.56	(32,363)	(113.95)	(0.46)	26.32	24.56	60.71
53s	82	10.98	(13,634)	(166.27)	(0.70)	21.43	23.81	40.00
53o	309	4.85	(30,649)	(99.19)	(0.45)	34.88	30.23	61.54
52s	94	-	(11,810)	(125.64)	(0.53)	-	-	-
52o	274	-	(31,570)	(115.22)	(0.50)	-	-	-
44	155	45.16	24,869	160.45	0.41	45.45	30.52	59.57
43s	102	15.69	(8,529)	(83.62)	(0.45)	32.65	16.33	62.50
43o	287	1.74	(33,979)	(118.39)	(0.50)	29.41	35.29	50.00
42s	92	4.35	(8,917)	(96.92)	(0.41)	40.00	20	100.00
42o	303	0.33	(33,508)	(110.59)	(0.50)	50.00	-	-
33	149	32.89	(4,708)	(31.60)	(0.17)	34.51	30.99	50.00
32s	96	1.04	(12,151)	(126.57)	(0.61)	16.67	66.67	-
32o	300	-	(34,920)	(116.40)	(0.50)	-	-	-

22	147	40.82	19,002	129.26	0.40	45.11	24.81	69.70
Total	31,530	21.08	(1,654,673)	(52.48)	(0.23)	38.77	33.12	56.78

High-Put $ in Pot								
Hand	Trials	Win %	Amount ($)	Avg $/Hand	BB/ Hand	Win % WSF	Went to SD (%)	Won at SD (%)
AA	153	84.97	101,869	665.81	2.86	84.87	54.61	73.49
AKs	99	65.66	32,047	323.70	1.53	65.66	60.61	63.33
AKo	299	62.88	75,306	251.86	1.02	62.88	61.87	63.78
AQs	103	64.08	18,769	182.22	0.93	64.08	48.54	64.00
AQo	299	56.52	20,947	70.06	0.39	56.52	49.5	58.11
AJs	93	60.22	17,266	185.66	0.72	60.22	52.69	61.22
AJo	293	53.24	16,867	57.57	0.35	53.24	39.25	60.00
ATs	107	61.68	28,554	266.86	1.28	61.68	53.27	75.44
ATo	237	49.79	13,985	59.01	0.19	49.79	43.04	60.78
A9s	93	46.24	1,021	10.98	0.21	46.24	38.71	55.56
A9o	193	51.3	23,031	119.33	0.35	51.30	43.01	59.04
A8s	72	44.44	3,880	53.88	(0.03)	44.44	44.44	50.00
A8o	269	41.26	(14,212)	(52.83)	(0.30)	41.26	39.03	45.71
A7s	84	38.1	(7,200)	(85.71)	(0.31)	38.10	36.9	45.16
A7o	250	38.4	(16,409)	(65.63)	(0.18)	38.40	33.2	59.04
A6s	83	42.17	4,114	49.56	0.44	42.17	42.17	60.00
A6o	224	43.3	7,833	34.97	0.06	43.30	35.27	62.03
A5s	73	54.79	7,458	102.16	0.65	54.79	39.73	65.52
A5o	209	42.11	(558)	(2.67)	(0.03)	42.11	35.89	62.67
A4s	75	48	11,696	155.94	0.66	48.00	34.67	69.23
A4o	194	39.69	(3,177)	(16.37)	(0.07)	39.69	32.99	59.38
A3s	70	30	(8,788)	(125.54)	(0.49)	30.00	44.29	48.39
A3o	205	34.15	(17,794)	(86.80)	(0.38)	34.15	32.68	49.25
A2s	71	47.89	(1,172)	(16.51)	0.10	47.89	36.62	57.69
A2o	164	39.63	(764)	(4.66)	(0.10)	39.63	35.98	59.32
KK	134	70.9	55,791	416.35	2.00	70.90	61.94	67.47
KQs	95	53.68	6,454	67.94	0.38	53.68	41.05	51.28
KQo	275	42.55	(876)	(3.18)	(0.09)	42.55	37.82	52.88
KJs	89	52.81	7,782	87.44	0.46	52.81	23.6	52.38
KJo	244	39.34	(9,363)	(38.37)	(0.20)	39.34	38.11	52.69
KTs	82	56.1	20,797	253.62	0.81	56.10	45.12	67.57
KTo	229	38.43	(6,067)	(26.49)	(0.25)	38.43	36.68	51.19
K9s	66	48.48	6,344	96.12	0.44	48.48	34.85	65.22
K9o	215	33.02	(7,139)	(33.21)	(0.32)	33.02	30.7	51.52
K8s	93	30.11	(18,534)	(199.28)	(0.93)	29.35	28.26	30.77
K8o	193	35.23	(9,528)	(49.37)	(0.21)	35.23	31.09	56.67
K7s	82	29.27	(7,726)	(94.22)	(0.32)	29.27	31.71	50.00

K7o	206	25.73	(17,260)	(83.79)	(0.49)	25.73	22.33	43.48
K6s	84	27.38	(10,228)	(121.76)	(0.55)	27.38	34.52	44.83
K6o	204	31.86	(12,480)	(61.18)	(0.16)	31.86	27.45	58.93
K5s	78	21.79	(14,293)	(183.24)	(0.80)	21.79	24.36	47.37
K5o	165	24.24	(18,031)	(109.28)	(0.54)	24.24	27.27	51.11
K4s	73	23.29	(5,633)	(77.16)	(0.27)	23.29	19.18	64.29
K4o	140	30.71	(7,003)	(50.02)	(0.23)	30.71	25	60.00
K3s	69	34.78	(1,041)	(15.09)	0.15	34.78	15.94	72.73
K3o	140	28.57	199	1.42	(0.13)	28.57	25.71	66.67
K2s	81	37.04	8,974	110.78	0.14	37.04	29.63	66.67
K2o	104	25.96	(14,310)	(137.59)	(0.45)	25.96	20.19	61.90
QQ	160	70	55,152	344.70	1.64	70.00	58.75	65.96
QJs	103	47.57	6,860	66.60	0.21	47.57	30.1	58.06
QJo	231	43.72	(8,846)	(38.30)	(0.10)	43.72	37.66	47.13
QTs	83	38.55	(9,692)	(116.77)	(0.44)	38.55	38.55	40.63
QTo	230	41.3	1,314	5.71	0.08	41.30	31.3	54.17
Q9s	75	41.33	8,295	110.60	0.26	41.33	33.33	64.00
Q9o	216	37.5	1,157	5.35	(0.07)	37.50	30.56	54.55
Q8s	60	20	(6,301)	(105.02)	(0.63)	20.00	21.67	38.46
Q8o	213	29.11	(11,368)	(53.37)	(0.32)	29.11	27.7	54.24
Q7s	81	32.1	(5,544)	(68.44)	(0.27)	32.10	24.69	55.00
Q7o	202	28.71	(26,856)	(132.95)	(0.45)	28.71	25.74	46.15
Q6s	77	31.17	967	12.55	(0.18)	31.17	35.06	51.85
Q6o	160	23.75	(19,615)	(122.59)	(0.58)	23.75	20	37.50
Q5s	70	32.86	(985)	(14.07)	(0.37)	32.86	22.86	50.00
Q5o	111	15.32	(22,071)	(198.83)	(0.87)	15.32	18.92	42.86
Q4s	59	25.42	(6,563)	(111.24)	(0.62)	25.42	20.34	58.33
Q4o	95	23.16	(7,951)	(83.69)	(0.43)	23.16	23.16	50.00
Q3s	62	29.03	(1,087)	(17.53)	0.11	29.03	20.97	76.92
Q3o	85	25.88	(7,879)	(92.69)	(0.41)	25.88	24.71	52.38
Q2s	50	26	(8,285)	(165.69)	(0.53)	26.00	24	50.00
Q2o	45	33.33	758	16.83	0.06	33.33	28.89	69.23
JJ	132	70.45	44,987	340.81	1.51	70.23	52.67	69.57
JTs	74	36.49	(6,510)	(87.97)	(0.64)	36.49	40.54	33.33
JTo	234	40.6	449	1.92	0.01	40.60	34.62	58.02
J9s	86	31.4	(9,451)	(109.89)	(0.40)	31.40	31.4	40.74
J9o	230	41.3	25,566	111.16	0.33	41.30	32.17	74.32
J8s	78	37.18	4,856	62.25	0.20	37.18	30.77	62.50
J8o	226	33.19	(16,282)	(72.04)	(0.41)	33.19	26.99	50.82
J7s	68	38.24	4,229	62.19	0.22	38.24	35.29	66.67
J7o	191	34.56	(1,599)	(8.37)	(0.09)	34.56	26.7	62.75
J6s	69	33.33	47	0.67	0.17	33.33	28.99	60.00
J6o	146	25.34	(15,104)	(103.45)	(0.49)	25.34	18.49	44.44
J5s	65	27.69	(5,990)	(92.15)	(0.16)	27.69	26.15	64.71

J5o	83	24.1	(12,103)	(145.81)	(0.53)	24.10	25.3	38.10
J4s	56	28.57	(2,719)	(48.55)	(0.35)	28.57	21.43	50.00
J4o	76	32.89	(3,620)	(47.63)	(0.17)	32.89	25	52.63
J3s	48	37.5	1,274	26.53	0.19	37.50	25	75.00
J3o	70	15.71	(14,541)	(207.73)	(0.86)	15.71	12.86	44.44
J2s	33	21.21	(4,161)	(126.09)	(0.38)	21.21	27.27	66.67
J2o	57	26.32	(5,263)	(92.33)	(0.52)	26.32	28.07	43.75
TT	124	57.26	27,764	223.90	0.79	57.26	52.42	55.38
T9s	91	42.86	551	6.05	0.18	42.86	34.07	54.84
T9o	220	37.27	(2,080)	(9.45)	(0.11)	37.27	30.91	58.82
T8s	76	32.89	(10,347)	(136.14)	(0.34)	32.89	31.58	54.17
T8o	227	38.77	8,299	36.56	0.08	38.77	31.72	61.11
T7s	83	33.73	(13,309)	(160.34)	(0.66)	33.73	20.48	41.18
T7o	203	29.06	(22,608)	(111.37)	(0.53)	29.06	26.11	47.17
T6s	70	28.57	(8,429)	(120.41)	(0.35)	28.57	18.57	61.54
T6o	153	26.14	(13,313)	(87.01)	(0.48)	26.14	24.84	36.84
T5s	50	26	(3,538)	(70.76)	(0.25)	26.00	28	57.14
T5o	52	28.85	(4,274)	(82.19)	(0.28)	28.85	13.46	57.14
T4s	31	12.9	(7,944)	(256.24)	(1.28)	12.90	19.35	33.33
T4o	28	25	(1,727)	(61.68)	(0.27)	25.00	14.29	50.00
T3s	21	19.05	(4,972)	(236.76)	(0.72)	19.05	19.05	50.00
T3o	7	28.57	894	127.71	(0.08)	28.57	14.29	100.00
T2s	18	38.89	1,709	94.94	0.49	38.89	11.11	100.00
T2o	5	20	(353)	(70.60)	0.09	20.00	20	100.00
99	147	55.1	24,565	167.11	0.53	55.10	47.62	67.14
98s	82	35.37	(1,398)	(17.04)	(0.08)	35.37	39.02	50.00
98o	223	30.94	(16,601)	(74.44)	(0.27)	30.94	25.56	47.37
97s	75	37.33	(4,227)	(56.36)	(0.24)	37.33	36	62.96
97o	199	23.12	(23,617)	(118.68)	(0.60)	23.12	23.62	48.94
96s	76	18.42	(14,088)	(185.36)	(0.85)	18.42	22.37	29.41
96o	153	31.37	(10,025)	(65.52)	(0.25)	31.37	26.8	63.41
95s	34	20.59	(3,949)	(116.15)	(0.44)	20.59	11.76	75.00
95o	23	39.13	1,109	48.22	0.23	39.13	30.43	57.14
94s	12	50	404	33.63	0.18	50.00	25	66.67
94o	7	-	(2,110)	(301.43)	(1.36)	-	-	-
93s	14	21.43	(3,304)	(236.00)	(1.20)	21.43	35.71	20.00
93o	7	42.86	481	68.71	0.35	42.86	28.57	100.00
92s	12	16.67	(1,121)	(93.42)	(0.61)	16.67	8.33	100.00
92o	3	33.33	197	65.67	1.32	33.33	33.33	100.00
88	143	48.25	10,702	74.84	0.19	48.25	42.66	59.02
87s	80	43.75	4,260	53.25	0.21	43.75	33.75	55.56
87o	238	36.13	(2,161)	(9.08)	(0.09)	36.13	34.87	49.40
86s	75	41.33	3,539	47.18	0.22	41.33	28	66.67
86o	226	28.32	(17,999)	(79.64)	(0.36)	28.32	22.57	50.98

85s	45	42.22	(5,202)	(115.60)	(0.31)	42.22	40	61.11
85o	27	37.04	(4,487)	(166.19)	(0.34)	37.04	25.93	28.57
84s	23	30.43	(4,156)	(180.70)	(0.63)	30.43	13.04	33.33
84o	11	27.27	(1,749)	(159.00)	(0.91)	27.27	18.18	-
83s	13	30.77	(917)	(70.54)	0.47	30.77	23.08	66.67
82s	10	20	(226)	(22.60)	(0.45)	20.00	20	50.00
82o	2	-	(500)	(250.00)	(1.00)	-	-	-
77	119	45.38	(2,767)	(23.25)	(0.06)	45.38	38.66	43.48
76s	66	33.33	(8,267)	(125.25)	(0.55)	33.33	34.85	43.48
76o	208	28.37	(15,022)	(72.22)	(0.34)	28.37	23.56	55.10
75s	68	36.76	129	1.90	0.08	36.76	27.94	63.16
75o	59	27.12	(9,617)	(163.00)	(0.38)	27.12	18.64	72.73
74s	38	28.95	(3,193)	(84.01)	(0.39)	28.95	23.68	55.56
74o	10	10	(4,653)	(465.30)	(1.95)	10.00	30	33.33
73s	9	11.11	(1,504)	(167.11)	(0.86)	11.11	11.11	100.00
72s	10	20	(1,507)	(150.70)	(0.55)	20.00	10	100.00
72o	1	-	(297)	(297.00)	(0.99)	-	100	-
66	130	50.77	11,575	89.03	0.40	50.77	36.92	66.67
65s	74	32.43	(7,204)	(97.35)	(0.38)	32.43	31.08	60.87
65o	154	30.52	(12,038)	(78.17)	(0.28)	30.52	31.17	58.33
64s	69	30.43	1,375	19.93	(0.09)	30.43	27.54	63.16
64o	44	13.64	(9,268)	(210.64)	(1.04)	13.64	27.27	33.33
63s	26	26.92	(6,383)	(245.50)	(0.69)	26.92	30.77	37.50
63o	4	50	244	61.00	0.12	50.00	50	50.00
62s	9	22.22	(1,256)	(139.56)	(0.56)	22.22	33.33	66.67
62o	2	-	(400)	(200.00)	(1.00)	-	-	-
55	160	50	25,913	161.95	0.59	50.00	40	65.63
54s	96	38.54	(818)	(8.52)	0.16	38.54	23.96	65.22
54o	114	26.32	(12,588)	(110.42)	(0.41)	26.32	24.56	60.71
53s	42	21.43	(9,169)	(218.31)	(0.88)	21.43	23.81	40.00
53o	43	34.88	181	4.21	(0.12)	34.88	30.23	61.54
52s	5	-	(960)	(192.00)	(1.00)	-	-	-
44	154	45.45	24,919	161.81	0.42	45.45	30.52	59.57
43s	49	32.65	(2,644)	(53.96)	(0.39)	32.65	16.33	62.50
43o	17	29.41	(2,139)	(125.81)	(0.54)	29.41	35.29	50.00
42s	10	40	1,488	148.80	0.37	40.00	20	100.00
42o	2	50	347	173.50	(0.26)	50.00	-	-
33	142	34.51	(4,058)	(28.58)	(0.15)	34.51	30.99	50.00
32s	6	16.67	(1,963)	(327.17)	(2.34)	16.67	66.67	-
32o	1	-	(100)	(100.00)	(1.00)	-	-	-
22	133	45.11	20,402	153.39	0.49	45.11	24.81	69.70
Total	17,136	38.78	19,424	1.13	(0.01)	38.77	33.1	56.80

Mid								
Hand	Trials	Win %	Amount ($)	Avg $/Hand	BB/ Hand	Win % WSF	Went to SD (%)	Won at SD (%)
AA	151	86.09	11,449	75.82	2.73	86.09	56.95	79.07
AKs	89	61.8	3,396	38.16	1.05	61.80	61.8	50.91
AKo	306	60.13	4,215	13.77	0.58	60.13	52.61	55.90
AQs	109	59.63	1,534	14.07	0.56	59.63	56.88	54.84
AQo	317	56.47	2,092	6.60	0.37	56.37	55.1	50.87
AJs	97	60.82	1,927	19.86	0.77	60.82	50.52	55.10
AJo	298	50.67	399	1.34	0.16	53.74	50.89	49.65
ATs	114	58.77	2,919	25.61	0.71	60.91	52.73	63.79
ATo	314	49.36	3,550	11.31	0.31	55.76	56.47	54.14
A9s	103	48.54	(496)	(4.82)	0.09	52.08	52.08	52.00
A9o	289	41.52	635	2.20	0.00	47.81	53.78	50.37
A8s	118	38.98	(2,130)	(18.05)	(0.42)	43.81	52.38	41.82
A8o	270	32.59	(2,992)	(11.08)	(0.45)	40.55	52.53	46.49
A7s	92	35.87	(820)	(8.92)	(0.22)	45.21	58.9	46.51
A7o	299	37.79	(2,476)	(8.28)	(0.24)	46.69	52.89	51.56
A6s	97	40.21	(15)	(0.16)	0.15	46.43	50	66.67
A6o	294	37.07	(2,132)	(7.25)	(0.17)	49.32	50.23	51.35
A5s	84	39.29	(453)	(5.40)	(0.34)	45.21	52.05	50.00
A5o	335	41.19	818	2.44	0.17	53.70	52.53	56.30
A4s	113	37.17	(1,130)	(10.00)	(0.31)	42.86	50	55.10
A4o	302	32.45	(2,262)	(7.49)	(0.31)	41.70	55.74	42.75
A3s	99	32.32	(628)	(6.34)	(0.30)	38.55	50.6	45.24
A3o	300	27	(1,845)	(6.15)	(0.46)	38.39	49.76	43.81
A2s	109	40.37	452	4.15	0.04	45.36	45.36	50.00
A2o	339	11.5	(3,639)	(10.73)	(0.47)	44.83	72.41	38.10
KK	142	79.58	10,401	73.24	2.29	79.58	55.63	72.15
KQs	111	51.35	1,852	16.69	0.41	51.82	42.73	55.32
KQo	326	40.8	(2,119)	(6.50)	(0.18)	46.18	46.18	48.12
KJs	88	46.59	(47)	(0.54)	0.12	50.00	36.59	53.33
KJo	285	44.56	2,607	9.15	0.27	49.42	42.41	66.97
KTs	103	50.49	918	8.91	0.50	59.09	31.82	64.29
KTo	291	37.11	(735)	(2.53)	(0.08)	43.03	39.04	56.12
K9s	108	37.96	(981)	(9.09)	(0.17)	45.56	37.78	47.06
K9o	307	29.32	(1,791)	(5.83)	(0.25)	38.30	34.89	54.88
K8s	85	44.71	1,121	13.19	0.27	50.00	28.95	54.55
K8o	311	28.62	(2,677)	(8.61)	(0.23)	37.24	29.71	52.11
K7s	107	21.5	(2,029)	(18.96)	(0.61)	25.56	37.78	44.12
K7o	312	23.08	(1,696)	(5.44)	(0.32)	32.29	26.46	54.24
K6s	103	30.1	1,572	15.27	(0.29)	34.07	36.26	54.55
K6o	333	19.52	(4,891)	(14.69)	(0.44)	29.15	34.08	52.63
K5s	103	32.04	439	4.26	(0.15)	35.11	32.98	61.29

K5o	302	19.21	(2,642)	(8.75)	(0.42)	29.74	28.21	49.09
K4s	109	30.28	31	0.28	(0.02)	33.67	24.49	87.50
K4o	322	10.25	(3,634)	(11.29)	(0.45)	26.83	23.58	58.62
K3s	116	29.31	552	4.76	0.02	33.33	24.51	76.00
K3o	311	6.75	(5,030)	(16.17)	(0.54)	24.42	26.74	39.13
K2s	120	22.5	(62)	(0.51)	(0.26)	27.27	29.29	44.83
K2o	307	2.28	(4,014)	(13.07)	(0.54)	17.95	17.95	28.57
QQ	151	70.86	4,174	27.64	1.39	70.86	64.9	62.24
QJs	99	45.45	948	9.58	0.31	48.39	44.09	53.66
QJo	306	37.58	(235)	(0.77)	(0.13)	43.07	38.95	51.92
QTs	98	41.84	698	7.12	0.29	50.62	45.68	62.16
QTo	349	39.83	290	0.83	(0.04)	44.13	43.17	55.15
Q9s	102	37.25	38	0.37	0.03	42.22	33.33	60.00
Q9o	294	32.31	(867)	(2.95)	(0.15)	36.82	32.95	57.65
Q8s	106	35.85	(184)	(1.73)	(0.24)	40.00	43.16	53.66
Q8o	355	23.38	(2,756)	(7.76)	(0.36)	31.09	31.46	44.05
Q7s	88	29.55	(923)	(10.48)	(0.29)	34.21	31.58	58.33
Q7o	332	18.98	(4,282)	(12.90)	(0.45)	29.72	29.72	47.62
Q6s	116	29.31	(662)	(5.71)	(0.30)	31.48	29.63	46.88
Q6o	305	14.1	(4,356)	(14.28)	(0.53)	25.75	25.75	41.86
Q5s	107	25.23	(1,054)	(9.85)	(0.37)	26.73	26.73	44.44
Q5o	305	11.8	(3,910)	(12.82)	(0.59)	22.78	27.22	44.19
Q4s	98	25.51	(396)	(4.04)	(0.34)	30.86	28.4	56.52
Q4o	317	5.99	(4,588)	(14.47)	(0.51)	21.59	22.73	45.00
Q3s	105	23.81	(152)	(1.44)	(0.15)	26.60	24.47	60.87
Q3o	289	4.5	(3,816)	(13.21)	(0.47)	26.00	24	58.33
Q2s	112	19.64	(83)	(0.74)	(0.30)	29.73	22.97	52.94
Q2o	344	2.62	(3,563)	(10.36)	(0.44)	45.00	30	66.67
JJ	139	66.19	6,842	49.22	1.29	66.19	66.19	58.70
JTs	113	39.82	257	2.27	(0.22)	42.86	38.1	42.50
JTo	303	31.35	(383)	(1.26)	(0.30)	35.45	38.43	49.51
J9s	107	46.73	1,120	10.47	0.27	52.63	55.79	58.49
J9o	305	34.43	867	2.84	(0.08)	38.32	34.31	53.19
J8s	92	34.78	100	1.08	0.01	40.00	37.5	50.00
J8o	290	25.17	(1,024)	(3.53)	(0.22)	36.32	32.34	53.85
J7s	103	36.89	(426)	(4.14)	0.03	39.58	35.42	52.94
J7o	299	21.4	(1,974)	(6.60)	(0.29)	34.22	27.81	50.00
J6s	96	27.08	(909)	(9.47)	(0.42)	32.10	34.57	50.00
J6o	302	9.6	(4,239)	(14.04)	(0.50)	25.22	27.83	43.75
J5s	102	31.37	889	8.71	0.12	39.02	35.37	68.97
J5o	305	7.21	(3,201)	(10.50)	(0.51)	22.22	24.24	54.17
J4s	102	26.47	(105)	(1.03)	(0.09)	31.76	20	58.82
J4o	316	3.8	(3,869)	(12.24)	(0.49)	18.75	20.31	53.85
J3s	110	18.18	(1,344)	(12.21)	(0.41)	29.41	17.65	58.33

J3o	301	0.33	(3,831)	(12.73)	(0.50)	10.00	10	100.00
J2s	93	7.53	(682)	(7.33)	(0.44)	23.33	43.33	46.15
J2o	317	-	(4,343)	(13.70)	(0.51)	-	-	-
TT	165	66.67	6,250	37.88	1.36	67.07	52.44	60.47
T9s	110	32.73	65	0.59	(0.15)	36.36	47.47	48.94
T9o	313	25.56	(2,582)	(8.25)	(0.36)	29.09	34.91	45.83
T8s	103	31.07	(1,490)	(14.46)	(0.47)	35.96	37.08	27.27
T8o	282	25.89	(4,085)	(14.49)	(0.45)	32.30	33.63	46.05
T7s	114	28.95	(1,418)	(12.44)	(0.33)	34.74	34.74	48.48
T7o	341	20.82	(3,402)	(9.98)	(0.47)	30.08	32.63	40.26
T6s	119	29.41	(986)	(8.29)	(0.25)	34.65	32.67	45.45
T6o	328	8.84	(4,699)	(14.33)	(0.50)	23.97	22.31	40.74
T5s	124	32.26	676	5.45	0.16	39.60	36.63	62.16
T5o	312	8.01	(3,481)	(11.16)	(0.49)	30.12	27.71	43.48
T4s	114	26.32	(676)	(5.93)	(0.11)	34.48	21.84	52.63
T4o	310	5.81	(4,126)	(13.31)	(0.50)	32.73	38.18	33.33
T3s	108	17.59	241	2.23	(0.24)	37.25	25.49	61.54
T3o	378	0.53	(5,132)	(13.58)	(0.51)	33.33	16.67	-
T2s	103	3.88	(1,046)	(10.16)	(0.47)	25.00	37.5	50.00
T2o	349	-	(4,277)	(12.26)	(0.50)	-	-	-
99	154	56.49	1,301	8.45	0.57	60.00	53.1	54.55
98s	99	34.34	(472)	(4.76)	(0.26)	39.53	36.05	48.39
98o	322	25.78	(4,354)	(13.52)	(0.42)	31.09	28.46	46.05
97s	108	37.96	72	0.66	0.07	42.71	35.42	58.82
97o	324	23.15	(3,646)	(11.25)	(0.47)	30.12	36.95	39.13
96s	106	26.42	(707)	(6.67)	(0.38)	30.77	25.27	65.22
96o	302	7.28	(3,519)	(11.65)	(0.50)	25.00	26.14	47.83
95s	104	25.96	(1,684)	(16.20)	(0.54)	30.00	31.11	42.86
95o	294	8.84	(1,909)	(6.49)	(0.31)	40.63	25	81.25
94s	102	15.69	(1,628)	(15.96)	(0.58)	28.07	33.33	42.11
94o	327	3.67	(4,291)	(13.12)	(0.47)	35.29	20.59	57.14
93s	111	2.7	(2,089)	(18.82)	(0.67)	11.11	18.52	-
93o	299	0.33	(3,745)	(12.53)	(0.50)	25.00	25	100.00
92s	98	2.04	(1,220)	(12.45)	(0.48)	28.57	28.57	50.00
92o	324	-	(3,929)	(12.13)	(0.50)	-	-	-
88	139	53.96	1,862	13.39	0.58	59.52	49.21	59.68
87s	99	28.28	(878)	(8.87)	(0.33)	34.15	32.93	40.74
87o	300	25.67	(2,816)	(9.39)	(0.44)	30.92	31.73	44.30
86s	94	29.79	(705)	(7.50)	(0.21)	32.94	27.06	47.83
86o	303	14.19	(1,961)	(6.47)	(0.45)	25.75	27.54	54.35
85s	105	28.57	516	4.91	(0.17)	32.26	32.26	53.33
85o	305	6.23	(4,101)	(13.45)	(0.53)	27.14	35.71	44.00
84s	114	17.54	(1,299)	(11.39)	(0.51)	24.39	28.05	43.48
84o	327	2.45	(4,226)	(12.92)	(0.51)	26.67	26.67	37.50

83s	108	8.33	(1,307)	(12.10)	(0.35)	40.91	18.18	75.00
83o	285	-	(3,579)	(12.56)	(0.50)	-	-	-
82s	99	-	(1,606)	(16.22)	(0.52)	-	-	-
82o	306	-	(4,298)	(14.05)	(0.50)	-	-	-
77	155	40.65	(285)	(1.84)	(0.17)	43.97	38.3	48.15
76s	115	31.3	(324)	(2.82)	(0.16)	35.29	35.29	61.11
76o	320	20.63	(4,049)	(12.65)	(0.39)	27.50	28.75	52.17
75s	97	31.96	751	7.74	0.10	37.35	36.14	56.67
75o	306	17.32	(3,677)	(12.01)	(0.46)	31.18	31.18	49.06
74s	116	25.86	(2,201)	(18.97)	(0.44)	29.70	28.71	37.93
74o	286	3.15	(3,401)	(11.89)	(0.49)	27.27	18.18	33.33
73s	103	9.71	(966)	(9.37)	(0.64)	19.23	26.92	21.43
73o	318	-	(4,024)	(12.65)	(0.50)	-	-	-
72s	94	2.13	(913)	(9.71)	(0.39)	33.33	33.33	100.00
72o	298	-	(3,786)	(12.70)	(0.50)	-	100	-
66	152	49.34	2,201	14.48	0.31	54.74	41.61	54.39
65s	116	31.9	248	2.14	(0.06)	37.76	29.59	55.17
65o	346	18.21	(4,984)	(14.41)	(0.56)	27.63	28.95	39.39
64s	124	25	(1,821)	(14.68)	(0.39)	31.31	27.27	48.15
64o	334	1.8	(4,487)	(13.43)	(0.59)	11.76	15.69	37.50
63s	115	17.39	(1,854)	(16.12)	(0.68)	25.00	23.75	26.32
63o	320	0.31	(4,063)	(12.70)	(0.49)	50.00	100	50.00
62s	109	1.83	(1,363)	(12.50)	(0.46)	22.22	22.22	100.00
62o	331	-	(4,206)	(12.71)	(0.51)	-	100	-
55	157	44.59	298	1.90	0.20	50.00	37.86	56.60
54s	111	33.33	80	0.72	(0.04)	38.14	29.9	51.72
54o	316	10.44	(3,107)	(9.83)	(0.51)	25.98	25.98	36.36
53s	102	25.49	(672)	(6.59)	(0.04)	36.62	26.76	63.16
53o	282	0.71	(3,595)	(12.75)	(0.48)	40.00	20	100.00
52s	103	4.85	(1,202)	(11.67)	(0.46)	25.00	20	50.00
52o	320	-	(3,900)	(12.19)	(0.50)	-	-	-
44	160	45	933	5.83	0.33	51.80	41.73	53.45
43s	115	19.13	(183)	(1.59)	(0.40)	29.73	44.59	39.39
43o	312	0.32	(4,331)	(13.88)	(0.49)	20.00	20	100.00
42s	113	3.54	(1,680)	(14.87)	(0.40)	28.57	28.57	75.00
42o	305	-	(3,755)	(12.31)	(0.50)	-	-	-
33	156	32.69	(1,558)	(9.99)	(0.28)	36.69	34.53	52.08
32s	113	1.77	(1,802)	(15.94)	(0.58)	11.11	5.56	-
32o	321	-	(4,214)	(13.13)	(0.50)	-	-	-
22	163	33.74	(956)	(5.86)	(0.27)	37.24	26.9	56.41
Total	34,548	22.1	(201,648)	(5.84)	(0.25)	39.82	38.22	51.93

							Went to	Won at
				Avg	**BB/**	**Win**		
Hand	**Trials**	**Win %**	**Amount ($)**	**$/Hand**	**Hand**	**% WSF**	**SD (%)**	**SD (%)**
AA	151	86.09	11,449	75.82	2.73	86.09	56.95	79.07
AKs	89	61.8	3,396	38.16	1.05	61.80	61.8	50.91
AKo	306	60.13	4,215	13.77	0.58	60.13	52.61	55.90
AQs	109	59.63	1,534	14.07	0.56	59.63	56.88	54.84
AQo	316	56.65	2,097	6.63	0.38	56.37	55.1	50.87
AJs	97	60.82	1,927	19.86	0.77	60.82	50.52	55.10
AJo	281	53.74	662	2.36	0.20	53.74	50.89	49.65
ATs	110	60.91	2,974	27.04	0.75	60.91	52.73	63.79
ATo	278	55.76	3,993	14.36	0.42	55.76	56.47	54.14
A9s	96	52.08	(396)	(4.13)	0.14	52.08	52.08	52.00
A9o	251	47.81	1,051	4.19	0.08	47.81	53.78	50.37
A8s	105	43.81	(1,936)	(18.44)	(0.41)	43.81	52.38	41.82
A8o	217	40.55	(2,337)	(10.77)	(0.44)	40.55	52.53	46.49
A7s	73	45.21	(574)	(7.87)	(0.14)	45.21	58.9	46.51
A7o	242	46.69	(1,744)	(7.21)	(0.18)	46.69	52.89	51.56
A6s	84	46.43	170	2.02	0.25	46.43	50	66.67
A6o	221	49.32	(1,135)	(5.14)	(0.06)	49.32	50.23	51.35
A5s	73	45.21	(298)	(4.09)	(0.32)	45.21	52.05	50.00
A5o	257	53.7	1,740	6.77	0.37	53.70	52.53	56.30
A4s	98	42.86	(926)	(9.45)	(0.28)	42.86	50	55.10
A4o	235	41.7	(1,480)	(6.30)	(0.25)	41.70	55.74	42.75
A3s	83	38.55	(402)	(4.84)	(0.26)	38.55	50.6	45.24
A3o	211	38.39	(778)	(3.69)	(0.44)	38.39	49.76	43.81
A2s	97	45.36	578	5.96	0.10	45.36	45.36	50.00
A2o	87	44.83	(456)	(5.24)	(0.38)	44.83	72.41	38.10
KK	142	79.58	10,401	73.24	2.29	79.58	55.63	72.15
KQs	110	51.82	1,867	16.98	0.41	51.82	42.73	55.32
KQo	288	46.18	(1,584)	(5.50)	(0.14)	46.18	46.18	48.12
KJs	82	50	(6)	(0.08)	0.17	50.00	36.59	53.33
KJo	257	49.42	2,958	11.51	0.36	49.42	42.41	66.97
KTs	88	59.09	1,131	12.85	0.67	59.09	31.82	64.29
KTo	251	43.03	(184)	(0.73)	(0.02)	43.03	39.04	56.12
K9s	90	45.56	(686)	(7.63)	(0.10)	45.56	37.78	47.06
K9o	235	38.3	(942)	(4.01)	(0.17)	38.30	34.89	54.88
K8s	76	50	1,261	16.59	0.36	50.00	28.95	54.55
K8o	239	37.24	(1,832)	(7.67)	(0.15)	37.24	29.71	52.11
K7s	90	25.56	(1,754)	(19.49)	(0.63)	25.56	37.78	44.12
K7o	223	32.29	(740)	(3.32)	(0.25)	32.29	26.46	54.24
K6s	91	34.07	1,742	19.15	(0.26)	34.07	36.26	54.55
K6o	222	28.83	(3,444)	(15.51)	(0.42)	28.83	33.78	52.00
K5s	94	35.11	540	5.74	(0.12)	35.11	32.98	61.29

(Table title: Mid-Put $ in Pot)

K5o	195	29.74	(1,358)	(6.96)	(0.38)	29.74	28.21	49.09
K4s	98	33.67	206	2.10	0.03	33.67	24.49	87.50
K4o	123	26.83	(1,299)	(10.56)	(0.37)	26.83	23.58	58.62
K3s	102	33.33	753	7.39	0.09	33.33	24.51	76.00
K3o	86	24.42	(2,118)	(24.62)	(0.66)	24.42	26.74	39.13
K2s	99	27.27	162	1.64	(0.21)	27.27	29.29	44.83
K2o	39	17.95	(905)	(23.20)	(0.79)	17.95	17.95	28.57
QQ	151	70.86	4,174	27.64	1.39	70.86	64.9	62.24
QJs	93	48.39	1,023	11.00	0.36	48.39	44.09	53.66
QJo	267	43.07	254	0.95	(0.08)	43.07	38.95	51.92
QTs	81	50.62	926	11.43	0.46	50.62	45.68	62.16
QTo	315	44.13	790	2.51	0.01	44.13	43.17	55.15
Q9s	90	42.22	301	3.34	0.10	42.22	33.33	60.00
Q9o	258	36.82	(345)	(1.34)	(0.10)	36.82	32.95	57.65
Q8s	95	40	(76)	(0.80)	(0.21)	40.00	43.16	53.66
Q8o	267	31.09	(1,802)	(6.75)	(0.31)	31.09	31.46	44.05
Q7s	76	34.21	(812)	(10.68)	(0.25)	34.21	31.58	58.33
Q7o	212	29.72	(2,835)	(13.37)	(0.42)	29.72	29.72	47.62
Q6s	108	31.48	(547)	(5.07)	(0.29)	31.48	29.63	46.88
Q6o	167	25.75	(2,654)	(15.89)	(0.55)	25.75	25.75	41.86
Q5s	101	26.73	(949)	(9.39)	(0.36)	26.73	26.73	44.44
Q5o	158	22.78	(2,351)	(14.88)	(0.67)	22.78	27.22	44.19
Q4s	81	30.86	(184)	(2.27)	(0.31)	30.86	28.4	56.52
Q4o	88	21.59	(1,668)	(18.96)	(0.55)	21.59	22.73	45.00
Q3s	94	26.6	(22)	(0.23)	(0.11)	26.60	24.47	60.87
Q3o	50	26	(645)	(12.91)	(0.35)	26.00	24	58.33
Q2s	74	29.73	318	4.29	(0.20)	29.73	22.97	52.94
Q2o	20	45	311	15.55	0.55	45.00	30	66.67
JJ	139	66.19	6,842	49.22	1.29	66.19	66.19	58.70
JTs	105	42.86	365	3.48	(0.20)	42.86	38.1	42.50
JTo	268	35.45	86	0.32	(0.27)	35.45	38.43	49.51
J9s	95	52.63	1,258	13.24	0.37	52.63	55.79	58.49
J9o	275	38.18	1,260	4.58	(0.04)	38.32	34.31	53.19
J8s	80	40	256	3.20	0.08	40.00	37.5	50.00
J8o	201	36.32	131	0.65	(0.10)	36.32	32.34	53.85
J7s	96	39.58	(350)	(3.65)	0.07	39.58	35.42	52.94
J7o	187	34.22	(657)	(3.51)	(0.16)	34.22	27.81	50.00
J6s	81	32.1	(745)	(9.20)	(0.41)	32.10	34.57	50.00
J6o	115	25.22	(1,823)	(15.85)	(0.51)	25.22	27.83	43.75
J5s	82	39.02	1,257	15.33	0.28	39.02	35.37	68.97
J5o	99	22.22	(936)	(9.45)	(0.52)	22.22	24.24	54.17
J4s	85	31.76	201	2.36	0.00	31.76	20	58.82
J4o	64	18.75	(765)	(11.95)	(0.47)	18.75	20.31	53.85
J3s	68	29.41	(900)	(13.23)	(0.36)	29.41	17.65	58.33

J3o	10	10	(207)	(20.70)	(0.55)	10.00	10	100.00
J2s	30	23.33	(30)	(1.00)	(0.31)	23.33	43.33	46.15
J2o	3	-	(230)	(76.67)	(1.50)	-	-	-
TT	164	67.07	6,255	38.14	1.37	67.07	52.44	60.47
T9s	99	36.36	213	2.15	(0.11)	36.36	47.47	48.94
T9o	275	29.09	(2,008)	(7.30)	(0.35)	29.09	34.91	45.83
T8s	89	35.96	(1,292)	(14.51)	(0.47)	35.96	37.08	27.27
T8o	226	32.3	(3,570)	(15.80)	(0.44)	32.30	33.63	46.05
T7s	95	34.74	(1,070)	(11.26)	(0.30)	34.74	34.74	48.48
T7o	236	30.08	(2,224)	(9.42)	(0.45)	30.08	32.63	40.26
T6s	101	34.65	(792)	(7.84)	(0.21)	34.65	32.67	45.45
T6o	121	23.97	(2,210)	(18.27)	(0.51)	23.97	22.31	40.74
T5s	101	39.6	977	9.67	0.31	39.60	36.63	62.16
T5o	83	30.12	(651)	(7.84)	(0.46)	30.12	27.71	43.48
T4s	87	34.48	(275)	(3.16)	0.01	34.48	21.84	52.63
T4o	55	32.73	(723)	(13.14)	(0.52)	32.73	38.18	33.33
T3s	51	37.25	916	17.96	0.04	37.25	25.49	61.54
T3o	6	33.33	(170)	(28.25)	(0.86)	33.33	16.67	-
T2s	16	25	19	1.19	(0.30)	25.00	37.5	50.00
T2o	1	-	(60)	(60.00)	(1.00)	-	-	-
99	145	60	1,419	9.79	0.64	60.00	53.1	54.55
98s	86	39.53	(261)	(3.03)	(0.22)	39.53	36.05	48.39
98o	267	31.09	(3,522)	(13.19)	(0.40)	31.09	28.46	46.05
97s	96	42.71	223	2.32	0.15	42.71	35.42	58.82
97o	249	30.12	(2,702)	(10.85)	(0.46)	30.12	36.95	39.13
96s	91	30.77	(484)	(5.32)	(0.36)	30.77	25.27	65.22
96o	88	25	(882)	(10.02)	(0.51)	25.00	26.14	47.83
95s	90	30	(1,453)	(16.15)	(0.55)	30.00	31.11	42.86
95o	64	40.63	831	12.98	0.37	40.63	25	81.25
94s	57	28.07	(982)	(17.22)	(0.64)	28.07	33.33	42.11
94o	34	35.29	(359)	(10.54)	(0.19)	35.29	20.59	57.14
93s	27	11.11	(1,054)	(39.04)	(1.21)	11.11	18.52	-
93o	4	25	(81)	(20.25)	(0.59)	25.00	25	100.00
92s	7	28.57	(103)	(14.71)	(0.23)	28.57	28.57	50.00
88	126	59.52	1,976	15.68	0.69	59.52	49.21	59.68
87s	82	34.15	(671)	(8.18)	(0.30)	34.15	32.93	40.74
87o	249	30.92	(2,086)	(8.38)	(0.43)	30.92	31.73	44.30
86s	85	32.94	(535)	(6.30)	(0.18)	32.94	27.06	47.83
86o	167	25.75	(484)	(2.90)	(0.40)	25.75	27.54	54.35
85s	93	32.26	672	7.23	(0.12)	32.26	32.26	53.33
85o	70	27.14	(1,217)	(17.38)	(0.64)	27.14	35.71	44.00
84s	82	24.39	(836)	(10.19)	(0.51)	24.39	28.05	43.48
84o	30	26.67	(577)	(19.24)	(0.64)	26.67	26.67	37.50
83s	22	40.91	(50)	(2.27)	0.25	40.91	18.18	75.00

83o	1	-	(45)	(45.00)	(1.50)	-	-	-
82s	3	-	(140)	(46.67)	(1.00)	-	-	-
77	142	44.37	(136)	(0.96)	(0.15)	43.97	38.3	48.15
76s	102	35.29	(88)	(0.86)	(0.11)	35.29	35.29	61.11
76o	240	27.5	(2,995)	(12.48)	(0.35)	27.50	28.75	52.17
75s	83	37.35	912	10.99	0.20	37.35	36.14	56.67
75o	170	31.18	(1,987)	(11.69)	(0.42)	31.18	31.18	49.06
74s	101	29.7	(2,015)	(19.95)	(0.43)	29.70	28.71	37.93
74o	33	27.27	(191)	(5.77)	(0.41)	27.27	18.18	33.33
73s	52	19.23	(314)	(6.03)	(0.78)	19.23	26.92	21.43
73o	1	-	(60)	(60.00)	(1.00)	-	-	-
72s	6	33.33	102	16.92	1.16	33.33	33.33	100.00
72o	1	-	(32)	(32.00)	(1.07)	-	100	-
66	137	54.74	2,421	17.67	0.40	54.74	41.61	54.39
65s	98	37.76	485	4.95	0.02	37.76	29.59	55.17
65o	228	27.63	(3,518)	(15.43)	(0.60)	27.63	28.95	39.39
64s	99	31.31	(1,549)	(15.64)	(0.36)	31.31	27.27	48.15
64o	51	11.76	(994)	(19.49)	(1.08)	11.76	15.69	37.50
63s	80	25	(1,354)	(16.93)	(0.75)	25.00	23.75	26.32
63o	2	50	9	4.50	0.75	50.00	100	50.00
62s	9	22.22	(76)	(8.39)	(0.06)	22.22	22.22	100.00
62o	1	-	(100)	(100.00)	(2.50)	-	100	-
55	140	50	492	3.51	0.29	50.00	37.86	56.60
54s	97	38.14	264	2.72	0.02	38.14	29.9	51.72
54o	127	25.98	(573)	(4.51)	(0.52)	25.98	25.98	36.36
53s	71	36.62	(215)	(3.02)	0.15	36.62	26.76	63.16
53o	5	40	(12)	(2.40)	0.43	40.00	20	100.00
52s	20	25	(63)	(3.13)	(0.31)	25.00	20	50.00
44	139	51.8	1,214	8.73	0.46	51.80	41.73	53.45
43s	74	29.73	420	5.68	(0.35)	29.73	44.59	39.39
43o	5	20	(31)	(6.20)	0.03	20.00	20	100.00
42s	14	28.57	(238)	(17.00)	0.28	28.57	28.57	75.00
33	139	36.69	(1,361)	(9.79)	(0.25)	36.69	34.53	52.08
32s	18	11.11	(479)	(26.60)	(1.00)	11.11	5.56	-
22	146	37.67	(700)	(4.79)	(0.25)	37.24	26.9	56.41
Total	19,168	39.83	(7,113)	(0.37)	(0.05)	39.82	38.22	51.93

Grinder								
Hand	Trials	Win %	Amount ($)	Avg $/Hand	BB/ Hand	Win % WSF	Went to SD (%)	Won at SD (%)
AA	92	72.83	15,577	169.32	1.70	72.83	64.13	59.32
AKs	67	59.7	3,790	56.57	0.86	59.70	58.21	56.41
AKo	173	63.01	15,739	90.97	0.94	63.01	54.91	61.05

AQs	70	52.86	17	0.24	0.14	52.86	54.29	47.37
AQo	175	56.57	10,346	59.12	0.73	57.89	43.86	66.67
AJs	55	63.64	7,317	133.04	1.31	64.81	42.59	65.22
AJo	184	51.09	8,202	44.57	0.62	55.95	44.05	68.92
ATs	62	56.45	1,469	23.69	0.36	58.33	45	55.56
ATo	201	44.78	4,693	23.35	0.23	51.74	50	56.98
A9s	72	51.39	1,502	20.85	0.58	58.73	46.03	68.97
A9o	176	36.36	2,469	14.03	(0.03)	47.76	40.3	59.26
A8s	66	34.85	107	1.62	0.14	40.35	31.58	50.00
A8o	189	31.75	136	0.72	0.04	49.59	41.32	54.00
A7s	41	43.9	99	2.40	0.33	48.65	37.84	57.14
A7o	180	28.33	(3,596)	(19.98)	(0.16)	45.54	33.93	55.26
A6s	46	32.61	(977)	(21.24)	(0.40)	39.47	26.32	60.00
A6o	167	22.16	(4,103)	(24.57)	(0.26)	41.11	37.78	52.94
A5s	71	47.89	2,083	29.34	0.58	53.97	49.21	61.29
A5o	204	24.02	(5,395)	(26.44)	(0.20)	42.98	39.47	60.00
A4s	70	34.29	(130)	(1.85)	(0.19)	38.10	36.51	52.17
A4o	177	22.03	(5,094)	(28.78)	(0.35)	38.24	50.98	46.15
A3s	64	40.63	(1,096)	(17.13)	(0.08)	44.07	47.46	53.57
A3o	190	21.05	(4,170)	(21.94)	(0.35)	43.96	42.86	46.15
A2s	58	32.76	(725)	(12.50)	(0.11)	35.85	32.08	76.47
A2o	172	21.51	(4,412)	(25.65)	(0.27)	43.02	38.37	57.58
KK	91	72.53	11,978	131.63	1.90	72.22	66.67	65.00
KQs	58	58.62	6,347	109.44	1.07	59.65	38.6	77.27
KQo	172	41.28	186	1.08	(0.03)	44.65	33.96	59.26
KJs	67	44.78	3,318	49.52	0.45	51.72	44.83	57.69
KJo	192	27.6	(5,136)	(26.75)	(0.42)	37.06	41.96	45.00
KTs	58	31.03	(849)	(14.64)	(0.15)	36.00	44	59.09
KTo	183	22.4	(8,310)	(45.41)	(0.34)	30.15	32.35	52.27
K9s	51	31.37	(796)	(15.61)	(0.18)	34.78	41.3	52.63
K9o	187	18.72	(3,918)	(20.95)	(0.30)	29.91	27.35	62.50
K8s	53	26.42	253	4.77	0.00	31.82	11.36	80.00
K8o	197	13.71	(8,032)	(40.77)	(0.37)	30.34	26.97	54.17
K7s	61	19.67	(1,000)	(16.39)	(0.35)	25.00	10.42	80.00
K7o	174	11.49	(4,365)	(25.09)	(0.36)	34.48	25.86	66.67
K6s	55	18.18	(1,517)	(27.58)	(0.47)	23.81	19.05	50.00
K6o	182	7.14	(8,344)	(45.85)	(0.50)	22.03	22.03	53.85
K5s	64	21.88	(3,459)	(54.05)	(0.62)	26.92	25	46.15
K5o	180	6.11	(9,333)	(51.85)	(0.53)	25.58	32.56	35.71
K4s	64	25	(2,963)	(46.30)	(0.23)	33.33	16.67	62.50
K4o	185	2.7	(8,577)	(46.36)	(0.52)	16.13	16.13	60.00
K3s	48	22.92	(491)	(10.23)	0.09	31.43	28.57	80.00
K3o	184	5.43	(8,323)	(45.23)	(0.49)	26.32	42.11	43.75
K2s	49	12.24	(2,522)	(51.46)	(0.34)	21.43	28.57	75.00

K2o	144	1.39	(5,464)	(37.94)	(0.48)	13.33	6.67	100.00
QQ	107	62.62	9,666	90.34	1.03	62.62	60.75	58.46
QJs	61	34.43	1,388	22.75	0.25	36.21	29.31	58.82
QJo	181	25.97	(1,057)	(5.84)	(0.11)	38.84	33.06	55.00
QTs	53	24.53	(4,655)	(87.83)	(0.61)	26.00	28	35.71
QTo	197	20.3	(6,135)	(31.14)	(0.36)	34.19	33.33	56.41
Q9s	65	36.92	(464)	(7.14)	0.16	40.00	31.67	52.63
Q9o	167	16.77	(2,692)	(16.12)	(0.25)	32.18	28.74	60.00
Q8s	50	24	313	6.26	(0.08)	28.57	38.1	62.50
Q8o	194	9.28	(11,988)	(61.79)	(0.57)	19.78	17.58	43.75
Q7s	56	19.64	(654)	(11.68)	(0.34)	33.33	15.15	40.00
Q7o	153	3.27	(7,631)	(49.88)	(0.55)	15.63	15.63	40.00
Q6s	58	22.41	1,503	25.91	(0.17)	31.71	26.83	72.73
Q6o	168	2.98	(7,196)	(42.83)	(0.55)	15.63	25	50.00
Q5s	49	16.33	(992)	(20.23)	(0.39)	22.22	16.67	33.33
Q5o	186	2.69	(8,293)	(44.59)	(0.53)	17.24	13.79	25.00
Q4s	54	16.67	(316)	(5.85)	(0.31)	26.47	35.29	58.33
Q4o	180	2.22	(8,003)	(44.46)	(0.54)	22.22	33.33	50.00
Q3s	44	13.64	(1,827)	(41.52)	(0.54)	28.57	42.86	44.44
Q3o	196	1.02	(7,428)	(37.90)	(0.49)	18.18	9.09	-
Q2s	61	8.2	(2,605)	(42.70)	(0.54)	25.00	15	33.33
Q2o	170	-	(7,030)	(41.35)	(0.51)	-	-	-
JJ	85	70.59	15,372	180.85	2.07	70.59	58.82	70.00
JTs	62	35.48	3,423	55.21	0.16	36.67	40	66.67
JTo	185	21.62	(9,368)	(50.64)	(0.41)	32.00	26.4	51.52
J9s	57	40.35	2,347	41.17	0.29	45.10	43.14	72.73
J9o	184	17.39	(2,892)	(15.72)	(0.28)	33.68	21.05	75.00
J8s	51	13.73	(4,101)	(80.41)	(0.91)	17.07	41.46	29.41
J8o	171	8.19	(8,606)	(50.32)	(0.50)	23.33	40	45.83
J7s	57	22.81	(963)	(16.89)	(0.23)	32.50	32.5	46.15
J7o	189	4.23	(8,112)	(42.92)	(0.48)	23.53	17.65	66.67
J6s	62	19.35	(504)	(8.13)	(0.16)	33.33	25	55.56
J6o	185	2.16	(8,794)	(47.54)	(0.54)	17.39	26.09	33.33
J5s	58	12.07	(2,714)	(46.78)	(0.45)	25.00	32.14	44.44
J5o	162	3.7	(6,332)	(39.09)	(0.50)	35.29	47.06	37.50
J4s	52	7.69	(2,364)	(45.46)	(0.57)	22.22	33.33	16.67
J4o	166	0.6	(8,543)	(51.46)	(0.54)	6.67	6.67	100.00
J3s	55	5.45	(1,906)	(34.65)	(0.52)	15.79	10.53	50.00
J3o	191	1.05	(6,580)	(34.45)	(0.46)	100.00	-	-
J2s	59	10.17	(116)	(1.97)	(0.16)	40.00	40	83.33
J2o	186	-	(8,135)	(43.74)	(0.54)	-	20	-
TT	92	53.26	3,478	37.80	0.55	53.26	47.83	54.55
T9s	60	26.67	(1,179)	(19.65)	(0.03)	31.37	33.33	58.82
T9o	161	16.77	(2,089)	(12.98)	(0.20)	39.13	28.99	65.00

T8s	51	35.29	102	1.99	0.06	36.73	18.37	66.67
T8o	162	11.11	(4,991)	(30.81)	(0.36)	29.03	16.13	60.00
T7s	64	18.75	(3,915)	(61.17)	(0.70)	23.08	25	53.85
T7o	188	7.45	(9,141)	(48.62)	(0.51)	26.42	24.53	53.85
T6s	66	31.82	3,368	51.02	0.32	41.18	35.29	55.56
T6o	161	4.97	(9,021)	(56.03)	(0.60)	25.00	28.13	33.33
T5s	57	10.53	(1,940)	(34.04)	(0.39)	35.29	17.65	33.33
T5o	158	1.9	(8,122)	(51.41)	(0.56)	25.00	41.67	40.00
T4s	62	6.45	(2,165)	(34.92)	(0.64)	14.29	10.71	33.33
T4o	185	0.54	(8,173)	(44.18)	(0.50)	20.00	20	100.00
T3s	75	8	(3,057)	(40.76)	(0.41)	21.43	32.14	44.44
T3o	183	0.55	(8,153)	(44.55)	(0.53)	14.29	14.29	-
T2s	60	1.67	(2,658)	(44.30)	(0.55)	9.09	9.09	-
T2o	178	0.56	(7,821)	(43.94)	(0.52)	20.00	20	-
99	82	53.66	507	6.18	0.49	54.32	39.51	56.25
98s	52	21.15	(3,023)	(58.13)	(0.59)	23.91	30.43	42.86
98o	183	13.66	(6,094)	(33.30)	(0.40)	30.12	18.07	60.00
97s	54	22.22	(4,648)	(86.06)	(0.71)	26.67	22.22	40.00
97o	180	7.78	(7,049)	(39.16)	(0.46)	25.00	30.36	58.82
96s	60	16.67	(1,332)	(22.20)	(0.59)	22.73	18.18	75.00
96o	180	5	(6,721)	(37.34)	(0.48)	23.68	28.95	45.45
95s	42	11.9	(1,904)	(45.33)	(0.49)	31.25	18.75	66.67
95o	143	3.5	(5,499)	(38.45)	(0.46)	50.00	10	-
94s	52	11.54	(1,693)	(32.56)	(0.34)	35.29	29.41	40.00
94o	192	0.52	(8,523)	(44.39)	(0.49)	16.67	33.33	50.00
93s	59	10.17	(2,315)	(39.24)	(0.39)	30.00	20	75.00
93o	185	0.54	(7,648)	(41.34)	(0.51)	14.29	-	-
92s	58	-	(3,065)	(52.84)	(0.59)	-	-	-
92o	179	0.56	(7,638)	(42.67)	(0.48)	25.00	25	100.00
88	84	35.71	(4,552)	(54.19)	(0.46)	38.46	52.56	51.22
87s	62	19.35	(1,626)	(26.22)	(0.36)	24.49	26.53	53.85
87o	168	10.71	(8,491)	(50.54)	(0.41)	26.09	31.88	54.55
86s	70	25.71	(1,838)	(26.25)	(0.52)	31.03	34.48	55.00
86o	192	10.42	(9,607)	(50.04)	(0.54)	30.30	16.67	27.27
85s	54	14.81	(2,084)	(38.59)	(0.42)	21.62	18.92	28.57
85o	141	4.96	(3,520)	(24.96)	(0.39)	41.18	41.18	71.43
84s	48	12.5	(1,324)	(27.57)	(0.27)	23.08	26.92	71.43
84o	162	1.23	(6,076)	(37.51)	(0.50)	28.57	28.57	50.00
83s	68	7.35	(2,194)	(32.26)	(0.48)	19.23	19.23	80.00
83o	134	0.75	(5,493)	(40.99)	(0.53)	25.00	25	-
82s	62	8.06	(2,271)	(36.62)	(0.36)	38.46	30.77	50.00
82o	171	0.58	(7,593)	(44.40)	(0.48)	50.00	50	100.00
77	95	52.63	6,488	68.29	0.76	53.26	52.17	62.50
76s	65	36.92	3,223	49.58	0.58	42.86	26.79	86.67

Hand	Trials	Win %	Amount ($)	Avg $/Hand	BB/Hand	Win % WSF	Went to SD (%)	Won at SD (%)
76o	160	9.38	(4,534)	(28.33)	(0.42)	33.33	26.67	58.33
75s	52	23.08	(563)	(10.83)	(0.25)	30.00	30	58.33
75o	167	4.79	(7,056)	(42.25)	(0.51)	26.67	33.33	40.00
74s	54	9.26	(2,814)	(52.10)	(0.52)	17.86	21.43	66.67
74o	168	1.19	(7,501)	(44.65)	(0.52)	22.22	22.22	50.00
73s	62	11.29	(845)	(13.63)	(0.19)	38.89	27.78	100.00
73o	149	-	(6,880)	(46.17)	(0.52)	-	-	-
72s	65	1.54	(3,522)	(54.18)	(0.65)	7.69	15.38	50.00
72o	145	-	(5,550)	(38.28)	(0.52)	-	-	-
66	94	42.55	1,641	17.46	0.28	45.45	31.82	64.29
65s	50	22	(1,524)	(30.48)	(0.33)	26.19	14.29	66.67
65o	198	3.54	(7,058)	(35.65)	(0.44)	28.00	12	100.00
64s	59	16.95	(1,279)	(21.68)	(0.40)	32.26	29.03	44.44
64o	161	2.48	(4,970)	(30.87)	(0.45)	28.57	35.71	80.00
63s	68	8.82	(1,726)	(25.38)	(0.39)	22.22	22.22	50.00
63o	160	0.63	(6,968)	(43.55)	(0.50)	20.00	-	-
62s	65	4.62	(2,837)	(43.65)	(0.45)	18.75	25	50.00
62o	173	-	(7,520)	(43.47)	(0.50)	-	-	-
55	72	41.67	2,035	28.26	0.24	46.88	28.13	72.22
54s	58	29.31	(2,421)	(41.74)	(0.17)	36.96	32.61	53.33
54o	189	2.12	(8,373)	(44.30)	(0.50)	15.38	11.54	33.33
53s	52	5.77	(4,588)	(88.23)	(0.97)	9.68	12.9	25.00
53o	196	1.02	(8,864)	(45.22)	(0.52)	33.33	33.33	-
52s	65	1.54	(3,311)	(50.94)	(0.65)	5.56	16.67	-
52o	175	0.57	(7,253)	(41.45)	(0.50)	20.00	20	100.00
44	93	32.26	(1,100)	(11.83)	(0.33)	36.59	29.27	58.33
43s	74	24.32	(122)	(1.64)	(0.15)	36.00	22	100.00
43o	168	1.19	(7,529)	(44.82)	(0.53)	33.33	16.67	-
42s	52	5.77	(1,831)	(35.20)	(0.43)	33.33	11.11	-
42o	177	0.57	(7,888)	(44.57)	(0.51)	33.33	-	-
33	85	25.88	(4,510)	(53.05)	(0.39)	32.35	25	35.29
32s	61	8.2	(1,412)	(23.15)	(0.37)	41.67	41.67	60.00
32o	195	-	(8,215)	(42.13)	(0.50)	-	-	-
22	100	26	(1,717)	(17.17)	(0.07)	34.21	26.32	55.00
Total	19,490	16.32	(460,127)	(23.61)	(0.27)	38.53	34.33	57.03

Grinder-Put $ in Pot								
Hand	Trials	Win %	Amount ($)	Avg $/Hand	BB/Hand	Win % WSF	Went to SD (%)	Won at SD (%)
AA	92	72.83	15,577	169.32	1.70	72.83	64.13	59.32
AKs	67	59.7	3,790	56.57	0.86	59.70	58.21	56.41
AKo	173	63.01	15,739	90.97	0.94	63.01	54.91	61.05
AQs	70	52.86	17	0.24	0.14	52.86	54.29	47.37

AQo	171	57.89	10,456	61.15	0.76	57.89	43.86	66.67
AJs	54	64.81	7,332	135.78	1.34	64.81	42.59	65.22
AJo	168	55.95	8,902	52.99	0.73	55.95	44.05	68.92
ATs	60	58.33	1,529	25.48	0.39	58.33	45	55.56
ATo	173	52.02	5,678	32.82	0.35	51.74	50	56.98
A9s	63	58.73	1,902	30.18	0.73	58.73	46.03	68.97
A9o	134	47.76	4,194	31.30	0.12	47.76	40.3	59.26
A8s	57	40.35	487	8.54	0.24	40.35	31.58	50.00
A8o	121	49.59	2,921	24.14	0.36	49.59	41.32	54.00
A7s	37	48.65	289	7.80	0.42	48.65	37.84	57.14
A7o	112	45.54	(431)	(3.84)	0.04	45.54	33.93	55.26
A6s	38	39.47	(727)	(19.13)	(0.38)	39.47	26.32	60.00
A6o	90	41.11	(763)	(8.47)	(0.05)	41.11	37.78	52.94
A5s	63	53.97	2,368	37.59	0.71	53.97	49.21	61.29
A5o	114	42.98	(1,820)	(15.96)	0.04	42.98	39.47	60.00
A4s	63	38.1	181	2.87	(0.16)	38.10	36.51	52.17
A4o	102	38.24	(2,294)	(22.49)	(0.25)	38.24	50.98	46.15
A3s	59	44.07	(786)	(13.32)	(0.04)	44.07	47.46	53.57
A3o	91	43.96	(640)	(7.03)	(0.19)	43.96	42.86	46.15
A2s	53	35.85	(410)	(7.74)	(0.08)	35.85	32.08	76.47
A2o	86	43.02	(782)	(9.09)	(0.05)	43.02	38.37	57.58
KK	91	72.53	11,978	131.63	1.90	72.22	66.67	65.00
KQs	57	59.65	6,362	111.62	1.10	59.65	38.6	77.27
KQo	159	44.65	826	5.20	0.01	44.65	33.96	59.26
KJs	58	51.72	3,638	62.72	0.60	51.72	44.83	57.69
KJo	143	37.06	(2,906)	(20.32)	(0.39)	37.06	41.96	45.00
KTs	50	36	(499)	(9.98)	(0.09)	36.00	44	59.09
KTo	136	30.15	(6,400)	(47.06)	(0.28)	30.15	32.35	52.27
K9s	46	34.78	(621)	(13.50)	(0.15)	34.78	41.3	52.63
K9o	117	29.91	(1,008)	(8.61)	(0.18)	29.91	27.35	62.50
K8s	44	31.82	518	11.77	0.10	31.82	11.36	80.00
K8o	89	30.34	(4,022)	(45.19)	(0.22)	30.34	26.97	54.17
K7s	48	25	(495)	(10.31)	(0.31)	25.00	10.42	80.00
K7o	58	34.48	(75)	(1.29)	(0.07)	34.48	25.86	66.67
K6s	42	23.81	(1,022)	(24.33)	(0.46)	23.81	19.05	50.00
K6o	59	22.03	(3,374)	(57.19)	(0.51)	22.03	22.03	53.85
K5s	52	26.92	(3,104)	(59.69)	(0.65)	26.92	25	46.15
K5o	43	25.58	(3,513)	(81.70)	(0.62)	25.58	32.56	35.71
K4s	48	33.33	(2,358)	(49.13)	(0.15)	33.33	16.67	62.50
K4o	31	16.13	(2,097)	(67.65)	(0.64)	16.13	16.13	60.00
K3s	35	31.43	(31)	(0.89)	0.30	31.43	28.57	80.00
K3o	38	26.32	(2,388)	(62.84)	(0.47)	26.32	42.11	43.75
K2s	28	21.43	(1,727)	(61.67)	(0.22)	21.43	28.57	75.00
K2o	15	13.33	(4)	(0.27)	(0.34)	13.33	6.67	100.00

QQ	107	62.62	9,666	90.34	1.03	62.62	60.75	58.46
QJs	58	36.21	1,488	25.65	0.29	36.21	29.31	58.82
QJo	121	38.84	1,408	11.64	0.08	38.84	33.06	55.00
QTs	50	26	(4,545)	(90.90)	(0.62)	26.00	28	35.71
QTo	117	34.19	(3,080)	(26.32)	(0.27)	34.19	33.33	56.41
Q9s	60	40	(184)	(3.07)	0.21	40.00	31.67	52.63
Q9o	87	32.18	149	1.71	(0.01)	32.18	28.74	60.00
Q8s	42	28.57	818	19.48	0.00	28.57	38.1	62.50
Q8o	91	19.78	(7,808)	(85.80)	(0.64)	19.78	17.58	43.75
Q7s	33	33.33	221	6.70	(0.23)	33.33	15.15	40.00
Q7o	32	15.63	(2,301)	(71.91)	(0.72)	15.63	15.63	40.00
Q6s	41	31.71	2,018	49.21	(0.03)	31.71	26.83	72.73
Q6o	32	15.63	(1,586)	(49.56)	(0.76)	15.63	25	50.00
Q5s	36	22.22	(492)	(13.65)	(0.34)	22.22	16.67	33.33
Q5o	29	17.24	(1,868)	(64.41)	(0.70)	17.24	13.79	25.00
Q4s	34	26.47	309	9.09	(0.20)	26.47	35.29	58.33
Q4o	18	22.22	(928)	(51.56)	(0.91)	22.22	33.33	50.00
Q3s	21	28.57	(1,032)	(49.14)	(0.58)	28.57	42.86	44.44
Q3o	11	18.18	(33)	(3.00)	(0.39)	18.18	9.09	-
Q2s	20	25	(785)	(39.25)	(0.62)	25.00	15	33.33
JJ	85	70.59	15,372	180.85	2.07	70.59	58.82	70.00
JTs	60	36.67	3,483	58.05	0.18	36.67	40	66.67
JTo	125	32	(7,048)	(56.38)	(0.37)	32.00	26.4	51.52
J9s	51	45.1	2,697	52.87	0.39	45.10	43.14	72.73
J9o	95	33.68	203	2.13	(0.08)	33.68	21.05	75.00
J8s	41	17.07	(3,656)	(89.17)	(1.01)	17.07	41.46	29.41
J8o	60	23.33	(4,641)	(77.34)	(0.49)	23.33	40	45.83
J7s	40	32.5	(503)	(12.58)	(0.12)	32.50	32.5	46.15
J7o	34	23.53	(1,622)	(47.69)	(0.37)	23.53	17.65	66.67
J6s	36	33.33	401	11.14	0.09	33.33	25	55.56
J6o	23	17.39	(2,254)	(98.00)	(0.83)	17.39	26.09	33.33
J5s	28	25	(1,599)	(57.09)	(0.40)	25.00	32.14	44.44
J5o	17	35.29	(322)	(18.94)	(0.52)	35.29	47.06	37.50
J4s	18	22.22	(1,094)	(60.78)	(0.71)	22.22	33.33	16.67
J4o	15	6.67	(1,933)	(128.87)	(0.90)	6.67	6.67	100.00
J3s	19	15.79	(611)	(32.16)	(0.55)	15.79	10.53	50.00
J3o	2	100	1,140	570.00	2.85	100.00	-	-
J2s	15	40	1,439	95.93	0.83	40.00	40	83.33
J2o	5	-	(255)	(51.00)	(1.70)	-	20	-
TT	92	53.26	3,478	37.80	0.55	53.26	47.83	54.55
T9s	51	31.37	(769)	(15.08)	0.06	31.37	33.33	58.82
T9o	69	39.13	1,186	17.19	0.21	39.13	28.99	65.00
T8s	49	36.73	147	2.99	0.08	36.73	18.37	66.67
T8o	62	29.03	(1,431)	(23.08)	(0.12)	29.03	16.13	60.00

T7s	52	23.08	(3,325)	(63.94)	(0.75)	23.08	25	53.85
T7o	53	26.42	(4,041)	(76.24)	(0.55)	26.42	24.53	53.85
T6s	51	41.18	3,918	76.81	0.56	41.18	35.29	55.56
T6o	32	25	(4,036)	(126.13)	(1.01)	25.00	28.13	33.33
T5s	17	35.29	(310)	(18.24)	(0.12)	35.29	17.65	33.33
T5o	12	25	(1,597)	(133.08)	(1.29)	25.00	41.67	40.00
T4s	28	14.29	(925)	(33.04)	(0.80)	14.29	10.71	33.33
T4o	5	20	(318)	(63.60)	(0.32)	20.00	20	100.00
T3s	28	21.43	(952)	(34.00)	(0.23)	21.43	32.14	44.44
T3o	7	14.29	(518)	(73.93)	(1.23)	14.29	14.29	-
T2s	11	9.09	(723)	(65.73)	(0.78)	9.09	9.09	-
T2o	5	20	(301)	(60.20)	(1.31)	20.00	20	-
99	81	54.32	557	6.88	0.50	54.32	39.51	56.25
98s	46	23.91	(2,728)	(59.30)	(0.60)	23.91	30.43	42.86
98o	83	30.12	(2,279)	(27.46)	(0.29)	30.12	18.07	60.00
97s	45	26.67	(4,303)	(95.61)	(0.75)	26.67	22.22	40.00
97o	56	25	(2,324)	(41.50)	(0.36)	25.00	30.36	58.82
96s	44	22.73	(852)	(19.36)	(0.62)	22.73	18.18	75.00
96o	38	23.68	(966)	(25.43)	(0.41)	23.68	28.95	45.45
95s	16	31.25	(584)	(36.50)	(0.47)	31.25	18.75	66.67
95o	10	50	(129)	(12.85)	0.02	50.00	10	-
94s	17	35.29	(308)	(18.12)	0.05	35.29	29.41	40.00
94o	6	16.67	(108)	(18.00)	(0.27)	16.67	33.33	50.00
93s	20	30	(590)	(29.50)	(0.18)	30.00	20	75.00
93o	7	14.29	(168)	(24.00)	(0.86)	14.29	-	-
92s	8	-	(680)	(85.00)	(1.19)	-	-	-
92o	4	25	27	6.75	0.23	25.00	25	100.00
88	78	38.46	(4,332)	(55.54)	(0.46)	38.46	52.56	51.22
87s	49	24.49	(1,151)	(23.48)	(0.32)	24.49	26.53	53.85
87o	69	26.09	(4,626)	(67.04)	(0.28)	26.09	31.88	54.55
86s	58	31.03	(1,353)	(23.32)	(0.52)	31.03	34.48	55.00
86o	66	30.3	(4,072)	(61.70)	(0.62)	30.30	16.67	27.27
85s	37	21.62	(1,489)	(40.24)	(0.39)	21.62	18.92	28.57
85o	17	41.18	1,455	85.59	0.42	41.18	41.18	71.43
84s	26	23.08	(469)	(18.02)	(0.08)	23.08	26.92	71.43
84o	7	28.57	349	49.86	(0.44)	28.57	28.57	50.00
83s	26	19.23	(529)	(20.35)	(0.46)	19.23	19.23	80.00
83o	4	25	(318)	(79.38)	(1.27)	25.00	25	-
82s	13	38.46	(376)	(28.88)	0.15	38.46	30.77	50.00
82o	2	50	57	28.50	0.95	50.00	50	100.00
77	93	53.76	6,588	70.84	0.79	53.26	52.17	62.50
76s	56	42.86	3,608	64.43	0.75	42.86	26.79	86.67
76o	45	33.33	(474)	(10.52)	(0.23)	33.33	26.67	58.33
75s	40	30	(128)	(3.20)	(0.17)	30.00	30	58.33

75o	30	26.67	(1,811)	(60.37)	(0.56)	26.67	33.33	40.00
74s	28	17.86	(1,739)	(62.09)	(0.53)	17.86	21.43	66.67
74o	9	22.22	(371)	(41.17)	(0.74)	22.22	22.22	50.00
73s	18	38.89	915	50.83	0.56	38.89	27.78	100.00
73o	1	-	(105)	(105.00)	(3.50)	-	-	-
72s	13	7.69	(1,267)	(97.46)	(1.27)	7.69	15.38	50.00
72o	5	-	(150)	(30.00)	(1.00)	-	-	-
66	88	45.45	1,801	20.47	0.34	45.45	31.82	64.29
65s	42	26.19	(1,199)	(28.55)	(0.29)	26.19	14.29	66.67
65o	25	28	(343)	(13.72)	(0.03)	28.00	12	100.00
64s	31	32.26	(319)	(10.29)	(0.31)	32.26	29.03	44.44
64o	14	28.57	590	42.14	0.10	28.57	35.71	80.00
63s	27	22.22	(196)	(7.26)	(0.21)	22.22	22.22	50.00
63o	5	20	(113)	(22.50)	(0.43)	20.00	-	-
62s	16	18.75	(692)	(43.25)	(0.30)	18.75	25	50.00
55	64	46.88	2,390	37.34	0.33	46.88	28.13	72.22
54s	46	36.96	(1,831)	(39.80)	(0.08)	36.96	32.61	53.33
54o	26	15.38	(1,693)	(65.12)	(0.49)	15.38	11.54	33.33
53s	31	9.68	(3,848)	(124.13)	(1.29)	9.68	12.9	25.00
53o	6	33.33	(579)	(96.50)	(0.86)	33.33	33.33	-
52s	18	5.56	(1,676)	(93.11)	(1.06)	5.56	16.67	-
52o	5	20	(218)	(43.60)	(0.32)	20.00	20	100.00
44	82	36.59	(700)	(8.54)	(0.31)	36.59	29.27	58.33
43s	50	36	899	17.97	0.02	36.00	22	100.00
43o	6	33.33	(1,049)	(174.83)	(1.27)	33.33	16.67	-
42s	9	33.33	(86)	(9.50)	(0.08)	33.33	11.11	-
42o	3	33.33	(78)	(26.00)	(0.87)	33.33	-	-
33	68	32.35	(3,945)	(58.01)	(0.36)	32.35	25	35.29
32s	12	41.67	638	53.17	0.17	41.67	41.67	60.00
22	76	34.21	(877)	(11.54)	0.07	34.21	26.32	55.00
Total	8,252	38.55	163	0.02	0.04	38.53	34.33	57.03

A Note on Post-Flop Play

When you have three-bet from the big blind with a small pocket pair you should continue to bet the flop and turn. This will do the most to protect your vulnerable, made hand. However, you should generally be prepared to fold if your opponent raises, especially if there are two or more overcards to your pair on the board.

Against certain opponents and on certain boards, it will be correct to call down even if you are raised. This is a tough spot for a pocket pair on a draw heavy board — if you always fold to a raise, you will sometimes be folding the winner, but if you always call-down, you will pay off too much. So use your knowledge of your opponent and the texture of the board to determine the frequency with which he might be bluffing or semi-bluffing.

An alternative line for playing pocket pairs 22-77 is to call pre-flop and then check raise on the flop. This line also works well and arguably gives better information on the flop for the same price. Varying your play between these two approaches will help with balance as well.

You may also choose to "donk check" a small pocket pair on the turn or the river. The "donk check" is when you have the betting lead out of position and check the following street. This is especially appropriate on the river. You are rarely going to get a better hand to fold or a worse hand to call when you bet a weak pair, so check-calling is often best.

When calling against one opponent in the big blind with a weak hand like

you should check-fold the flop unless you make a pair or a good draw. When you do flop one of these hands, you should generally check raise the flop. With a pair, this is for value, and with a draw, this is to increase your fold equity. The one exception is when you flop a decent hand like middle pair (e.g., you hold J♣9♠ on a K♠J♦6♥ flop), where your opponent is likely to have three or fewer outs if behind, and you do not want to take him out of the lead because he will frequently bluff on all three streets.

Defending When The Small Blind Calls

When a player in late position open-raises and the small blind calls, you can call liberally because of the good pots odds — 5-to-1. However, since the pot is now multi-way, you should avoid playing hands with poor reverse implied odds such as A2o-A7o and K2o-K9o. Although many of these hands are good defending hands when heads up, in a multi-way pot you will be less able to control how many bets it costs to go to the showdown, and less likely to win without a showdown or unimproved.

For example, you hold

in the big blind. An aggressive player open-raises on the button, and the small blind folds. You should definitely call. If you flop top pair with a weak kicker, you can check and call all three streets and see the showdown for a total of 3 big bets (0.5 big bets each pre-flop and flop and 1 big bet each turn and river). However, if the small blind calls, you should fold a hand like A♦4♥ because you may be forced to play a big pot with a marginal hand, especially if your opponents play aggressively.

For example, you hold K♦8♣ in the big blind. A tight-aggressive player open-raises on the button, the loose-aggressive small blind calls, and you (incorrectly) call. The flop comes K♣T♥4♣, giving you top pair. The small blind bets, you call, the button raises, the small blind calls, and you call. The turn is the

127

6♦, the small blind checks, you check, the button bets, and the small blind raises. Since the small blind is loose-aggressive, he could be raising with a wide range of hands: a set, two pair, a flush draw, a straight draw, a pair of tens, pocket jacks or queens, or a king with a weaker kicker. Because of the small blind's wide range, you should still call down. Moreover, since the pot has now gotten large, the board is very coordinated, and you may currently have the best hand, you should consider three-betting to protect your hand. So it may cost you 4.5 to 5.5 big bets to get to the showdown with a marginal hand — 50 to 80 percent more costly than if the pot had been heads up.

On the other hand, you should call much more liberally with hands that have good implied odds such as pocket pairs and suited connectors because you may hit a big hand and win a big pot. This includes hands like 65s, JTo, or K5s.

When to Three-Bet
From the Big Blind Versus
a Steal and Small Blind Cold-Call

When an aggressive player open-raises from late position and the small blind calls, you should three-bet with your stronger hands against a typical stealer: 99+, AJs+, AQo+, and KQs. Obviously, you should three-bet more liberally if the raiser over-steals, and less often if he under-steals. Finally, you should be more inclined to three-bet if your opponents play tight post-flop, because the value of having the initiative is greater.

A typical button stealer raises 41.2 percent of his hands, with an approximate range of 22+, A2s+, A2o+, K2s+, K7o+, Q5s+, Q9o+, J8s+, J9o+, T8s+, T9o, 97s+, 98o, 86s+, 75s+, and 65s. It is difficult to put the small blind on a hand range, but on average it should be tighter than the button's stealing range. In a multi-way pot, deception value is somewhat less important than equity concerns because you get more value from your value bets. This includes jamming pre-flop or flop bets with an equity advantage. We suggest three-betting with any hand that has over 40 percent equity versus the two ranges as a baseline, and leaning towards three-betting with reverse implied odds and showdown-value type of hands like pairs and hands containing an ace. Simply calling with a strong hand like

that receives good implied odds is a good play, and allows for a credible semi-bluff on the flop or the turn if action dictates a good opportunity to do so.

Adjusting for opponent and game tendencies is always important. However, although it is difficult to put the small blind on a hand range, assume he will cold call with the following A2s-A6s, K4s-K7s, Q7s+, J8s+, T8s+, 97s+, 86s+, 75s+, 64s+, 54s, A5o-A8o, K8o-KTo, QTo+, JTo, T9o, and 98o — about 19 percent of hands, but not the top 19 percent.

Against this range and the button's stealing range, your equity with various hands is as follows:

22 = 30.2%	88 = 41.9%	AA = 72.2%
33 = 31.6%	99 = 45.9%	AKo = 46.4%
44 = 33.0%	TT = 50.8%	AKs = 49.1%
55 = 34.7%	JJ = 54.6%	JTo = 31.0%
66 = 36.7%	QQ = 58.6%	JTs = 34.3%
77 = 38.9%	KK = 63.8%	

When the
Small Blind Has a Big Hand

It should also be noted that some players *only* smoothcall from the small blind when they hold a monster, such as aces, kings, or queens. In that case, you should fold all unpaired, offsuit hands except for ace-king. But you should still call liberally with hands that have good implied odds — even four-trey suited is better than a 5-to-1 underdog against a typical steal (40 percent) and aces, kings, or queens.

Defending the Big Blind When the Small Blind Three-Bets

When a steal has been attempted and the small blind three-bets, you should tighten up considerably. Unless the small blind is very aggressive, we would play only 66+, AJs+, AQo+, and KQs. Even though you are getting approximately 3.5-to-1 on your call, the threat of domination is too great to play ace-jack offsuit or worse. Also, these odds assume the original stealer will just call — if he four-bets, you get only 3-to-1, and have significantly less equity against the combined ranges. However, getting four-bet by the stealer is less of a concern if he steals aggressively since he will have a wide range of hands, many of which will not be strong enough to four-bet. The exception is if he is a maniac and may four-bet with a wide range as well (in which case you are getting worse odds to play initially, but your equity will be better against his range).

Assuming the small blind will three-bet with the following range: 22+, A5s+, A8o+, K9s+, KTo+, QTs+, QTo+, and JTs, your equity against both players with various hands will be as follows (assuming an average 40 percent steal range from the original raiser):

66 = 34.0%	AJo = 36.6%
55 = 32.4%	KQs = 36.1%
AJs = 39.8%	KJs = 34.0%
ATs = 37.3%	KQo = 32.8%
AQo = 39.6%	

When to Four-Bet

Against a typical three-bet from the small blind, you should four-bet with QQ+, AQs+, and AKo. Whether to four-bet with TT, JJ, and AQo is a close decision (in the scenario described) and can be done occasionally to mix up your play. Against an aggressive button stealer and an aggressive small blind three-bettor, four-betting with hands as weak as 88, KQo, AJo, and A9s is viable as well.

When Holding a Pocket Pair

When holding a pocket pair, you are 7.5-to-1 to flop a set. Since you will sometimes flop a set and lose, you should only call if you can expect that the final pot will provide an overlay. In general, we will call with any pocket pair if we expect the final pot will be ten times our original investment (minus our investment in that pot). Since you have to call 2 small bets to see the flop, we recommend that you only call if you expect the pot to be 20 small bets (10 big bets) or more.

As a base guideline, we recommend that you call with 66+ and fold 22-55. If your opponents play very aggressively post-flop, you can relax your calling requirements since your implied odds and the final pot size will be greater. Conversely, if your opponents play passively and have tight opening standards, you should play fewer hands and fold sixes and sevens.

When the Small Blind is Passive

If the small blind is passive (i.e. will only three-bet with 88+, ATs+, and AJo+), you should tighten up since a three-bet here is likely to mean he has a very big hand. We would only play 99+, AQs+, and AQo+, and would four-bet with QQ-AA, AKs, and occasionally AKo. With eights and ace-jack suited you have about

30 percent equity and poor implied odds given the small blind's range. With ace-jack offsuit, you only have about 26 percent equity and a large threat of domination.

When the
Small Blind is Very Aggressive

If the small blind is very aggressive, you should four-bet far more liberally in an attempt to force out the original stealer which creates dead money in the pot, and buy the button for the rest of the hand. The button will rarely fold, but when he does it is a major coup, and since your capping range has good equity, you do not lose too much when he calls. We would four-bet on average with 88+, AJo+, ATs+, and KQs, and add hands like ace-nine suited and king-queen offsuit against even looser players.

Defending
with Pocket Pairs

When facing a steal raise in the big blind and holding a pocket pair, you must decide whether to call or three-bet.[7] (You definitely should not fold except perhaps deuces and treys in the very specific circumstances of being against an extremely tight cutoff opener.) For the sake of balance, you should mix up your play between calling and three-betting, but certain factors may make one play much better.

There are two sources of value in three-betting pre-flop. First, there is a straight equity value. Most pocket pairs have an equity edge against the range of a typical steal (i.e. 40 percent stealing range), so raising allows you to build the pot while you are a favorite. You should be more inclined to raise for this reason with your larger pairs — sixes or better.

Second, there is also value in taking the initiative and increasing your folding equity. For this reason, you should be more inclined to raise against a tight-aggressive player since he is more likely to fold later in the hand. It should also be noted that you can achieve the same goals at the same cost by calling pre-flop and check-raising any flop. You should use this line to mix up your play against tight-aggressive opponents.

Against a loose-aggressive player, your pre-flop equity edge is likely greater with a pocket pair (since he will steal with more hands), so you should three-bet more liberally. However, a loose-aggressive player is more likely to go to showdown, so folding equity becomes less important. Also, a loose-aggressive player is

---

[7] When defending your small blind with a pocket pair, you should almost always three-bet. For more on this see "Defending from the Small Blind" in Part Three of this book.

more likely to bluff all three streets. For these reasons, you should three-bet with a pair of sixes or better against a loose-aggressive opponent, but just call with weaker pairs hoping to induce bluff(s). (But keep in mind that when you do only call with the small pairs, you are giving your opponent more free cards to beat you.)

For example, a loose-aggressive opponent open-raises on the button, and you call in the big blind with

The flop comes

Your opponent bets, and you call. The turn is the 4♦. He bets, and you call. The river is the 3♠. He bets, and you call. He shows the

(or AK, AQ, AJ, A♥X♥, etc.), and you win. Check-raising at any point in this hand has the benefit of sometimes folding a 6-out hand like A♣5♦, or maybe folding a better pair like 5♠5♥. However, it also runs the risk of getting three-bet by better hands or being three-bet semi-bluffed (especially on the flop). (But if your opponent does slow down and takes a free card, that free card could beat you where he might have folded to your bet.)

If you have deuces on a draw-heavy board against an opponent who would bet all three streets, you should just check and call if you think it is rare that you will ever get a better hand to fold (and this is generally the case). The reason is that you will win the same when you are best, but you lose more when behind because your opponent can play future streets perfectly. He can call if he is getting the correct odds to draw and raise if his draw comes in, or fold on the river if he misses.

In the Q♥J♥ example above, if you knew *exactly* what your opponent had, the correct line would be to check raise the turn and then check call the river. However, when you do not know what your opponent has, check-calling is a safer play on the turn against an opponent who will bet for you. If you strongly suspect your opponent holds a draw, check-raising on the flop or the turn, and then check-calling when out of position on the river is a strong play.

Against certain opponents, it may be correct to fold a low pocket pair on a later street, even though you just called pre-flop. For example, a tight-aggressive opponent open-raises in the cutoff, and only you call in the big blind with 3♦3♠. The flop comes K♠9♣5♥. Your opponent bets, and you call. The turn is the 4♦. If your opponent bets, you should probably fold. On such a dry flop, it is likely that your opponent is betting a made hand on the turn since he cannot have a draw and he would probably check ace-high. If your opponent would bet AQ-A8 on the turn but check the river, you could check-call the turn and then check-fold the river unimproved. You will catch a trey on the river 4.5 percent of the time, and sometimes you will be ahead on the river when your opponent checks. Against some aggressive players this parlay is enough to call on the turn as well, even on a scary board.

Ultimately, whether you should call on the turn depends on whether you can narrow your opponent's range if he bets the turn.

With some players, you really cannot, and others you definitely can.

Here are typical ranges and your equity after the turn with the pair of treys. We can assume that the flop action does not narrow the villain's hand range at all:

Cutoff opener's range: 33+, A2s+, A7o+, K6s+, KTo+, Q8s+, QTo+, J8s+, JTo, T8s+, 97s+, 87s, and 76s.

- Your equity on the turn before any action takes place: 45.2 percent.

- Number of his hands you beat: 158.

- Average equity versus those hands: 83.1 percent.

- Number of his hands you are behind: 146.

- Average equity versus those hands: 4.2 percent.

Button opener's range: 22+, A2s+, A3o+, K2s+, K7o+, Q5s+, Q9o+, J7s+, J9o+, T7s+, T9o, 97s+, 98o, 86s+, 75s+, and 65s.

- Your equity on the turn before any action takes place: 40.4 percent.

- Number of his hands you beat: 202.

- Average equity versus those hands: 83.8 percent.

- Number of his hands you are behind: 243.

- Average equity versus those hands: 4.3 percent.

Why It Is Better to Defend with Queen-Seven Offsuit than King-Deuce Offsuit

Even though king-deuce offsuit is about a 3-to-2 favorite over queen-seven offsuit pre-flop, you should be more inclined to defend your big blind with the queen-seven. (The empirical analysis from our players' databases showed actual results were better with queen-seven offsuit as well.) The primary reason for this is domination, and, out of position, the effects of domination are magnified by poor implied odds. Here are the equity values against a few different stealing ranges:

35.3 percent: 55+, A2s+, A4o+, K3s+, K8o+, Q5s+, Q9o+, J7s+, J9o+, T7s+, T9o, 97s+, 87s.

- King-deuce offsuit has approximately 39 percent equity, and

- Queen-seven offsuit has approximately 37 percent equity.

40 percent: 44+, A2s+, A3o+, K2s+, K7o+, Q4s+, Q8o+, J7s+, J8o+, T7s+, T9o, 97s+, 87s.

- King-deuce offsuit has approximately 40 percent equity, and

- Queen-seven offsuit has approximately 38 percent equity.

45.4 percent: 22+, A2s+, A2o+, K2s+, K6o+, Q5s+, Q8o+, J6s+, J8o+, T7s+, T8o+, 97s+, 98o, 86s+, 76s.

- King-deuce offsuit has approximately 40 percent equity, and

- Queen-seven offsuit has approximately 39 percent equity.

From a purely "hot-and-cold" equity standpoint (i.e. there is no play after the flop), you would prefer to have the king-high hand. However, the queen-seven plays better after the flop, winning more bets on average when ahead and losing less when behind — enough to offset the equity difference in the two hands.

King-deuce offsuit is dominated by AK, A2, and KQ-K3 — 144 combinations of hands, almost all of which will be within the stealing range for most players. The only hands that king-deuce offsuit dominates are Q2, J2, T2, ... 32 — hands with which even the most aggressive players will probably not steal.

On the other hand, queen-seven offsuit is dominated by A7, K7, AQ, KQ, and QJ-Q8 — 96 hands. Queen-seven offsuit dominates Q6-Q2, J7, T7, 97, and 87 — some of which will be within an aggressive player's stealing range, especially the suited combinations.

Also, king-deuce offsuit is dominated by any pair (72 combinations), whereas queen-seven offsuit is dominated only by pairs sevens and higher (42 combinations). Moreover, queen-seven offsuit is only a slight underdog to pairs smaller than sevens (30 combinations).

In addition to domination concerns, your post-flop equity is better with queen-seven offsuit. Your post-flop equity will be very similar for both hands if you pair your high card (i.e. king or queen). You will almost always be way ahead or way behind — you (or your opponent) will have 2, 3, or (rarely) 5 outs. However, if you pair your deuce holding king-deuce offsuit and take the lead, your opponent will virtually always have at least 6 outs (the only exception being when you have him reverse dominated). If you pair your seven and take the lead with queen-seven offsuit, your opponent is far more likely to have 3 or fewer outs.

When you do not flop a pair, there will be far fewer flops to profitably call a continuation bet with king-deuce offsuit — in fact, you should almost always fold. However, with queen-seven offsuit, you may be able to call a continuation bet on a flop like J♥5♣2♠ or 9♠6♥2♠, because it is far more likely that both of your "pair" outs will be good.

Furthermore, it is impossible to flop top or middle pair with your bottom card when holding king-deuce offsuit. So you will not be able to bet and raise with confidence when you do flop the best hand, so you will not win as much and be less able to protect your hand.

For example, an aggressive player open-raises on the button. The small blind folds, and you call with

The flop comes

You check raise the flop with the intention of check-calling both the turn and river to induce bluffs. However, the turn is the T♥, putting three hearts on board. You now realize if you are ahead and your opponent has a heart in his hand, he has 15 outs, so you decide to lead the turn, and he raises. This is a very difficult spot because he could have a lone A♥ or K♥, a flush, a set, two-pair, or just be making a free showdown play with one pair. You should probably fold, but there is a chance that you are folding the best hand. If you were in this same spot with a pair of sevens, it would be much easier to call down, avoiding the risk of folding the best hand.

Finally, it should be noted that a pair of deuces is more likely to be counterfeited by the river than a pair of sevens, further lowering your post-flop expectation with king-deuce offsuit.

Defending
From the Small Blind

When in the small blind and someone has open-raised from late position (cutoff or button), there are three important things to keep in mind. They are:

1. You are not getting very good odds (3.5-to-1.5 in a typical 1-2 blind structure).

2. You are in the worst possible position for all subsequent rounds. And,

3. You are not closing the pre-flop action.

Given these factors, you should not play many hands. On average, playing about 20 percent of your hands seems right. Also, the vast majority of the time (i.e. roughly 95 percent) you play, you should three-bet. Again, it is almost always good to force out the big blind, creating dead money in the pot. In fact, the only hands it is optimal to cold call with here are aces and kings. However, for the sake of balance, you could also occasionally cold call with a hand like QJs, JTs, 77, and 88. Alternately, you could decide to never cold call with anything, including aces and kings, so there would be no need to balance.

There are two reasons to three-bet when defending your small blind. They are:

1. You are more likely to force out the big blind and create an overlay with his money already in the pot.

2. You will gain the initiative and win more pots without a showdown when both you and your opponent miss the flop.

Some argue that you should only call in the small blind with hands that have good implied odds such as

especially against a loose big blind who is unlikely to fold even if you three-bet. However, the fold equity you create for later in the hand by three-betting outweighs the implied odds consideration even against loose players. Also, against a big blind who will call 2 bets cold with a wide range, you should three-bet because your hand figures to have an equity edge against his calling range.

It should also be noted that drawing hands play poorly out of position. So even though a hand like 8♦7♦ looks inviting, you should not defend your small blind with it because of your poor position and the fact that the pot will be 3-handed or heads-up post-flop. Instead, you should be more inclined to play hands that have showdown value and/or reverse implied odds because they benefit from more bets going into the pot pre-flop. Also, since the pot will likely be heads up and will not go to the showdown too often, the implied odds will be smaller and thus less important than the money already in the pot.

As always, the most important factor to consider in this situation is your two cards. However, you should also be aware of the opener's position and how often he attempts to steal. His position is important because it will tell you the relative likelihood that he has a premium pocket pair, and help you refine his range. If both of your cards are below your opponent's pair, you are thoroughly dominated and will likely lose a big pot if you flop top or middle pair.

Assuming a button raiser tries to steal the blinds around 40 percent of the time, the following hand range is a good set of guidelines for three-betting from the small blind:

22-QQ, A6s+, A8o+, K9s+, KTo+, QJo, and JTs

Over time, you should adjust from these guidelines based on your reads and your results — removing hands that perform poorly and adding more hands if similar ones perform well.

Against an opponent who raises too liberally (attempts to steal more than 45 percent of the time), you should play more hands. You should also play more hands against a player who plays poorly post-flop since there is always value in being in a pot with them.

A Note on Post-Flop Play

If you three-bet from the small blind and get the pot heads up, you should bet virtually every flop because the pot offers 7-to-1 immediate odds. Many players check their strong hands in this situation. However, this looks suspicious and you sacrifice the chance to win a big pot when your opponent flops a good, second-best hand. With a strong hand against a hyper-aggressive player, you should be even more inclined to bet because of the chance he will raise you with a marginal or weak hand, allowing you to three-bet or check raise the turn.

If you three-bet from the small blind, the big blinds folds, and the original raiser caps, you should check every flop because it is always better to check raise your strong hands assuming the pre-flop capper will bet 100 percent of flops. If your opponent bets, you have three options. They are:

1. **Fold.** You should do this when the flop is horrible for your hand.

2. **Call.** The pot is offering you 9-to-1 odds and you have good implied odds, so any reasonable draw is worth at least a call.

3. **Check raise.** You should do this with your strong hands because it builds a big pot early (tying your opponent to it) and, if you wait until the turn to check raise, your opponent may check behind which would be a disaster.

Part Three

Playing Heads-Up Post-Flop

Playing Heads-Up Post-Flop

Introduction

Playing heads-up post-flop often requires a completely different strategy than playing multi-way. (We should note that whenever we say "playing heads-up," we mean playing heads-up post-flop, i.e. exactly two players see a flop, and not playing at a table with only two players). In tight-aggressive and/or short-handed games, many of the pots will be two-handed on the flop. In this section, we recommend specific lines which can be very effective, and explain in what circumstances they should be used. The first approach we recommend, the bet/bet line, highlights the importance of aggression. On most boards, when you are in the betting lead, you should continue betting the flop and turn because there is a significant chance that your opponent will fold.

Likewise, most of your opponents will be playing more aggressively, so you must learn to use their aggression against them. This often means you should play passively. The "Turn Value Check" is a great example of when passive play can be profitable. Also, when you hold a strong hand, you can use your opponent's aggression to punish them with check-raises.

Finally, when up against one opponent, you will be able to win more pots without a showdown. So you should be willing to bluff and semi-bluff more often.

The following chapters present important concepts and specific playing lines that, when used correctly, should yield good results when heads-up. These ideas are important in tough games, and you may want to read them more than once to have a clear understanding of everything stated.

The Bet-Bet Line

When heads-up post-flop and the pre-flop aggressor, you should bet every flop. This applies whether you are in or out of position. There may be some very obscure exceptions to this, but betting 100 percent of the time would be at most a small mistake.[8] You might slowplay against a tight player with a monster, such as

on a

flop. However, if that is the only time you check, it will be transparent and a difficult play to balance. You would give up too much value by sometimes checking this flop when you have nothing because your opponent is unlikely to call.

Against passive-to-typical opponents, you should usually bet the turn as well unless it is obvious from the board that your opponent has caught a piece of the flop and will not fold to a bet. With a strong hand, you should bet in an attempt to get action.

---

[8] An exception would be when you have the 6♠5♠ and the flop is the T♥9♣8♥.

For example, you open-raise A♥K♣ in the cutoff. The button and small blind fold and the big blind calls. The flop comes A♦7♥6♠, you bet, and your opponent calls. The turn is a K♦. You should bet because checking gives up too much value. Also, you want to protect your hand if your opponent has a good draw.

If you have nothing, you should usually bluff because of the pot odds. Also, if you check the turn and bluff the river, you are much more likely to be called.

For example, you open-raise with K♥4♥ on the button. The small blind folds and the big blind calls. The flop comes T♦7♥2♠, you bet, and your opponent calls. The turn is a T♣. You should bet against most opponents because the pot is offering you 3-to-1, and you can make a pretty safe fold if check raised.

With a strong draw, you should usually bet as a semi-bluff. Many players will check behind with strong draws to take a free card. However, by doing so, you forgo any chance to win without hitting your draw. Against an opponent who will call with almost anything (like king-high or better), it may be correct to take a free card. However, such opponents are rare at mid-to-high stakes since they go broke quickly.

Against aggressive opponents, it may be correct to check behind to induce a bluff with a draw that has some showdown potential, such as an ace-high flush draw. (For more on this, see the chapter entitled "The Turn Value Check" in Part Three of this book.)

Responding to Check-Raises on the Flop

If you have a strong hand and an aggressive opponent check-raises, you can either three-bet or wait for the turn to raise. Against an opponent who may fold to a three-bet, you should wait until the turn to raise. Also, on a very coordinated flop, you should be more inclined to wait until the turn as long as the turn does not complete any draws your opponent could have.

If you have a marginal hand and an aggressive opponent check raises, you should generally call down. You could potentially raise the turn for a free showdown. However, if your opponent may three-bet the turn as a bluff or semi-bluff, you should not raise for a free showdown since you may have to lay down the best hand in a fairly large pot. You should also be less inclined to make the free showdown raise on a coordinated board because it is more likely your opponent could three-bet and you can't fold since it might be a semi-bluff.

If you have a strong draw and an aggressive opponent check raises, you should generally wait until the turn and raise as a semi-bluff. This is because there is a chance your opponent is bluffing and will fold to a turn raise. This line may sacrifice some equity compared to a flop reraise because your draw is stronger with two cards to come, but it has more bluffing equity because a turn raise demands more respect than a flop three-bet.

If you have a very strong hand and a passive opponent check raises, you should three-bet because your opponent is likely to have a hand with which he is willing to give a lot of action.

If you have a marginal hand or strong draw and a passive opponent check-raises, you should evaluate your number of outs and the pot size, and proceed accordingly. Your bluffing equity in this instance is lower because a passive opponent is more likely to have a real hand, so just calling to hit your draw (as opposed to semi-bluffing) is usually best.

Responding to Check-Raises on the Turn

If you have a strong hand and an aggressive opponent check-raises, you should three-bet as your hand is likely best. Also, if your opponent has a decent hand, he will call down; or with a draw, he will call to try and catch on the river.

If you have a marginal hand and an aggressive opponent check raises, you should call down, especially on a draw heavy board. For example, if you hold

and the board is

you should generally be committed to seeing the showdown since your opponent could be semi-bluffing with a number of different straight or flush combinations that you are ahead of.

If you have a strong draw and an aggressive opponent check raises, you should call to hit your draw. Against the most aggressive opponents, however, you might three-bet as a semi-bluff (or raise the river as a bluff) since it is possible that they check-raised as a pure or semi-bluff, and will fold to any further aggression.

If you have a strong hand and a passive opponent check-raises you should call down or three-bet depending on the strength of your hand. For example, if you hold A♥T♣ on a T♥9♣4♣8♦ board you should just call down against a turn check-raise from a passive opponent. On the other hand, if you hold 9♣9♦ on that same board, you have an easy three-bet on the turn.

If you have a marginal hand and a passive opponent check-raises, it is generally time to fold unless you think you have enough outs to justify chasing. For example, if you hold 6♣6♠ on an A♣T♦7♠4♦ board, you can safely fold to a check-raise from a passive opponent.

If you have a strong draw and a passive opponent check-raises, you should call to hit your draw, but be prepared to fold the river unimproved.

Betting The
River as a Pure Bluff

Assume you open-raise with 7♣6♣ on the button, and only the loose-passive big blind calls. The flop comes J♥T♥2♠, the big blind checks, you bet, and he calls. The turn is a 3♠, he checks, you bet, and he calls. The river is a 4♦. Should you bet again?

In order for this river bet to be profitable, your opponent needs to fold only 20 percent of the time. So in this example, you should definitely bet. The coordinated nature of the board makes it likely enough that your opponent had a draw and will fold. Second-level thinking may dictate that your opponent thinks you had a draw and call down with a higher frequency. Against better players, especially those who go to the showdown more often, checking and giving up on the river in this spot is a good play.

On the other hand, if the board were very uncoordinated — for example, K♠8d♦2♣5♥3♠, you should give up and not bet against most opponents. It is too likely your opponent has a pair and will call. When you play aggressively, many opponents will call down with any pair, especially heads-up post-flop.

The Turn Value Check

When in position against aggressive opponents, it can be profitable to check the turn with marginal/good hands like second or third pair. Although you may be giving a free card, the gains outweigh the costs against the right players and in the right situations. There are three sources of value in "The Turn Value Check." They are:

1. Avoid a check-raise when behind.

2. Avoid folding the best hand when your opponent check-raises as a bluff or semi-bluff (which is a disaster).

3. Induce a river bluff when ahead.

Example No.1: Avoid a check-raise when behind. You open-raise with

on the button. Only the aggressive big blind calls. The flop comes

155

you bet, and he calls. The turn is a Q♥. If he checks, you should check. Because of the coordinated board and an aggressive opponent, you would have to call down if he check raises. However, usually when he check raises, he will have you beat. Checking this turn gets you to the showdown cheaply when behind, and gives you a free card.

Example No. 2: Avoid folding the best hand when your opponent check raises as a bluff or semi-bluff. You open-raise with 6♥6♣ in the cutoff. Only the aggressive big blind calls. The flop comes J♦T♦3♠, you bet, and he calls. The turn is a K♦. If he checks, you should check. Because the flop contains three overcards to your pair, you probably should fold if your opponent had raised. However, an aggressive opponent may check raise as a semi-bluff. Checking this turn avoids giving him a chance to push you off the best hand (or the chance of spiking a six).

Example No. 3: Induce a river bluff when ahead. You open-raise with T♥8♥ on the button. Only the aggressive big blind calls. The flop comes: Q♦T♣5♦, you bet, and he calls. The turn is a 4♥. If he checks, you should check. An aggressive opponent will bet almost any river card with a hand like nine-eight or even king-high, allowing you to gain an extra bet.

Obviously, all these factors favor checking against aggressive opponents. Against passive opponents, you should be more inclined to bet because if check raised you are likely way behind and you have an easy fold. Also, passive opponents may "chase" draws with few outs or call down with weak hands like king-high. Thus, you should bet your mediocre made hands for value against them.

Although giving a free card is a concern, against the right opponent the benefits from checking outweigh the cost of a free card. Even if your opponent has 6 outs, you are giving him a 12.5 percent (=⅛) chance to win. Most heads-up post-flop pots will be

4 big bets on the turn, thus giving a free card to 6 outs costs ½ of a big bet.

$$0.5 \text{ big bets} = (0.125)(4 \text{ big bets})$$

Since your opponent will miss his 6-outer 87.5 percent of the time, if you induce a bluff 57 percent of the time when he misses, checking the turn is break-even in terms of only inducing bets versus losing the existing pot.

$$0.5 \text{ big bets} = (0.875)(0.57)(1 \text{ big bet})$$

This is because the gain from inducing a bluff when he misses (if he does so 57 percent of the time) is exactly equal to the cost of giving a free card on the turn. Although some opponents will not bluff the river 57 percent of the time (but some will even more), when you add the value gained from:

1.   Avoiding a check-raise when behind,

2.   Avoiding laying down the best hand to a check-raise bluff or semi-bluff, and

3.   The times you benefit from the free card.

it is clear that checking is correct against aggressive opponents. If the pot is much bigger than 4 big bets, you should be more inclined to bet.

You should also be more inclined to bet with a weaker made hand or as a bluff since it is easier to fold to a check-raise. Also, with a strong draw (8 or more outs), you should bet because your opponent only needs to fold more than 17.5 percent of the time (or less with more than 8 outs) for betting to have positive expected value in a 4 big bet pot. However, if check raised, you obviously have to call.

The Lead Check-Raise Line

When in the lead (i.e. the last raiser preflop) and out of position, you should bluff every missed flop when heads up (and most 3-handed pots as well) because the pots odds are greater than the odds that most opponents will call.

For example, you open-raise with

from the cutoff, the button calls, and the blinds fold. The flop comes

leaving you with king-high and no draws. You should bet anyway. There are 5.5 small bets in the pot and your options are either check-folding or betting and folding to a raise. You need to get a better hand to fold here just 16 percent of the time to be profitable. 16 percent of the time you win 5.5 small bets for a profit of .88 small bets and 84 percent of the time you lost 1 small bet for a lost of .84 small bets. Additionally, an opponent may sometimes just call and let you catch a king on the turn. Plus, you may also win even if you are called when the turn goes check-check. If your opponent calls your flop bet, and the turn does not give you a pair or a decent draw, you should generally plan to check and fold.

Although this strategy is optimal, many aggressive opponents will bet the turn with any two cards when checked to, forcing you to occasionally fold the best hand (such as king-high in the above example). However, the probability that you are best does not justify a call-down based on the effective odds. In the specific example above, it is unlikely the villain called without a pair. The only non-pair hands he might call with are king-jack (you are behind) and queen-jack (you are ahead). Those hands might just call on the flop, and both would probably fold to a turn bet if unimproved. But against your opponent's flop calling range, you are definitely not getting the correct odds to bet again.

In order to balance this strategy and exploit your opponents' tendencies, you should frequently check raise the turn with your strong hands against aggressive opponents. If you sometimes give up on the turn with your weaker hands, aggressive opponents will bet almost every time you check to them. Using this approach extracts the maximum from aggressive opponents with your strong hands.

For example, you open-raise with A♠J♦ from the cutoff, the aggressive button calls, and the blinds fold. The flop comes A♦Q♥6♠, giving you top pair with a decent kicker. You bet and your opponent calls. The turn is the 2♦. You should check raise. If your opponent has nothing and bets the turn as a pure bluff, you earn an extra bet since he would have folded had you bet. If he has a decent draw (which is possible on this turn, but relatively unlikely versus a flop like J♥T♣6♥), a check-raise charges him two bets for the river card, getting more money in the pot while you are ahead. If he has a marginal made hand which he would like to showdown, you also earn an extra bet — he would just call down if you had bet the turn. Since your opponent did not three-bet pre-flop, you should not worry that he has ace-king or ace-queen, which makes a turn check-raise an even better play here.

Deciding whether to check or bet the river will depend on the river card and the timing of your opponents play on the turn. If he calls quickly on the turn, I would be more likely to suspect a draw and check-call the river. (You should check-call the river versus likely draws, and value bet versus likely made hands.)

You should be less inclined to use this approach when the board is very coordinated. For example, if you have

and by the turn the board is

you should bet to avoid giving a free card to an opponent with a lone club, and also because you are more likely to get called down lightly because your opponent might put you on the lone club.

The Check-Raise Lead Line

When you flop a strong made hand out of position and against an aggressive opponent, you should usually take control of the hand by check-raising the flop and then leading both the turn and the river. This gives you the opportunity to get as many bets in as possible.

The exception to this is when you figure to be either way ahead or way behind an aggressive opponent. For example, you have defended your big blind with

and the flop comes

The only viable alternative to check-raising the flop with a strong to very strong made hand would be to check-call the flop and then check raise the turn. This line has the added benefit of offering balancing for the time you check raise the turn as a semi-bluff.

However, there are a few drawbacks to this play. If, when out of position, you check-call the flop and attempt to check raise the turn, one of two negative things can happen. They are:

1. Your opponent could check behind on the turn and then call or fold to your river bet. In this case, you have somewhat wasted your strong hand by not getting good value.

    It's true that if you do check raise the flop, as we suggest, sometimes you will get an immediate fold or a fold on the turn after you lead. But overall on average, more money will go into the pot with a wider range of hands by playing it fast and then leading the turn out of position.

    When your flop check-raise gets three-bet and you have a strong to very strong hand, similar logic applies in deciding whether to four-bet and lead the flop, or to call and attempt a check-raise on the turn. Generally, you want to cap and lead if your sole objective is to get the most money into the pot as possible. (However, at this point you may be worried about being behind, which changes things.)

2. You force your opponent into more correct folds on the turn.

    When You Check Raise the Turn: When you defend your big blind versus a steal raise there is now 4.5 small bets in the pot. If you check-call the flop and then check the turn there is now 6.5 small bets in the pot, and the stealer has to invest 2 small bets more if he now bets. If you check raise, he is now getting 12.5-to-2 or 6.25-to-1 odds if he wants to call, but your turn check-raise play has shown a decent amount of strength. It would show even more strength on boards without many draws. Thus, it's better to check raise the turn with a strong hand if the flop had many draws on it.

    When You Check Raise the Flop: When you defend your big blind versus a steal raise, check-raise the flop and then lead the turn, your opponent is getting 10.5-to-2 or 5.25-to-1 odds to call, so his odds are slightly worse. In addition, you have shown much less strength as people correctly consider a flop check-raise range to be much wider than that of a turn check-raise. You will get more call-downs in this case on average.

When you flop a strong-marginal made hand, out of position, and against a passive opponent, you should also check-raise the flop and lead the turn. In this case, it is just basic value betting. Also, if your hand is marginal, you can easily fold if your passive opponent raises on the turn or river.

When you flop a strong draw, it is sometimes best to use this approach because your bluffing equity is low and your showdown equity and implied odds are highest on the flop as opposed to the turn. You should also be more inclined to use this line when the flop and turn cards may scare your opponent, or if your opponent is tight-passive because he may fold immediately to your flop check raise and may not bet the turn if you only check-call the flop. However, this is not the only line you should use when you semi-bluff since you should mix up your play and keep your opponents guessing. (See the "Check-Call Lead Line" and the "Check-Call/Check-Raise Line" also in Part Three of this book for other good semi-bluffing approaches.)

The Check-Call Lead Line

As a Semi-Bluff

Although this line is the least expensive way to semi-bluff, you should use it rarely because it is usually sub-optimal to play most made hands this way. If you frequently use this line to semi-bluff, your observant opponents will pick up on this betting pattern. Occasionally, you should use this approach with a made hand when out of position, and out of the lead against a passive opponent. (See below for more on this.) Likewise, you should use this line as a semi-bluff when out of position and out of the lead against a *passive* opponent. Sometimes you may use this approach when the turn card improves your hand into a strong made hand as you want the opportunity to bet and three-bet if you are raised.

This line is particularly useful when you pick up a strong draw on the turn *and* the turn brings a "scare card." For example, a tight-passive player open-raises from late-middle position, and only you call in the big blind with

The flop comes

You check, your opponent bets, and you call because you have one overcard, a gutshot, and a backdoor flush draw. Also, since your opponent is passive, you may get a free card on the turn. The turn is the A♥. This would be a good time to lead as a semi-bluff. If your opponent has a weak hand like a pair of nines or lower, he may fold because of the ace (on the turn), and your draw is strong enough that getting raised is not too expensive as you likely have 12 outs. An alternative flop play would be to check raise, but check-calling the flop and opting to make a decision on the turn is a good approach as well.

The reason you should use this line against a passive opponent (as opposed to check-raising the turn) is because he will be more likely to check behind on the turn, eliminating the possibility of the turn check-raise and your opportunity to semi-bluff. Also, a passive opponent is less likely to raise even if he has a relatively strong hand, meaning the chances are lower you will pay 2 big bets for your draw if he does not fold.

With a Made Hand

Although it is almost always optimal to check raise the flop with a strong hand heads-up post-flop — see the chapter entitled "The Check-Raise Lead Line" for more on this — you should sometimes use the check-call lead line with a strong hand to balance your semi-bluffs. Otherwise, your observant opponents will realize that whenever you use this approach, you are semi-bluffing. Additionally, you can add the turn lead to your arsenal with hands where you improve to a strong hand on the turn — the most common example being a pocket pair where you spike a set.

Against a passive opponent, you should sometimes use this line with a marginal made hand. Then if he raises, you can easily fold. Also, you should be more inclined to use this line when the turn card may be a "scare card" for your opponent.

For example, assume a passive player open-raises on the button and only you call in the big blind with 7♠6♠. The flop comes 9♦7♣3♥. You check, your opponent bets, and you call. The turn is the A♠. Since your opponent could have a hand like KQ, KJ, KT, QJ, QT, or JT, you should bet to prevent him from taking a free card. If he raises, you can safely assume he has an ace or better and make an easy fold. Also, since you bet out when the ace hit, your opponent may sometimes fold a pair better than your sevens.

The Check-Call/Check-Raise Line

As a Semi-Bluff

Against typical aggressive opponents, you should check raise turn cards that give you a strong draw (such as a flush draw or open-ended straight draw).[9] This will usually occur when you have called the flop with a weak draw, like two overcards or an inside straight draw and one overcard, and the turn card improves to a draw with 8 or more outs.

For example, assume an aggressive player opens for a raise on the button. The small blind folds, and you call in the big blind with

---

[9] If you have a very strong draw on the flop, you should usually check raise the flop to try and take control of the hand. (For more on this, see the chapter entitled "Playing Fast on the Flop Versus Waiting for the Turn" in Part Three of the book.)

The flop comes

You check, your opponent bets, and you call because you have two overcards and an inside straight draw. The turn is the K♥. This would be a great spot to check-raise as a semi-bluff. Because your opponent is aggressive, he may be betting the turn with nothing and will have to fold to your check-raise. Also, because the king may be a scare card for your opponent, he may fold a ten, eight, trey, or any pocket pair lower than kings.

Alternately, many players check raise the flop with in the above situation, which is also a valid line as well, but check-calling the flop and then making a decision on the turn is also a viable play depending on your opponent's tendencies. If your opponent frequently makes a continuation bet on the turn, you can give his bet less credit and set him up for a lot of turn check-raises. If your opponent will fold ace-high hands after a turn bet, this is a good play.

In addition, it should be noted that, against a passive opponent, you should generally lead turn cards that give you a strong draw. The reason for this is that your opponent may check-behind on the turn and take away your opportunity to semi-bluff. Getting a free card here is not terrible, but we think the opportunity to get some better hands to fold at a reasonable price is worth more than a free card.

The price you are paying to semi-bluff the turn is complicated to calculate because you can get called or raised, and you also have to make some assumptions about river action. But with a strong draw, you can estimate the lower bound of your equity pretty well. Thus, you are not paying a full bet because even if called or raised you expect to win those bets when your draw does come in or you successfully bluff on the river.

With a Made Hand

When it appears that the turn card has given you the best hand against an aggressive opponent, you should generally go for a check-raise. For example, assume an aggressive player opens for a raise from the cutoff. The small blind folds, and you call in the big blind with

The flop comes

You check, your opponent bets, and you call with two overcards. The turn is the Q♥. You should check raise. (Again it should be noted that you should lead this turn against a passive opponent because of the risk he will check behind causing you to lose too much value with a strong hand.)

The reason for using this line is that it will win the maximum when your hand is best and does the most to protect your hand if your opponent is drawing. If an aggressive opponent has nothing, he will usually bet the turn because you have shown no strength by just calling the flop. Although he will fold to your raise, you gain an extra big bet by allowing him to bet the turn — if you had led the turn, he would have folded.

If your opponent has a marginal made hand and value bets the turn, your check-raise may collect two big bets on the turn and another on the river. Since you will also be semi-bluffing with this line, your opponents may sometimes call you down with marginal holdings.

If your opponent has a strong draw, he will usually bet the turn as a semi-bluff. Check-raising allows you to charge him two big bets to see the river card.

If your opponent has a very strong hand (such as a set, a straight, or a flush), you will lose an extra bet because he will three-bet your check-raise. However, when playing heads up, you should not play timidly out of fear of running into very strong hands. Of course, if the board is very scary (e.g., it contains four cards to a straight or flush), you may not want to make this play with a hand like top pair.

The Check-Raise/Check-Call Line

When out of position you flop a weak made hand. Against an aggressive opponent, you can sometimes check raise the flop and then check-call both the turn and river. The reason for this is that against an aggressive opponent you want to get to the showdown as cheaply as possible. If you continue betting after the flop, you will have a difficult decision if your opponent raises on the turn or river since aggressive players have wide ranges for making an outright bluff or marginal semi-bluff. Also, you will avoid paying extra bets when he has the better hand. Finally, you will also induce more bluffs.

You should be more inclined to use this line when the board is coordinated since your opponent may semi-bluff. When you are out of position with a coordinated board, you forfeit charging a draw in favor of being passive to avoid paying extra versus better hands, and simultaneously gain extra bets from worse hands by inducing bluffs. With a marginal made hand, two of the three general reasons for betting:

1.   Getting worse hands to call, or

2.   Getting better hands to fold

decrease in value, and the two general reasons for being passive:

1.   Inducing bluffs from worse hands that would fold to a bet, and

2.   Avoiding raises from better hands

increase in value.

For example, assume an aggressive player open-raises from the cutoff and only you call in the big blind with

(or A♠3♦ or K♣3♣). The flop comes

You check, your opponent bets, and you raise. The turn is the 6♦. Since your opponent is aggressive, you can check-call both the turn and river.

If you had lead the turn and he raised, you would not know if he has a queen, a pocket pair, two diamonds, KJ, KT, JT, or a complete bluff. Thus, you should probably call down, but will not feel good about it. To avoid this tough decision and possibly induce a bluff, check-call both the turn and river. In these cases your equity is pretty good and you are likely ahead against his range of hands, and the way to get the most money against aggressive opponents is to play passively.

Playing Fast On The Flop Versus Waiting for The Turn

With a Strong Made Hand

When you flop what figures to be the best hand heads up, you must decide whether to put in heavy action or wait for the turn to raise. In general, we recommend that you put your action in immediately because several good things can happen. First, your opponent may "sandbag" with a good, second-best hand and wait until the turn to raise, which will allow you to three-bet and maximize the value from your strong hand. For example, an aggressive player open-raises in the hijack and only you call in the big blind with

The flop comes

In this scenario, you should try to check raise the flop. If your opponent has a hand like ace-king or a pair of aces, he may three-bet, which is fine because it gives you the chance to four-bet.

Alternately, he may just call your check-raise and raise any turn card, which is also good because it allows you to three-bet the turn.

Second, your opponent may play back at you with a drawing hand. This allows you to re-raise with your strong hand and charge him the maximum to draw. For example, if you hold A♥A♠ on a K♦Q♦4♥ flop against an opponent who will play drawing hands aggressively, you should be willing to put in a lot of action since you may be able to charge him 4 or 5 bets to see the turn if he continues to play back at you.

Third, if you are out of position and are waiting to go for a check-raise on the turn, your opponent may check behind and take a free card. This forces you to miss a lot of value.

On the other hand, when the board is very coordinated you may want to wait until the turn card to put in an extra bet or raise. For example, if you hold A♣A♠ on a 9♥8♥3♥ flop, your equity changes dramatically between the flop and turn card. If the turn card is a safe one, such as the 2♣ in this example, you can then put in an extra bet or raise.

If the turn card is not safe, you have a choice to make. Both folding or calling might make sense depending on your opponent and the specifics of the situation. You should not, however, take this concept too far and wait for the turn every time the flop is slightly (as opposed to heavily) coordinated. For example, if you held A♣A♠ on a T♥7♥2♠ board, you should be more inclined to put in action on the flop, especially against an aggressive opponent who will play back at you with a drawing hand.

With a Very Strong Draw

When you flop a very strong draw — 12 or more outs, you should be more inclined to put in action on the flop because you are usually a favorite or a very slight underdog at that point, even against a top-pair or overpair type hand. Putting in heavy action on the flop allows you to increase your fold equity on a turn bet, while at the same time costing you nothing or very little because you have so much equity in the pot.

For example, a tight-aggressive player opens on the button, the small blind folds, and you call in the big blind with

The flop comes

giving you a flush draw and an open-ended straight draw. At this point you should check raise because your hand is a favorite even if your opponent has a pair of aces. If your opponent three-bets your check-raise, you should be willing to four-bet because of your equity, especially against tight-aggressive players who will three-bet with overcards or ace-high, and fold to a turn bet if you lead after four-betting the flop.

Some passive opponents, however, will almost never three-bet the flop and fold to a turn bet. In that case, you may still want to four-bet to push your equity edge, but should not bet the turn as a semi-bluff. On the other hand, you may not want to four-bet the flop and check the turn because doing so may give your hand away. It should also be noted that some passive opponents will not give heavy action on the flop without a very strong hand (such as a set or two pair). In that case, you are a not a favorite even with a very strong draw, and should slow down.

Why the "Free Card" Play May Have Negative Expectation in Tight-Aggressive Games

In a loose-passive game it is usually correct to raise the flop with a draw in late position. This play gets its value from three sources. They are:

1. Since the game is loose, there will be many players in the pot. If two or more opponents call your raise, it is immediately profitable if you have eight or more outs.[10]

2. Since the game will be passive, there is a good chance that everyone will check to you on the turn allowing you to check behind earning the "free card." (This play has the most value with 3 to 5 players in the pot.)

3. The looser the game, the more likely hands will be showndown. So bluffing goes down in value.

Higher-stakes games tend to be tighter and more aggressive. In tight games, there will be fewer people in each pot and you will

---

[10] With 8 clean outs, you will win 34 percent of the time. If both opponents call, you are only investing 33.33 percent of all the bets going in; thus, you are profiting.

get less equity value for your raise.[11] Also, against aggressive opponents, it is more likely that someone will three-bet and lead the turn, charging you an extra big bet to see the turn and river.

Further, in tight-aggressive games, you have more bluffing equity (because your opponents are more likely to fold to aggression). When you raise the flop and check the turn, your sacrifice virtually all of your bluffing equity (since you would never play a strong hand this way).

For example, you hold

in the cutoff. A loose-aggressive opponent open-raises from early position. A loose-passive (bad) player cold-calls in middle position. You call, and everyone else folds. The flop is

The pre-flop raiser bets, and the loose-passive player calls. You should just call. With only two opponents, your equity edge is razor thin. Also, if the aggressive opponent has an ace, he is likely to three-bet and lead the turn, which would be a small disaster.

---

[11] Your "equity" value is the immediate profit you get from getting more money into the pot. For example, if you bet with 25 percent equity and 5 opponents call, you profit 0.5 bets because your 25 percent share of the 6 total bets is worth 1.5 bets.

Now, assume the turn is a 9♠. The pre-flop raiser bets, and the loose-passive opponent folds. This would be a good time to raise as a semi-bluff. Assuming you have 9 clean outs, if your opponent folds a better hand more than 10 percent of the time, raising is more profitable than calling.[12]

Had you raised the flop for a free card, on the turn you would probably still have two opponents. So a semi-bluff would have much less value because the probability that both opponents will fold is a fraction of what it is against only one opponent. By just calling the flop, you are giving yourself two options to play the turn. If both players are still in the hand, you have decent implied odds and can play straight-forwardly with your draw by just calling a turn bet or checking if given the chance. If you hit your draw on the river you will collect a few more bets on average with two players still in. If, on the turn, there is only one player left when it is your action, you can now make a semi-bluff raise because of the increased chance the hand will be won without a showdown. If you hit your draw, the hand gets relatively easy to play (regardless of whether you are against one or two opponents).

There is also an additional, little-known cost associated with the free card play. Raising on the flop for a free card can actually decrease your implied odds when you hit your draw on the turn card. For example, you hold A♥J♥ on the button. A loose-aggressive opponent open-raises from early position. A loose-passive (bad) player cold-calls in middle position. You call, and

------

[12] EV of calling = 0.2 [probability of hitting your draw] × 7 big bets [current pot size plus 1 river big bet] + 0.8 [probability of missing your draw] × (-1 big bet) [cost of calling] = **0.6 big bets**.

If your opponent folds 10 percent of the time, EV of raising = 0.1 [probability of opponent folding] × 6 big bets [current pot size] + 0.9 [probability of opponent calling] × (0.2) [probability of hitting draw] × 8 big bets [current pot size plus 1 turn big bet and 1 river big bet] + 0.8 [probability of missing your draw] × (-2 big bets) [cost of raising] = **0.6 big bets**

both blinds fold. The flop is K♥7♥4♠. The pre-flop raiser bets, the loose-passive player calls, you raise, and they both call. The turn is the 2♥. Both opponents check, you bet, and they call. At this point, you have the nuts (and, based on the action, it is likely that your opponents are drawing dead) in a 9.75 big bet pot.

If you had just called the flop and the pre-flop raiser had led the turn, it is likely that the loose-passive player would have called. You then could have raised the turn, potentially trapping your opponents for 2 big bets each on that round. Playing the hand this way would yield a pot of 11.25 big bets after the turn for an additional gain of 1.5 big bets.[13]

Since you will hit your flush draw on the turn about 20 percent of the time, raising for a free card costs 0.3 big bets.

$$0.3 \text{ big bets} = 1.5 \text{ big bets (bets gained when you hit)}$$
$$X\ 0.2 \text{ (probability you hit)}$$

But a successful free-card play saves you 0.5 big bets when you do not hit your draw on the turn, which is 80 percent of the time, so it is worth 0.4 big bets.

$$0.4 \text{ big bets} = 0.5 \text{ big bets (savings when you get free card)}$$
$$X\ 0.8 \text{ (prob you miss your draw and realize your savings)}$$

---

[13] It should also be noted that if there are more players in the pot, then the cost associated with decreasing your implied odds is greater. However, the immediate equity edge you gain from your flop raise will be greater. Thus, if the pot is 4 or 5-handed and you think there is a reasonable chance that you will get a free card — or that all your opponents will call several bets on the flop, you should go ahead and raise for a free card. In fact, even if you are three-bet and everyone calls, you should four-bet the flop for value which may cause everyone to check to you on the turn, where you can then take a "free" card.

So,, the cost of decreasing your implied odds does not, by itself, outweigh the gains of a successful free card play. However, when combined with the chance that your opponent will three-bet the flop when you raise, and the lost bluffing equity on the turn for those times you are facing only one opponent, it becomes clear that raising for a free card is not always the best play in tight-aggressive games.

The Free Showdown Play

When in position and heads-up post-flop, it is often correct to raise the turn with the intention of checking the river unimproved. You should make this play when you have a marginal made hand and some of the following conditions are true:

1. Your opponent may be bluffing or semi-bluffing.

2. Your opponent may fold a better hand.

3. You do not have many outs, making it easier to fold to a three-bet.

4. Your opponent rates to have six or more outs. And,

5. Your opponent is unlikely to bluff the river if you just call.

With a marginal made hand against an aggressive opponent who will bet the turn as a bluff or semi-bluff, you want to get to the showdown because of the good pot odds. However, it is usually better to raise the turn with the intention of checking the river because it costs the same number of bets as calling down but does more to protect your hand. When the board is coordinated, you should be even more inclined to raise for two reasons. First, it is more likely that your hand is good since your opponent could be semi-bluffing. Second, when your opponent is behind, he will have more outs on average, which increases the value of protecting your hand.

For example, you open-raise with

in the hijack. Only the aggressive big blind calls. The flop comes

you bet, your opponent raises, and you call. The turn is the 3♣, and your opponent bets. Since he could be semi-bluffing with KQ, Q9, 98, or any two diamonds, you should raise here because, if you are ahead, he likely has as many as 14 or 15 outs.

Also, since your opponent could be semi-bluffing, you want to showdown your pair of sixes. If he three-bets the turn or leads the river, it is usually safe to fold since most players will not do so (after you have raised) with a hand you beat. However, a few opponents may make one of these plays as a semi-bluff. You should be aware of who they are and be more inclined to just call-down rather than making a free showdown play against them.

You can also three-bet the turn as a free showdown play against an opponent who will check raise the turn as a semi-bluff. For example, you open-raise with 8♦7♦ in the cutoff. Only the very aggressive big blind calls. The flop comes Q♣7♠T♣, you bet, and he calls. The turn is the J♣, you bet, and he raises. You should three-bet with the intention of getting a free showdown. If your opponent four-bets the turn or leads the river, you should fold since very few players will go that far with a bluff or semi-bluff.

This is certainly a debatable play, but there are some definite positives to making it. They are:

1. The biggest positive is that sometimes you will get a better hand to fold. Jack-x and ten-x are hands that might fold to the turn three-bet, which is a major victory.

2. You do not really have many good alternatives. Getting raised on the turn is always a tough spot because it does indicate a strong hand. Your alternatives would be to fold immediately, risking folding the best hand against lots of open-ended-straight or flush draws or, simply calling down which is viable but allows some hands that are ahead (that might have folded) to the turn three-bet to beat you.

The board in this example is certainly scary and you would have to rely on your overall read of the player to make this play, but it is one that can be added to your arsenal and should make you more difficult to read. If it seems that your opponents are always folding correctly to your turn and/or river three-bets (because they always represent monsters), then maybe a three-bet for a free showdown at some point is the right play.

Again, one benefit of the free showdown play is that you may get your opponent to fold a better hand. As another example, you open-raise with 5♠5♦ on the button. Only the tight-aggressive big blind calls. The flop comes T♠9♠3♦, you bet, your opponent raises, and you call. The turn is the A♣, and your opponent bets. You should raise in this situation not only because you may have the best hand, but your opponent may fold a hand like a pair of nines which would be a huge win.

There is one particular situation in which you do not want to make a free showdown play. When you are playing against a very loose-aggressive opponent who could be bluffing with very few outs (based on your hand and the board), you want to encourage him to bluff again on the river, earning you an extra bet. If you raised and he was bluffing, he will make an easy fold. You should also be less inclined to raise for a free showdown when the board is not coordinated since your opponent will have fewer outs on average.

For example, you open-raise with

on the button. Only the very loose-aggressive big blind calls. The flop comes

you bet, your opponent raises, and you call. The turn is the 2♦, and your opponent bets. You should just call down because, if ahead, your opponent usually has at most 3 to 5 outs. Also, if he is bluffing, he will likely bet again on the river, but just fold the turn if you raised. Here, the value gained from his possible river bluff exceeds the value of protecting your hand against his 3 to 5 outs.[14]

---

[14] See the chapter entitled "The Turn Value Check" in Part Three of this book.

Counters to the Free Showdown Play

The Turn Three-Bet Semi-Bluff

If you think your opponent frequently makes a free showdown play, you should occasionally three-bet the turn as a semi-bluff. However, you should only make this play if the circumstances are ideal. There are two prerequisites:

1. You should have a very strong draw — 13 outs or more. And,

2. Your opponent should be a tight-aggressive player.

Strong Draw

You should have a strong draw because your opponent will rarely fold in a large pot since he is getting good effective odds to call down. Also, your opponent may four-bet. Although getting four-bet is a disaster, it is less of one if you have many outs. Moreover, you will frequently have an 8 to 9 out draw on the turn and bet at the pot. If you were to three-bet semi-bluff with these weaker draws often, your opponents would become more likely to call you down, eliminating the folding equity needed to make the play have positive expected value.[15] If you have a good read that your opponent is making a free showdown play, then you can three-bet semi-bluff the turn with an 8 to 9 out draw, although you should be sure that you have not been caught doing this recently.

---

[15] This is a metagame rationale and applies less to games in which you are new or against players with whom you have no history.

Alternately, even if you have a draw with 13 outs, but your opponent is very unlikely to fold or has recently seen you make this play, you should not three-bet semi-bluff.

Tight-Aggressive Opponent

Your opponent should be both tight and aggressive when you three-bet the turn as a semi-bluff. If your opponent is loose, he will be far too likely to call you down to make this play profitable. If your opponent is passive, he will be less likely to raise the turn for a free showdown. In other words, he will be far more likely to have a big hand. Even if you have seen a passive player make a free showdown play before, you should not three-bet as a semi-bluff because they do not do it often enough to make the play profitable.

Example: The tight-aggressive button opens for a raise, the small blind folds, and you call in the big blind with

The flop is

giving you a flush draw and an open-ended straight draw. Your opponent bets, you check raise, and he calls. The turn is the J♦, you bet, and your opponent raises. If you think he may be raising for a free showdown, you should three-bet as a semi-bluff. If called on the turn, you should probably bet again on the river because he only needs to fold a little more than 10 percent of the time for betting to be profitable. If your opponent four-bets the turn, you should call and check-fold the river if you do not hit your flush or straight.

Playing When You Are
Way Ahead or Way Behind
(But Don't Know Which)

Discussion

Heads up, you will often flop a hand where you can be fairly certain that either you are well ahead and your opponent usually has very few outs, or you are behind and usually only have 2 to 3 outs. For example, the button open-raises, and only you call in the big blind with

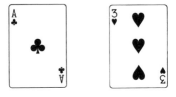

The flop comes

If your pair of aces is best, you have a huge edge. On the other hand, if you are outkicked, you have only 3 outs to improve. (Sometimes you can split if your opponent's kicker is counterfeited.) A related situation would be where you are either

way ahead or way behind is when you hold a big pocket pair and a single overcard flops. For example, Q♥Q♦ on a K♦8♣3♠ flop.

Against aggressive opponents — particularly tight-aggressive — in this scenario, you should often play passively and check-call all 3 streets. The reason is if you did raise with the best hand, your opponent could make an easy fold, winning you the minimum when ahead, but losing you more when behind.

Many players in this situation like to lead out on the river after check-calling the flop and the turn. This is a close decision, but check-calling should be considered as an option. It is tempting to think that you missed a bet when the river goes check-check, but it is a relatively narrow range of hands that you beat which will just call your river bet or would not have bet after you checked. By betting, you miss value from getting hopeless hands to bluff, and by check-calling you may save money by avoiding a raise from stronger hands.

When you flop top pair with aces or kings, you should be more willing to play passively for two reasons. The first commonly-known reason is that your opponent is less likely to have overcard outs. However, another little known reason is that if you hold aces or kings with a weak kicker you are more likely to be way ahead or way behind than with queens or jacks. This is because many opponents will not play hands like Q2-Q8 or J2-J8, but they will play any ace or any king, particularly in a steal situation.

When to Raise

There are five factors, with the first three being fairly obvious, to consider when deciding to raise even though you may be way ahead or way behind. They are:

1. You should be more willing to raise the better your kicker is because it is more likely that you are ahead and additionally, more likely you will get paid off by worse hands.

2.   You should be more likely to raise if your opponent plays loose post-flop since he is more likely to call down with a hand you beat.

3.   You should raise more often the more aggressive your opponent is because it is more likely that he is betting a worse hand. However, you may want to encourage bluffs from hopeless hands as well so you need to find a balance between inducing bluffs versus betting for value. As a simple illustration, you want to find a raise somewhere with ace-queen on an ace-x-x board, but encourage bluffs with ace-four on that same board. With ace-queen, you are going to get called down by all aces, and with ace-four, you save bets against better aces when you don't raise.

4.   You should be more likely to raise earlier in the hand the wider your opponent's range is since you will have more of an edge against his possible hands. For example, if you call in the big blind with K♥5♥ and the flop comes K♣9♦4♠, you should be more willing to get aggressive if your opponent open-raised on the button versus two seats off-the-button. Likewise, you should be more inclined to raise an opponent who plays very aggressively pre-flop.

5.   You should be more likely to raise if the board is coordinated for two reasons:
     A.   Your opponent will, on average, have more outs if you are ahead, and
     B.   Your opponent will be more likely to call down with a marginal hand since it looks like you might be semi-bluffing. For example, an aggressive player open raises on the button, and only you call in the big blind with K♠8♥. The flop comes K♦J♠5♣. You check and call. The turn is the T♦. You could check raise here because your opponent might put you on a flush and straight draw and call you down with any pair or even ace-high.

Knowing When
Ace-High Is No Good

Against the most aggressive opponents you should often show down hands as weak as ace-high when heads-up post-flop. However, there are times when, based on the texture of the board and the betting, you can be certain that your opponent has at least a pair.

For example, you open raise with

in the hijack. Only the tight-aggressive big blind calls. The flop comes

you bet, and your opponent check raises. At this point, you know that your opponent's two most likely hands are either a pair or an open-ended straight draw (i.e. 54, 85, or 98). Since he may be semi-bluffing and you have up to 6 outs if behind, you call. The turn is the 2♣, your opponent bets, and you call because there is a reasonable chance that you are still best.[16] The river is the 8♦, and your opponent bets again. Now, you can be fairly certain that you are behind and safely fold. If your opponent was semi-bluffing with five-four, he just made a straight. If he was semi-bluffing with eight-five or nine-eight, the river just gave him a pair of eights. It should also be noted that some tight-aggressive players will play a weaker ace-high this way. However, they will generally check the river with those hands hoping to get a free showdown or induce a bluff.

---

[16] Raising the turn for a free showdown would also be a viable play.

Making Thin Value Bets

An additional way to profit from an aggressive hold 'em strategy is to make thin value bets when you know your opponent will call down with a wide range of hands. Since you will often be bluffing and semi-bluffing, your opponent should be willing to see a showdown against you with hands as weak as ace-high, and sometimes even worse. This will create many situations where you can bet a hand as weak as bottom pair (or even an unimproved ace-king) for value.

For example, you open-raise in the cutoff with

and only the big blind calls. The flop comes

you bet, and he calls. The turn is the 2♠, you bet, and he calls. The river is the J♣. Against most opponents, you should bet for value.

Since there was a flush draw on the flop, your opponent is likely to call you down with sixes down through fours, a weaker seven, a pair of treys, a pair of deuces, or even ace-high. Also, on this particular board, you can be almost certain that your pair of sevens is good. Since your opponent did not raise the flop or turn, he is very unlikely to have a full house, a jack, two pair, aces down through queens, tens down through eights, or a pair of sevens with a better kicker.

If your opponent is very aggressive, you might not want to value bet the river to avoid a bluff check-raise. (If he is maniacal you can bet the river to induce a bluff-raise.) However, against such opponents, it is usually better to check behind on the turn with a marginal pair hoping to induce a river bluff. So it should be rare that you are forced to consider making a marginal value bet against them.

Calling Down With Outs

When an aggressive opponent's bet or raise forces you to decide whether or not you should make a tough call-down with a marginal made hand, you should be far more inclined to call down if you have outs to improve.

For example, you open-raise with

on the button, and only a tight-aggressive player in the big blind calls. The flop comes

the big blind checks, you bet, and he calls. The turn is the 3♦, you bet, and your opponent check raises. Here, your opponent could be semi-bluffing with a flush draw or straight draw, so there is a reasonable chance that you still have the best hand. Also, if your opponent was slowplaying with a top pair hand like KQ, QJ, or Q9, you have 5 outs to beat him — a little more than an extra 10 percent chance that you will win the pot. Even if your opponent has two-pair, you still have 2 outs to improve to the best hand if the river is another five, which adds an extra 5 percent to your chances of winning. When you combine the probability that you currently have the best hand with your chances of improving, calling your opponent's turn check-raise is clearly the correct play.

If you do not improve on the river, you have to make a decision based on your opponent's tendencies. If he is the type of player that will follow through on a turn semi-bluff by betting the river, you should probably call another bet. Otherwise, you can safely fold.

Similarly, you should be more willing to make tough, ace-high call-downs when you have other outs, such as an inside straight draw. For example, if you have A♣T♠ on a board of K♠Q♣8♣4♥. Not only do you have 3 outs to the nuts — the J♣ is probably a clean out for you the vast majority of the time, and any ace may give you the best hand as well. Since you have up to 7 outs to win and some chance of currently having the best hand, you should call a turn bet or raise here in any reasonably-sized pot.

Part Four
Semi-Bluffing

Semi-Bluffing

Introduction

In tough hold 'em games, your opponents will usually be more willing to fold compared to a typical small-stakes game. Accordingly, making well-timed semi-bluffs will produce a nice profit and even the loosest players will fold enough hands to make semi-bluffing worthwhile. However, simply firing whenever you hold a flush draw or straight draw will not be profitable. You must use hand reading skills to pick your spots.

Other times, if you think you may have the best hand as well as a good draw, checking and calling may be a better play than semi-bluffing, especially against aggressive opponents. In addition, when playing multi-way, you should be even more selective with your semi-bluffs, carefully balancing the current size of the pot, the probability that all of your opponents will fold, and your implied odds.

The following chapters outline some important concepts that will help you determine when and how to semi-bluff profitably. They are important to your overall success in tough games.

Semi-Bluffing
Heads-Up Post-Flop

When playing heads-up post-flop, you should semi-bluff fairly frequently. If you fail to do so, two things will happen. They are:

1. If you simply check and call with your drawing hands and fold on the river if you do not improve, your opponent will be able to win a large number of pots by taking the lead in the betting — sometimes winning with a hand that is worse than yours.

2. You will become very easy to read. Whenever you bet or raise, your opponent will know that you have a strong hand and will be able to make easy decisions based on the strength of his hand.

It should be noted that some opponents will go to the showdown far too often, particularly against only one player. Against these opponents, you should be less inclined to semi-bluff because they may call down with hands as weak as queen-high. It is also possible to setup a river bluff by playing the flop and turn passively against these types.

We recommend five different lines for semi-bluffing — three to be used when out of position and two to be used when in position.

Out of position, you can semi-bluff by:

1. Jamming the flop and leading the turn.

2. Check-calling the flop and check-raising the turn — the "Check-Call/Check-Raise Line." And,

3. Check-calling the flop and leading the turn — the "Check-Call/Lead Line."

In position, you can semi-bluff by:

1. Jamming the flop and betting the turn if your opponent checks to you. And,

2. Calling the flop and raising the turn.

We recommend that you vary how you semi-bluff to keep your opponents guessing. However, in certain situations, you should be more inclined towards certain lines. For example, with your stronger draws — e.g., a flush draw with overcards, a flush draw and a gutshot, or a flush draw and a pair, you should be more inclined to jam the flop because it is likely that you are a favorite at that point. Thus, you will be more likely to profit from bets going in on the flop.

When your opponent has raised pre-flop from a late, or stealing, position, you should be more inclined to raise or check-raise the turn as a semi-bluff. The reason for this is your opponent will be more likely to have a hand he will fold, such as a small pocket pair or a single overcard. Also, you should use this approach more against a tight-aggressive opponent, especially if he's tight post-flop. That's because an aggressive opponent is often more likely to have a weak hand and be making a continuation bet when he bets the turn. So you must evaluate the relative tightness or looseness of these mistakes and adjust accordingly.

We also recommend that for each line you use to semi-bluff, you use that same line with your stronger hands for balancing purposes. Otherwise, an observant opponent will easily be able to determine when you are semi-bluffing. For this reason, you should rarely use the "Check-Call/Lead Line" as a semi-bluff even though it is the least expensive way to make this play. That's because with a made hand it is usually optimal to check raise the flop when out of position.[17]

Also, it should be noted that hand reading becomes important when deciding to semi-bluff. For example, if your opponent has raised preflop from an early position and the flop contains an ace, you should rarely play in this fashion. It is very likely that your opponent has a big pocket pair or an ace, neither of which he will be likely to fold heads-up.

---

[17] See the chapter entitled "The Check-Call/Lead Line" in Part Three of this book.

Deciding Whether to Semi-Bluff with Showdown Value

When heads up post flop with a strong draw that also has showdown value, such as an ace-high flush draw, whether or not you should bet depends largely on your opponents tendencies. It is common knowledge that semi-bluffing has positive expected value if your opponent folds a small percentage of the time — roughly 10 to 20 percent depending on the pot size and your number of outs. However, you do not gain nearly as much unless your opponent folds a better hand than you currently have. This is particularly true against an aggressive opponent who will fold if you bet, but will bluff if you check to him.

For example, you open-raise in the cutoff with

and only the loose-aggressive big blind calls. The flop comes

giving you the nut flush draw. The big blind checks, you bet, and he calls. The turn is the T♦, and he checks. Since your opponent is loose-aggressive, you should check behind. Even though you often have the best hand, and you have nine outs to the nuts, you should not bet because your opponent probably will not fold a better hand. Also, your opponent may check raise, forcing you to pay two bets to hit your draw.

If your opponent has nothing, he will fold to your turn bet. But if you check behind on the turn, he may bluff the river, allowing you to gain an extra bet. Additionally, he may improve on the river with a card that also completes your draw, in which case you will frequently win two bets on the river.

If your opponent was loose-passive, you should be more inclined to bet the turn because betting does more to protect your hand which is still often best. Also, a loose-passive opponent is less likely to raise the turn. He will probably only make this play with top pair or better. Finally, a passive opponent is far less likely to bluff the river, so there is little value in inducing a bluff. If you bet the turn and your loose-passive opponent raises, you should assume he has at least a pair and fold any non-ace or non-heart river.

If your opponent was tight-passive, you should be more inclined to check behind on the turn. This is not because you may induce a bluff, but rather it is more likely that you are behind since he called a flop bet. This is particularly true on a king-high flop since he could not have called a flop bet with two overcards.

There may be situations, such as a queen-high flush draw, where you think you may have the best hand, but it is so weak that you cannot pay a bet to see the showdown. In this situation, you should be more inclined to semi-bluff the turn. If you were to check behind (on the turn) with a queen-high flush draw against an aggressive opponent, they would often bet the river with worse hands. However, you will generally not be getting good enough odds to call a river bluff, so by not semi-bluffing the turn, you forfeit all chance to win the pot without hitting your draw. We should note however that if the board or situation indicates that your aggressive opponent is likely to check-raise, then you should not semi-bluff and take the free turn card.

Against a passive opponent, you should generally check-behind with a queen-high flush draw or similar holding if the pot is small since they will rarely bet the river with a worse hand. As an example, against a passive opponent who takes every ace to the showdown, you should not bet a queen-high flush draw. (However, if the pot is large, you should be more inclined to semi-bluff if there is a reasonable chance he will fold a better hand.)

Semi-Bluffing a Loose Player

Consider the following hand: A loose-aggressive player open-raises on the button, the small blind calls, and you call in the big blind with

The flop comes

giving you a flush draw. The small blind and you both check, the button bets, and you both call. The turn is the 2♣. The small blind and you both check, the button bets, and the small blind folds. At this point, you must decide whether you should check raise as a semi-bluff. You know that, in general, your opponent needs to fold a relatively small percentage of the time for a raise to have positive expected value. However, will a loose player fold often enough for a raise to be more profitable than calling? Also, does the risk of my aggressive opponent three-betting destroy the potential extra profit?

To answer these questions, it is helpful to completely dissect your opponent's hand range. Since your opponent is loose and aggressive, we will make the following assumptions:

1. He will open-raise from the button with about 50 percent of his hands: 22+, A2s+, A2o+, K2s+, K5o+, Q2s+, Q7o+, J4s+, J7o+, T6s+, T7o+, 96s+, 98o, 86s+, 76s, and 65s.

2. He will bet every hand on the turn after both you and the small blind check.

3. He will call down with ace-high or better.

4. He will call a turn raise with any flush or open-ended straight draw. And,

5. He will three-bet with top-pair/good-kicker (i.e. ace-king, or king-queen), aces, or any two pair or better.

Based on these assumptions, we know our opponent has 536 possible hands after he bets the turn. Of those 536 hands, he will call a turn raise with 381 of them:

> QQ-TT, 88, 66-44, AQ-A2o, KJ-KTo, K8o, K6-K5o, Q9o, Q7o, J9o, J7o, T9-T7o, 98o, A♠J♠-A♠2♠, K♠J♠-K♠T♠, K♠8♠, K♠6♠, K♠4♠-K♠3♠, J♠T♠-J♠6♠, J♠4♠, T♠9♠-T♠6♠, 9♠8♠, 9♠6♠, 8♠7♠-8♠6♠, 7♠6♠, 6♠5♠, A♥Q♥-A♥2♥, Q♥9♥, Q♥7♥, Q♥2♥, J♥9♥, J♥7♥, T♥9♥-T♥7♥, 8♥7♥-8♥6♥, 7♥6♥, A♦Q♦-A♦2♦, K♦J♦-K♦T♦, K♦8♦, K♦6♦-K♦3♦, Q♦9♦, Q♦7♦, Q♦2♦, J♦9♦, J♦7♦, T♦9♦-T♦7♦, 8♦7♦-8♦6♦, 7♦6♦, A♣Q♣-A♣3♣, K♣J♣-K♣T♣, K♣8♣, K♣6♣-K♣3♣, Q♣9♣, Q♣7♣, J♣9♣, J♣7♣, T♣9♣-T♣7♣, 8♣7♣-8♣6♣, and 7♣6♣.

Also, he will three-bet your turn raise with 62 of his hands:

> AA, KK, 99, 77, 22, AKo, KQo, K9o, K7o, A♠K♠, K♠2♠ 9♥7♥, A♦K♦, K♦Q♦, K♦9♦, K♦7♦, K♦2♦, 9♦7♦, A♣K♣, K♣Q♣, K♣9♣, K♣7♣, and 9♣7♣.

From the data above, we can conclude that your opponent will fold 93 of his hands

$$93 = 536 - 381 - 62$$

In other words, if you check raise the turn, he will fold 17.35 percent of the time, call 71.08 percent of the time, and three-bet 11.57 percent of the time. For this analysis, we will assume you have 9 outs to hit your flush — you will hit 19.57 percent of the time and miss 80.43 percent of the time — and that you will collect one extra big bet on the river when you do hit.[18] Since there are 5.5 big bets in the pot after your opponent bets the turn, we calculate the expected value of raising to be 0.77 big bets.

$$0.7671 \text{ big bets} = (0.1735)(5.5 \text{ big bets})$$
$$+ (0.7108)\big[(0.8043)(-2 \text{ big bets}) + (0.1957)(7.5 \text{ big bets})\big]$$
$$+ (0.1157)\big[(0.8043)(-3 \text{ big bets}) + (0.1957)(8.5 \text{ big bets})\big]$$

Now, we must compare the expected value of raising to the expected value of calling, which is calculated as 0.47 big bets.

$$0.4674 \text{ big bets} = (0.8043)(-1 \text{ big bets}) + (0.1957)(6.5 \text{ big bets})$$

Therefore, when compared to calling, it is more profitable to raise the turn as a semi-bluff even though your opponent is loose and aggressive, and will call down and/or three-bet with a fairly wide range. This is true for this hand and many others like it.

---

[18] For completeness, it should be noted that we have ignored the possibility that you will hit your flush and lose to a higher flush or full house — which will happen rarely but be expensive. However, this is somewhat offset by the fact that you may catch a queen or five on the river and improve to the best hand.

Semi-Bluffing Multi-Way

In general, you should be less inclined to semi-bluff in multi-way pots for a couple of reasons.[19] First, it is far less likely that two or more opponents will fold than it is that one opponent will fold. For example, assume you are in a pot against two opponents, (A and B). If there is a 20 percent chance that opponent A will fold and a 20 percent chance that opponent B will fold, there is only a 4 percent chance that both opponents will fold (since 0.04 = (0.2)(0.2)).[20]

Furthermore, when you hold a strong draw multi-way, in comparison to heads-up post-flop, your implied odds will have more value relative to the current pot odds, particularly on the flop. In other words, if you bet or raise on the flop and drive out one or more of your opponents, you are actually reducing your implied odds when you do hit in order to slightly increase your chances to win a relatively small pot.

For example, a tight-aggressive player opens in the hijack, the button cold-calls, you call in the small blind with

and the big blind calls. The flop comes

---

[19] That is not to say you should not bet and raise for value with your strong draws in multi-way pots.

[20] This, of course, assumes that your opponents' folding are independent events which is not always the case.

you and the big blind check, and the hijack bets. Many players may want to semi-bluff raise here and represent an ace, which may force out the big blind and get the hijack to fold a lot of king-x and queen-x hands as well as some small-to-medium pocket pairs. However, at this point, the pot is still relatively small, so winning it now is less valuable than keeping both players in (increasing your implied odds the times you do hit your draw). Also, if either of your opponents has an ace, they are unlikely to fold and you will probably have to pay even more bets to draw to your flush.

It should be noted that the pot will usually be large if four or more players are in and someone has raised pre-flop. However, the probability that you will get all of your opponents to fold will be minuscule. While it is possible that you may be able to force several opponents out of the pot with a turn raise (particularly facing them with calling two big bets cold), if the turn bettor has led into a field of many players it increases the chance he has a strong hand, which he intends on taking to the showdown.

For example, you are dealt 8♣7♣ in the big blind, three players limp, the small blind raises, and everyone calls. The flop comes Q♣5♣2♠. The small blind bets, and you call, as do two of the three limpers. The turn is the 9♥, and the small blind bets again. In this spot, if you raised you may get the two remaining limpers to fold hands like middle pair or even a queen with a weak kicker. However, the fact that the small blind raised pre-flop and has bet into a large field twice means that he is very likely to have a strong hand, at least top pair with a good kicker — a hand he most likely will not fold. If the small blind is very aggressive, it might make sense to raise, but such opponents and situations will be rare. You get more value on average on the turn from this strong draw by just calling and hoping to hit on the river, which you will do about 26 percent of the time.

Betting and Raising for Value with Strong Draws

The fact that you usually should not semi-bluff when multi-way should not deter you from betting or raising with strong draws when you have an equity edge, particularly on the flop. For example, if you have the nut flush draw against five opponents on a non-paired flop, you profit from every bet and raise since you will hit your flush far more than one in five times.

You may also be able to push very strong draws, such as an open-ended straight flush draw, on the turn if there are multiple opponents. However, when raising your draws for value, make sure that your raise is not likely to drive out opponents yet to act, because that can potentially destroy your equity edge. In this situation, you are trying to make "pull" bets and raises that are designed to keep people in, as opposed to "push" bets and raises which attempt to knock players out.

On the flop, an interesting situation sometimes arises when you call an initial bet with a strong draw, and the player directly on your left raises and gets a number of callers. In this spot, you can three-bet because everyone is tied to the pot. This also has the benefit of representing a huge hand, and actually creates a scenario where you may want to semi-bluff the turn and/or bluff the river into multiple opponents because you have a reasonable chance to get your opponents to make some big folds given your flop play.

Part Five

Miscellaneous Topics

Miscellaneous Topics

Introduction

We have covered a lot of material so far and have focused on what we feel are the most important concepts for playing in tough hold 'em games. But this is by no means an exhaustive text on limit hold 'em, since volumes upon volumes could be written about various aspects of the game and the resulting strategy.

However, not everything we wanted to say fit nicely into one of the previous sections. In addition to some new theoretical concepts, the following chapters contain important practical advice concerning topics such as turning pro and bankroll requirements. Make sure you read them carefully.

Playing Multi-Way

When playing multi-way, many of the principles for playing heads-up post-flop do not apply. Here are five things to consider:

1. The value of a hand, like unimproved ace-high, decreases significantly since it is much more likely that at least one of your opponents will flop a pair or better.

2. You should bluff far less because it is much less likely to work. For example, if you take a flop with two opponents, each of whom will fold 30 percent of the time after the flop, the probability that both will fold is 9 percent.[21]

3. Since bluffing is less likely to succeed, value betting becomes more important. This is because it is more likely that one of your opponents will have a hand with which he will call-down (although they may call down less liberally which is why you should avoid very thin value bets with a hand like bottom pair). Also, since pots will be larger on average, you should value bet more in order to protect your hand.

4. Checking to induce bluffs has less value for two reasons. First, as mentioned above, betting to protect your hand is more important since pots tend to be larger. Second, your opponents will be less likely to bluff into a field of two or more players. And,

5. Many multi-way pots will become so big that you must make an extra bet or raise to maximize your chances to win.

---

[21] This, of course, assumes that your opponents' folding are independent events.

213

Implied Fold Equity

In limit hold 'em it's occasionally correct to bet or raise as a bluff or semi-bluff even though your bet does not have immediately positive expected value. By showing aggression on the current street, you greatly increase the probability that your opponent will fold on a later street. Thus, the combination of the two bets creates a positive return.

The most obvious example occurs when you open-raise pre-flop with a marginal hand, one of the players in the blinds calls, and three low cards flop. Since your opponent will have frequently either flopped a pair or more likely two overcards, he will not fold to a flop bet often enough to show an immediate profit. However, by betting the flop, you continue to represent a strong hand and preserve the right to successfully bluff again on the turn.

For example, you open-raise with

on the button, and only the tight-aggressive big blind calls. The flop comes

Even though there are very few hands the big blind will call with pre-flop and fold to a flop bet, you should still bet. There is too good a chance that he will hold nothing after the turn and be forced to fold if you bet again.

Implied fold equity may also dictate that you make a very marginal semi-bluff on the turn against a tight-aggressive player because of the chance that he may fold if you fire again on the river. For example, you hold K♥2♥ on a board of Q♦J♦7♥6♥. Even though there are a large number of draws your opponent may hold (thus greatly decreasing the likelihood that he will fold), you may still want to semi-bluff because he will fold a lot of hands on the river if he does not hit his draw.

Furthermore, you can use implied fold equity to guide your pre-flop decisions. For example, you open-raise with K♠T♠ in the cutoff, the button folds, a tight-aggressive player three-bets from the small blind, and the big blind folds. If your opponent does not go to the showdown too often (roughly less than 37 percent of the time), you should strongly consider four-betting because doing so will greatly increase the chance that he will fold a better hand post-flop. In this example, a large portion of your opponent's range consists of small-to-medium pairs and ace-high hands. If he has a pocket pair and an ace flops, he will likely fold most of them post-flop. Also, if he has only ace-high and you continue to show aggression, it's likely he will eventually fold if he does not improve.

Weighted Implied Odds

With a hand that has multiple ways of improving to be likely best, but is currently unlikely best, it is often necessary to weigh the calculation of your implied odds based on the strength of the hands to which you are drawing. For example, you open-raise with

on the button, the aggressive small blind three-bets, the big blind folds, and you call. The flop comes

giving you two overcards and a gutshot straight draw. The small blind bets, and you stop to calculate your pot odds and implied odds. Your pot odds are 8-to-1, but knowing your implied odds is not so straightforward.

Your implied odds on your gutshot are great. If you catch a seven, you will hold the absolute nuts and it is likely that your opponent will be drawing dead. On the other hand, if you spike an eight or a nine, you will be uncertain if you have the best hand. Even if you are best, your opponent is likely to have a 6 out redraw. In this case, your implied odds are much worse.

Your total implied odds can be estimated by weighting your implied odds for each draw by the relative probability that you will hit that draw. In our example, you have 4 outs to a straight and 6 outs to hit an overcard.[22] Thus, the gutshot straight draw represents 40 percent of your draw and the overcards represent 60 percent. In other words, your total implied odds are:

(0.4)(implied odds on gutshot) $+ (0.6)$(implied odds on overcards)

If we assume your opponent has the following hand range: 66+, A7s+, K9s+, QTs+, JTs, A9o+, KTo, and QJo, you will hit one of your overcards but still be behind roughly 50 percent of the time, in which case you have negative implied odds. The other 50 percent of the time, your opponent will have a 6-out redraw, which means he will have 13 percent equity (for his 6 outs) on the turn bet.

Assuming there is an average of 1 big bet in implied odds when a nine or eight turns, and approximately 1.5 big bets when a seven turns, your weighted implied odds are 0.522 big bets:

$$0.522 \text{ big bets} = (0.4)(1.5 \text{ big bets}) + $$
$$(0.6)\left\{(.50)(-1 \text{ big bet}) + (.50)\left[\begin{array}{l}(.87)(1 \text{ big bet}) \\ + (.13)(-1 \text{ big bet})\end{array}\right]\right\}$$

not nearly as attractive as they may have initially seemed, but arguably enough to call a flop bet from the small blind.

---

[22] This is actually an overestimation of the number of outs you have because of the probability that it will not give you the best hand, but discounting it is not important for our analysis of implied odds because you will likely go to the showdown if you hit any of those 6 outs.

This equation shows that you will win on average an extra 1.5 big bets when you hit your straight, lose 1 big bet 50 percent of the time you hit an eight or a nine, and win less than 1 big bet the times that you hit your overcard and it is good.

Since you are in position, we can estimate the last term with reasonable accuracy by assuming that the villain will lead on the turn when an eight or a nine falls 100 percent of the time. At this point, you would just call, and if you are ahead, your opponent will fire unimproved on the river sometimes and sometimes he will check. If you are behind, you will improve on the river sometimes, but sometimes you will not and lose 2 big bets from your decision point.

Using these assumptions, we can see that calling a flop bet here, which is common practice for almost all players, is actually a close decision. Ultimately, the implied odds on the gutshot, particularly because you are in position, will depend upon your opponent and could be higher. We also advocate calling on this flop, but it is important to note how close the decision actually is.

It should be noted that your weighted implied odds are even worse against an opponent who plays (correctly) tight and will fold his 6 out re-draw on the turn. They are also worse against an aggressive opponent because you may be compelled to call down (or at least see the river card) even when he puts in more action on the later streets.

Bankroll Management and Risk of Ruin Considerations

Bankroll and risk considerations are unique to every individual. If you are playing as a pro, you have two objectives when considering what limits to play. You want to maximize your earn rate while minimizing your risk. Unfortunately, the higher limits, at which you maximize your earn rate, carry more risk than the lower limits, at which you earn less. Of course, if you have a large edge in a smaller game and a small edge in a higher game, your overall earn may be higher and your risk lower in the smaller game.

In the past, the standard yardstick for a limit hold 'em bankroll has been 300 big bets. This number is based on the relatively low risk of ruin, assuming that your win rate is somewhat positive and follows the normal distribution. The risk of ruin, or the probability of going broke can be expressed as follows:

$$\text{Pr(going broke)} = e^{[(-2BW)/(V)]}$$

where:

B is the bankroll,

W is the win rate, and

V is the variance which is equal to the standard deviation squared.

For example, for a good player in a good live game, a typical win rate is 1 big bet per hour and a typical standard deviation is 10 big bets per hour. Based on these assumptions, we can calculate the risk of ruin for various size bankrolls as follows:

Bankroll (Big Bets)	Risk of Ruin
50	36.80%
100	13.50%
200	1.80%
300	0.25%

With the rise of Internet poker, it is also useful to understand your risk of ruin in terms of your win rate per 100 hands and standard deviation per 100 hands. This allows you to compare Internet and live games, where the number of hands you can play in one hour is vastly different.

For example, Stox's win rate over his past 300,000 hands is 0.82 big bets/100 hands with a standard deviation of 17.65 big bets/100 hands. Therefore, his risk of ruin, assuming a 300 big bet bankroll would be 20.61 percent.

$$.2061 = e^{[((-2)(300)(.82)/(17.65)(17.65)]}$$

In Stox's case, the risk of ruin is much higher because his edge is smaller in the high-stakes games relative to his variance (1 big bet per hour approximately equals 3 big bets per 100 hands). Also, his standard deviation is higher due to the aggressive nature of the games and the fact that he often plays short-handed. In general, short-handed and aggressive games have higher variance, and passive, full-ring games have lower variance. So if you're playing in tough or short-handed games, 300 big bets is not enough to assure survival, even if you play very well.

Going Pro

Becoming a professional poker player
is easy, all you have to do is quit your day job.

Although it is easy to become a professional poker player, becoming successful is another matter. This is not to say you have to play the highest limits or be one of the best in the world to be considered successful. Certainly, there are many players who grind out a decent living playing several tables at limits as low as $2-$4 and $3-$6. A successful pro, in our opinion, is someone who relies on and realizes income from playing poker in order to pay for everday expenses.

Deciding whether or not you should go pro is a personal decision based in large part on your poker skill, the overall quality of current poker games, your prediction of future game quality, your alternative possiblities, and your overall temperament and risk tolerance. The following are some questions (though certainly not exhaustive) that are important when deciding whether to turn pro:

1. **Do you have at least 6 to 12 months of living expenses (over and above your playing bankroll)?** Preferably, you have a lot more than just this, our minimum recommendation. Especially in live play, an expert poker pro can experience a period of several months where he or she loses money. Being on a short bankroll, and in a downswing, can be incredibly stressful. You can mitigate this stress, and improve your performance, by being sure that you have a large cushion to fall back on during the rough stretches.

2. **Do you have a sufficient bankroll to comfortably play a limit that can support you?** The variance in limit hold 'em is extreme. A player who wins 1 BB/100 hands with a

standard deviation of about 17 BB/100 hands has a 22 percent chance of going broke starting with a 300 big bet bankroll. In today's more aggressive games, winning 1BB/100 hands over a large sample at any mid-or-high stakes game is a very good accomplishment, and probably puts you in the top 10 percent of players for that limit.

3. **Do you have the mind set and ability to grind out your hours and hands even when things are not going your way?** People usually find it very easy to play the hours they need to when they are doing well, but when running poorly, they have a harder time focusing and grinding without tilt.

4. **Are you good enough?** Are you a solid winner at the limits you play, and are those limit high enough to support your lifestyle? Determining if you are a winner at the limits you play is not an easy task. If you have won 2 BB/100 hands over only 25,000 hands, it is very difficult to say what your true winrate is, or even to approximate it with any degree of accuracy. There are players with discrepancies of 3 BB/100 hands between 100,000 hand samples. An example is the person who played 100,000 hands and won 3 BB/100 hands, and for the next 100,000 hands, he broke even, and there are many players like this. You are much more likely to determine if you are a winner in a game by recognizing mistakes your opponents make, understanding how you profit from those mistakes, and not making mistakes yourself, than from statistics alone.

5. **Can you find enough games to play in and do you foresee that continuing in the future?** If you mostly play live poker, not only is it important to have a casino nearby, but it must consistently spread the limits you play, and those games must be soft enough so that you have an edge. If you are playing at a table with 6 players equal in ability, you are all losing

money to the rake or time charge. If you play poker online, your games should be going most of the time and, again, they must be soft enough for you to have an edge.

As a final note, there are few things better than being a successful poker pro. But actually getting there is difficult, and failing as a pro can be hard to accept. Poker can fit beautifully into your schedule as a supplementary source of income, and we would suggest most winning players pursue this route if it is an option.

Many people will have stretches where they make much more money playing poker than at their "normal" job. They may become tempted and think it can continue indefinitely, or even increase their income if they were to devote their attention to poker full-time. However, there is something to be said for having some diversification in your income stream, and if poker happens to be part-time and much more lucrative than your real job, that is a good problem to have.

Being a
Student of the Game

In order to succeed at any form of poker, you must be willing to constantly evaluate and improve your own game. Presumably, many of your opponents are working to improve their game, so you may fall behind if you get too complacent. Unfortunately, the variance in limit hold 'em can convince many players that they play "perfectly" when they are running hot, causing them to think they have nothing left to learn about the game. Conversely, when running bad, even the best players will think they might be making significant mistakes and start to re-evaluate their games.

Aside from playing experience, the best way to improve at any form of poker is to discuss hands and situations with other good players. The recent rise of Internet forums, especially those at www.twoplustwo.com, has been a great resource for this, and is likely a major reason why the games have gotten much tougher in recent years. However, it is also important to find someone that you trust who is a better player than you are.

When discussing hands, it is important to pause the hand at your decision point. Make sure you include only the information you had at the time of the decision, as that is the only way you will be equipped to follow similar strategy in the future. The next card that falls, or a player read you developed after the hand should have no effect on the analysis you make for a particular decision, and disclosing future action will influence the analysis and advice that others may give you about the hand.

We also recommend that you set up a formal process for reviewing some key hands at least once a week. Whether you are discussing these with a coach or other players on an Internet forum, getting different perspectives on how to play them will be invaluable. Finally, when reviewing hands, if you are having difficulty in deciding what is the right play, you should do the math. Work hard to think about what range of hands your opponent could have, what your equity is against his range, and what he will do with each of the hands he holds — i.e. how likely is he to fold or bluff? Most decisions become more clear once you have crunched the numbers, although getting there may be difficult.

Part Six

Hands with Stox

Hands with Stox
Introduction

We have selected the hands in this section because they highlight important concepts for succeeding in tough hold 'em games. In most of the hands, Stox played well and they contain plays you should seek to emulate. However, in some of the hands, Stox made mistakes which we thoroughly analyze, and hope you'll learn by example not to repeat.

The first set of hands involve Stox's attempt to steal the blinds and his subsequent post-flop play. The second and third sets show how Stox plays when defending his blinds. And the last set addresses some important miscellaneous concepts. Finally, many of these hands involve multi-way pots. We felt hand examples were the best way to cover more complex scenarios presented when playing multi-way.

Stealing Hands

Hand No. 1

Limit: $20-$40; four players

Pre-flop: Stox is on the button with 3♣3♦
Action: Cutoff folds, Stox raises; small blind three-bets; big blind folds, Stox calls

Flop: (7 Small bets) T♥8♥2♠ (two players); small blind bets; Stox calls.
Turn: (4.5 big bets) 4♣ (two players); small blind bets, Stox raises, small blind folds.

My pre-flop raise is standard with a pair of treys on the button. I would also open with deuces here 100 percent of the time. Some of the time, four-betting with treys can be a good play, particularly against players who are less showdown bound. Alternately, you can call and make a decision about your play on the flop. Either is fine, and folding, of course, is not an option.

The flop is good for me. There are no paint cards, and an undercard to my pair. I definitely could have raised the flop because I have an equity advantage against my opponent's hand range, but I think it is better to call and raise any non-ace turn. (If the flop had contained an ace, I would have immediately folded after getting three-bet pre-flop.)

The turn is another safe card, and I raise for a free showdown. Raising is better than calling down because the pot is worth protecting, and getting six-out draws to fold combined with the possibility of sometimes getting a better hand to fold is worth the risk of having to fold to a three-bet and foregoing a potential river bluff or the chance to spike a trey. Also, after my turn raise, my opponent will probably only bet the river when I am behind, so I can safely fold if that happens.

The flush draw on board makes the free showdown play riskier for two reasons. They are:

1. My opponent may think I have a flush draw. Thus, he will be less likely to fold a better hand.

2. My opponent may have the flush draw and three-bet as a semi-bluff, forcing me to fold the best hand (although such an opponent is rare).

On the other hand, with a draw on the board, my opponent will have more outs on average, so I should be more inclined to raise to protect my hand, and I may actually get some additional value out of a looser call on the turn because of the draw on board. Overall, with the flush draw on board my turn raise is a marginal play, but I still like it for a free showdown, especially when there are no paint cards, and taking the small risk of folding the best hand to a three-bet semi-bluff from a flush draw is justifiable. If there was no flush draw on board, a turn raise would most likely be best.

Hand No. 2

Limit: $150-$300, six players

Pre-flop: Stox is in cutoff with A♥Q♦
Action: UTG raises, hijack folds, Stox three-bets, button folds, small blind four-bets (cap), big blind folds, UTG calls, Stox calls

Flop: (13 Small bets) A♦4♦2♠ (three players)
Action: Small blind bets, UTG folds, Stox calls

Turn: (7.5 big bets) 6♦ (two players)
Action: Small blind checks, Stox checks

River: (7.5 big bets) A♣ (two players)
Action: Small blind bets, Stox raises, small blind folds

Pre-flop is an easy three-bet versus all raisers who are three seats off the button. A decent range to put a solid player on would be basically what we recommend: 44+, A7s+, A9o+, K9s+, KQo, QTs+, J9s+, T9s, and 98s. (This is 15.5 percent of the hands.)

Ace-queen offsuit has 54 percent equity against this range. Ace-jack has 50 percent equity, but plays even worse because of the threat of domination from JJ+, AQs+, and AQo+.

So while we say ace-queen offsuit is an "easy" three-bet against a solid raiser who is three seats off the button, we still would muck ace-jack against that same player. 50 percent equity is usually enough to three-bet when in position and likely to be heads-up post-flop. But since you are not on the button (allowing more players behind you to have a big hand) and ace-jack offsuit faces domination concerns, we would muck it in this situation. Ace-queen is dominated by QQ+, AKs, and AKo which is 2.6 percent of the hands, while ace-jack is dominated by JJ+, AQs+, and AQo+ or 4.2 percent of the hands, and those hands make up approximately 30 percent of the opening hands that a solid player raises with 3 seats off the button.

The small blind caps pre-flop and will probably lead 100 percent of flops, so we cannot narrow his range from pre-flop when he bets the flop. Against a 6-handed under the gun (3 off the button) raise, and a cutoff three-bet, a reasonable small blind will have a narrow capping range. However, it may not be as narrow as you might think since many players find it difficult to fold a pretty good hand from the small blind even when faced with a strong three-bet. Once the small blind caps, a decent estimate for his range is TT+, ATs+, AQo+, and KQs.

Given that we have ace-queen offsuit and the UTG raiser's range is 44+, A7s+, A9o+, K9s+, QTs+, J9s+, T9s, 98s, the pre-flop equity distribution is as follows:

UTG = 31.5%
Stox = 26%
Small Blind = 42.5%.

Once the flop comes and the UTG player folds, the equity distribution changes to:

Stox = 67.4%
Small blind = 32.6%.

In other words, the flop is good for me, and I am definitely seeing the showdown. Once it is heads up, I am either way ahead or way behind the small blind's range. Thus, even though the pot is big, raising to protect my hand is worth less than getting the right amount of bets in on the turn and river.

After the small blind checks the turn, his most likely holdings are JJ-KK, but he may be trying to check raise with AA, AK, or AQ. While he may call a turn and river bet with JJ-KK, he also may fold. So it seems best to check the turn and see what the river brings. This is a close decision, and I potentially miss value from hands that would payoff on the turn and the river. Conversely, I avoid checkraises from AA, AK, and 66.[23] In addition, my river bet will get called down more lightly on the river because of my turn check, or I may get to raise the river if my hand improves to a flush or three aces.

Although this play is conservative, it might win an extra bet from a lower pocket pair (77-TT). The fact that there is a flush draw on the turn makes my check a bit more questionable since

---

[23] Although if I am sure that these are the only hands with which he will check raise, I can fold immediately.

there are plenty of worse hands that will call a turn and river bet, and against the better hands, betting is somewhat less expensive because of my flush redraw. My play basically relies on my read that this opponent can correctly fold a pocket pair below an ace to a turn bet after the pre-flop and flop action, but will likely bet the river if the turn goes check/check because he thinks it has value.

When the river pairs the ace, the chance that the small blind has an ace greatly decreases. Thus, my raise, hoping that he will view it as a bluff and pay off with TT-KK.

Note: This hand illustrates some important principles. However, it should not be viewed as the clearly better way to play this particular hand.

Hand No. 3

Limit: $150-$300; five players

Pre-flop: Stox is in cutoff with A♠T♥
Action: Hijack raises, Stox three-bets, button folds, small blind four-bets (cap), big blind folds, hijack calls, Stox calls

Flop: (13 Small bets) 9♥3♣2♦ (three players)
Action: Small blind bets, hijack calls, Stox folds

In this hand, a loose-aggressive player open-raises from the hijack, and I three-bet in the cutoff with A♠T♥ because my hand should be a favorite against his range and I have a good chance to get it heads-up post-flop with a loose player which always has value. However, when the small blind, who is a solid winning player, caps out of position, he has a pretty strong hand — 99+, AQs+, AQo+, and maybe AJs.

Even though the flop gives me two overcards, it appears that I have at most three outs (likely even 2.5 on average) because of the small blind's pre-flop play, and I do not know which outs are good. If I do have odds to draw (which most likely is not the case), it is by a very slim margin. Also, my implied odds are likely negative here, so my hand is folded.

Hand No.4

Limit: $150-$300, three players, Stox has $17,463 in chips, small blind has $1,191 in chips

Pre-flop: Stox is on the button with J♥7♥
Action: Stox raises, small blind three-bets, big blind folds, Stox calls

Flop: (7 Small bets) J♠T♣3♦ (two players)
Action: Small blind bets, Stox calls

Turn: (4.5 big bets) 5♣ (two players)
Action: Small blind bets, Stox calls

River: (6.5 big bets) 9♥ (two players)
Action: Small blind bets $291 (all-in), Stox calls $291

Showdown: Small blind shows Q♠9♣

As a default, jack-seven suited is the worst suited jack with which I will open-raise on the button. In this hand, my raise gets three-bet pre-flop, so I have to respect the possibility of a better jack or overpair. But more importantly, my opponent has just enough money to put in one bet on each street. Often someone with a short stack is gambling — either they want to double up or bust and get it over with.

In this particular hand, I had the good fortune of flopping top pair, but any pair would be strong enough to call down with because my opponent would play both ace-king and ace-queen like this. (Notice my opponent three-bet with Q♠9♣, definitely a questionable play and probably not something he does regularly, but he was likely on tilt.)

So the only decision in this hand was whether to raise the turn or call down. Against most hands in my opponent's range, it does not matter as all the money will go in either way. I do think there are slightly more junk hands that would fold to a turn raise but still bet the river versus hands that would call a turn raise but check-fold the river unimproved. So against my opponent's entire range it appears that calling down was the best option. (However, it would be better to raise the turn if he might fold six outs.)

Hand No. 5

Limit: $150-$300, four players

Pre-flop: Stox is on the button with A♣2♦
Action: Stox raises, small blind folds, big blind calls

Flop: (4.5 Small bets) J♦6♦5♦ (two players)
Action: Big blind checks, Stox bets, big blind raises, Stox calls

Turn: (4.25 big bets) 2♥ (two players)
Action: Big blind bets, Stox raises, big blind calls

River: (8.25 big bets) A♥ (two players)
Action: Big blind checks, Stox bets, big blind folds

The pre-flop play is close. If the blinds are loose defenders and play well post-flop, folding is a decent option. Over 316,000 hands of limit hold 'em with limits ranging from $30-$60 to $1,000-$2,000 (with the majority being $100-$200 and above), open-raising ace-deuce offsuit from the button in a 3-or-more-handed game has been a small loser.[24] Notice the smaller number of trials because I do often fold in this situation:

> A2o: 89 trials — losing 0.06 big bets per hand
> A3o: 279 trials — winning 0.29 big bets per hand
> A4o: 260 trials — losing 0.17 big bets per hand
> A5o: 276 trials — winning 0.3 big bets per hand
> A6o: 274 trials — winning 0.15 big bets per hand.

No other unsuited ace loses money in this spot. But even over 316,000 hands, sample size and related variance is a big issue for such a specific query in limit hold 'em.

Calling the check-raise on the flop is close. I might be ahead of a straight draw, or even a K♦X or Q♦X type hand. Overall, there are a large number of very dirty outs, and paying the 7.5-to-1 price to see a turn card in position is what I elected to do.

On the turn, once I make a pair, my raise is for a free showdown since it is my belief I can fold to a three-bet given my weak hand strength and marginal redraws. The river is an easy value bet after making two pair.

Hand No. 6

Limit: $150-$300, four players

Pre-flop: Stox is on the button with Q♦5♦
Action: Cutoff folds, Stox raises, small blind three-bets, big blind calls, Stox calls

Flop: (9 Small bets) 7♠5♣4♣ (three players)
Action: Small blind bets, big blind calls, Stox raises, small blind calls, big blind calls

---

[24] Flat calling is an option against loose bad players.

Turn: (7.5 Small bets) 8♠ (three players)
Action: Small blind checks, big blind checks, Stox checks

River: (7.5 Small bets) 2♣ (three players)
Action: Small blind checks, big blind checks, Stox checks

Showdown: Small blind shows A♥9♠, big blind folds

As my default, queen-five suited is the worst suited queen to open-raise with on the button. The turn is the big decision here, and I think my checking is a big mistake. Two overcards is the most likely holding for both of my opponents, and on this board with my weak hand, I can safely fold to a check-raise as it is my opinion even aggressive players probably will not check raise with a flush draw on a board that also has four cards to a straight. As the hand played out, I gave a free card to two opponents when a bet would have either gotten folds or charged 3 to 6 out draws — both of which are much better than checking. Betting on the flop and turn both for value and to protect your hand should go up in frequency as more players are in the pot.

Hand No. 7

Limit: $150-$300, three players

Pre-flop: Stox is on the button with Q♣5♣
Action: Stox raises, small blind folds, big blind three-bets, Stox calls

Flop: (6.5 small bets) 7♠6♥4♥ (two players)
Action: Big blind bets, Stox calls

Turn: (4.25 big bets) K♠ (two players)
Action: Big blind bets, Stox raises, big blind calls

River: (8.25 big bets) 9♦ (two players)
Action: Big blind checks, Stox bets, big blind raises, Stox folds

This hand is a semi-bluff gone wrong, but I still think it's played correctly. Giving up and checking the river is an option because, once my opponent calls the turn raise with the king on the board, it is unlikely he has a hand that will fold to a river bet. Also, because of his three-bet pre-flop, it is almost impossible that he has a hand worse than queen-high. Jack-ten suited would be the one possiblity.

The specific hands that might fold to a river bet would be A♥X♥ or A♠X♠ but certain opponents will call down with those hands a fair amount. A better queen with a flush draw (queen-jack suited or queen-ten suited) is also possible, and my opponent would almost certainly fold those hands to a river bet. The king may have been a bad card to semi-bluff, and if the turn were an ace, I would not have raised but would have called and bet the river if my opponent checked.

Hand No. 8

Limit: $75-$150, six players

Pre-flop: Stox is in the cutoff with K♥J♦
Action: The first two players fold, Stox raises, button three-bets, small blind folds, big blind calls, Stox calls

Flop: (9.5 small bets) J♥8♣5♣ (three players)
Action: Big blind checks, Stox checks, button bets, big blind raises, Stox three-bets, button four-bets (cap), big blind calls, Stox calls

Turn: (10.75 big bets) 7♥ (three players)
Action: Big blind checks, Stox checks, button bets, big blind calls $122.50 (all-in), Stox calls

River: (16.25 big bets) 2♠ (three players with one player all-in)
Action: Stox checks, button bets, Stox calls

Showdown: Button shows A♣J♣

My pre-flop open-raise is completely standard, and I think the button three-bets with a fairly wide range: 44+, A7o+, A4s+, KQo, and KQs. The flop gives me top pair with a good kicker. When the big blind check raises, he is likely to have a hand like middle pair or a worse jack and is trying to shut me out of the pot. I three-bet to try to force out the button and push my edge since my hand is likely ahead at this point.

When, the button four-bets, I think he has a set, an overpair, or two clubs — less likely given his pre-flop range. Against this range, my hand is a significant underdog, but the pot is laying me odds to call. Also, I know it's likely to only cost two big bets to get to the showdown since the third player is all-in.

This was a tough hand, and it is difficult to find a fold anywhere given the flush draw on the flop. Some players will four-bet this flop as a semi-bluff 3-handed because they feel like they are even money on the draw (2-to-1 to complete on the flop) and they get some folding equity out of the four-bet. Additionally, some players will four-bet a worse jack on the flop because they will read the big blind's check-raise for a marginal made hand and put me on a possible draw. If a club, queen, or ace fell on the turn or river, I can fold. But as the hand played, it appears a call-down is necessary because of the pot size.

Hand No. 9

Limit: $150-$300, five players

Pre-flop: Stox is in the hijack with Q♣Q♠
Action: Stox raises, next three players fold, big blind calls

Flop: (4.5 small bets) J♠J♦5♣ (two players)
Action: Big blind checks, Stox bets, big blind calls

Turn: (3.25 big bets) 3♠ (two players)
Action: Big blind checks, Stox bets, big blind calls

River: (5.25 big bets) K♥ (two players)
Action: Big blind checks, Stox bets, big blind calls

Showdown: Big blind mucks A♥T♠

In this hand, the only interesting decision is at the river. The pre-flop raise is certainly standard, and the flop and turn bets are for value. On the river, I should bet only if my hand is a favorite the times that my opponent calls. My opponent will probably call with any pair. I lose to any jack, 33, 55, KK, or AA, none of which are very likely since he has not put in a raise. I also lose to any king, but beat any pocket pair below tens and any five or any trey. If my opponent will call with all of those hands, I am probably enough of a favorite to bet for value. But this particular opponent is showdown bound and, thus, may call me with ace-high. Therefore, it is my opinion the river is a clear value bet.

Hand No. 10

Limit: $150-$300, four players

Pre-flop: Stox is cutoff with Q♠T♠
Action: Stox raises, button folds, small blind three-bets, big blind folds, Stox calls

Flop: (7 small bets) A♠K♦2♠ (two players)
Action: Small blind bets, Stox calls

Turn: (4.5 big bets) 8♣ (two players)
Action: Small blind bets, Stox raises, small blind calls

River: (12.5 big bets) K♥ (two players)
Action: Small blind checks, Stox bets, small blind calls

Showdown: Small blind shows A♥9♣

On the flop, my equity is very good. I have 12 outs to the virtual nuts, but if my opponent has me beat, he is not very likely to fold. This is a hand where it may be better to raise the flop and bet the turn, then give up on the river if called down and my draw misses. My preference is to bet the turn rather than check for the free card. The strength of my draw is such that I am willing to risk the turn check-raise in return for getting pairs below king-x to fold and getting an extra bet on the river when my hand improves and gets called down.

Hand No. 11

Limit: $150-$300, three players

Pre-flop: Stox is on the button with Q♦T♦
Action: Stox raises, small blind three-bets, big blind calls, Stox
   calls

Flop: (9 small bets) Q♥8♣2♦ (three players)
Action: Small blind bets, big blind raises, Stox calls, small blind
   calls

Turn: (7.5 big bets) 4♦ (three players)
Action: Small blind checks, big blind bets, Stox calls, small blind
   raises, big blind folds, Stox calls

River: (12.5 big bets) 2♥ (two players)
Action: Small blind bets, Stox calls

Showdown: Small blind shows A♣A♦

In this hand, the small blind is a solid winner, and the big blind is the soft spot. The pre-flop raise is very standard. On the flop, my decision is whether to call or three-bet. In hindsight, I think not three-betting was a mistake because it would have allowed me to get a better read on the small blind and possibly given me the option to take a free card on the turn. The thought process behind my flop call should have been to raise a safe turn card and force out the small blind by facing him with two bets cold. This also allows me to fold to a three-bet or take a free showdown. Picking up the flush draw (on the turn) complicates matters slightly because I do not want to get three-bet and my penalty is now less from letting a third player see a river card cheaply.

Once the small blind check raises the field on the turn, I would have folded without the flush draw. Given the action thus far, the small blind's raise almost always means a big hand, but this particular player is aggressive enough to make this play with a hand as weak as ace-queen.

The river presents a tough decision. My opponent's play so far indicates that he has a monster, but the pot is offering me over 13-to-1. Since he could have played this way with A♦K♦ or A♦J♦, I make a crying call because of the pot size. My biggest mistake was not three-betting the flop, but given my thought process, it is somewhat defensible.

Big Blind Defense Hands

Hand No. 12

Limit: $50-$100, five players

Pre-flop: Stox is in the big blind with 3♠2♠
Action: The hijack folds, cutoff raises, button folds, small blind calls, Stox calls

Flop: (6 small bets) T♥9♠4♠ (three players)
Action: Small blind bets, Stox calls, cutoff folds

Turn: (4 big bets) J♥ (two players)
Action: Small blind bets, Stox calls

River: (6 big bets) K♥ (two players)
Action: Small blind checks, Stox bets, small blind calls

Showdown: Small blind shows J♠ T♣

Pre-flop, the pot is offering me 5-to-1 immediate odds closing the action, making it close to play any two suited cards. I will flop two pair, a flush, trips, or quads 4.54 percent of the time and a flush draw 10.94 percent of the time. Here, I called with 3♠2♠ because my opponents are not solid players, increasing my implied odds.

Since my betting opponent was loose-bad, my decision was not to semi-bluff raise the turn as I judged the range of hands he calls with to be very wide. Somehow, I could not help betting the river when checked to with my three-high.

However, my opponent played this hand well, inducing a river bluff from me when the backdoor flush and fourth straight card gets there. On a scary board like this, my opponent has an interesting decision that is very opponent-dependent. In his position, I would bet-call against a loose-aggressive player — betting to induce a bluff-raise. Against a tight-aggressive player, my play is to check-call, and against a passive player, I would bet-fold.

Hand No. 13

Limit: $150-$300, five players

Pre-flop: Stox is in the big blind with 5♣5♦
Action: UTG raises, three players fold, small blind calls, Stox calls

Flop: (6 small bets) T♦8♠8♥ (three players)
Action: Small blind checks, Stox bets, UTG calls, small blind calls

Turn: (4.5 big bets) Q♥ (three players)
Action: Small blind checks, Stox checks, UTG bets, small blind folds, Stox folds

Pre-flop, my call is standard in a 3-handed pot. (I might reraise if the small blind had folded.) On the flop, I figured to be best and bet out to gain information about my opponents' hands.

The turn is a tough spot. I do not like to give my opponent an invitation to steal, even though it is 3-handed. Also, the pot is a decent size which makes me more inclined to bet. So even though the UTG's turn bet carries more weight since the flop was multi-way and two players called my bet, he still may bet with many hands that my pair beats, specifically AK, AJ, and KJ. Instead of folding, I could have called the turn and called any non-broadway river. Ultimately, check-folding appears best since my opponent open-raised from under the gun.

Hand No. 14

Limit: $75-$150, six players

Pre-flop: Stox is in the big blind with 8♦7♣
Action: The first player folds, hijack raises, the next three players fold, Stox calls

Flop: (4.5 small bets) 7♦7♠2♠ (two players)
Action: Stox checks, hijack bets, Stox raises, hijack three-bets, Stox four-bets (cap), hijack calls.

Turn: (6.25 big bets) K♥ (two players)
Action: Stox bets, hijack raises, Stox calls

River: (10.25 big bets) 8♥ (two players)
Action: Stox bets, hijack calls

In this hand, the pre-flop decision is close. A typical open-raise from the hijack at this limit represents about 25 percent of the hands: 33+, A2s+, A8o+, K7s+, KTo+, Q9s+, QTo+, J9s+, JTo, T8s+, 98s, and 78s. Against this range, eight-seven offsuit has approximately 35 percent equity and it plays well post-flop because it is connected and not very likely to be dominated since the raiser will rarely hold an eight or a seven. Against someone who plays tighter pre-flop or very well post-flop, I would fold here. Also, eight-six offsuit and seven-six offsuit will be discarded in this spot.

The flop is great. My equity is now 94 percent versus his pre-flop range. With such a big edge, my decision is whether to check-raise the flop and lead the turn, or to check-call the flop and go for a check-raise on the turn. Waiting until the turn to raise is a mistake because the benefits to playing fast on the flop outweigh the extra small bet you gain if a turn check-raise succeeds.

Check-raising the flop has the following benefits:

1. It avoids the possibility of my opponent checking behind on the turn since I will bet the turn.

2. It's more likely to get called down by a wider range because opponents generally give less respect to a flop check-raise than to a turn check-raise.

3. It creates the opportunity to get in extra action on the turn. Many opponents will just call the flop with a strong hand, such as an overpair, planning to raise the turn in which case I can three-bet.

On the other hand, waiting until the turn to check raise has the following benefits:

1. It gains extra bets from an opponent who would fold to a flop check-raise or a turn bet, but who will fire a "second barrel" bluff on the turn.

2. It gains one extra small bet from showdown bound players who will call down versus either line.

In general, with a monster hand against only one opponent, it is better to play it fast on the flop, especially if the board is coordinated since your opponent may think you have a drawing hand. The opportunity to build a big pot and avoid the turn being checked through outweigh the benefits of waiting for the turn to check raise.

In this hand, however, I get more action than expected. I get to cap the flop, which is great. After that, my opponent still raises my turn bet. At this point, I have to be concerned that he may have a very strong hand, such as a pair of kings or a better seven. Although those hands are not likely given the board, the seven in my hand, and his pre-flop range,[25] there are not many hands that would play this way that I beat — maybe aces (with no spade) looking for a free showdown or hands with the K♠. However, it's my opinion that not three-betting the turn is the correct play because:

1. If my opponent is bluffing, he will fold to my three-bet.

2. If my hand is second best, my opponent will four-bet, and I will not be able to fold in this big pot forcing me to pay 2 more big bets to get to the showdown.

3. I must be ahead well over 50 percent of the time here (i.e. I have negative implied odds), but once he raises the turn, my opinion changes.

The river decision is also interesting. Although the 8♥ improves my hand, it is not by much since I am still behind to kings and king-seven suited. On the other hand, if my opponent was raising the turn with aces or K♠X♠, he will likely call a river bet but check if I check. Furthermore, he could possibly raise with ace-seven suited. I think the decision is close between bet-call and check raise. However, the problem with going for a check-raise is that he may check behind or three-bet, neither of which is a good result.

Hand No. 15

Limit: $300-$600, six players

---

[25] Even though I thought hands like 22, A7o, or K7o were not in his pre-flop range, I should reconsider given the flop and turn action.

Pre-flop: Stox is in the big blind with 9♥9♦
Action: The first player folds, hijack raises, cutoff calls, the next two players fold, Stox three-bets, hijack calls, cutoff calls

Flop: (9.5 small bets) A♥T♥9♠ (three players)
Action: Stox bets, hijack folds, cutoff raises, Stox three-bets, cutoff four-bets (cap), Stox calls

Turn: (8.75 big bets) 7♥ (two players)
Action: Stox bets, cutoff raises, Stox three-bets, cutoff calls

River: (14.75 big bets) 2♣ (two players)
Action: Stox bets, cutoff calls

Showdown: Cutoff mucks A♣9♣

In this hand, the hijack is a tight-solid player. His opening range is approximately: 44+, A2s+, A8o+, K8s+, KJo+, Q9s+, QJo, J9s+, T8s+, 98s, and 78s. The cutoff is a loose, bad player. His cold-calling range is a bit wider than the hijack's opening range.

With 9♥9♦ in the big blind, my decision is whether to call or three-bet. Since it is very unlikely that a pre-flop three-bet will get either opponent to fold a better hand post-flop, my strategy is to only raise if I have an equity advantage. Against their hand ranges, a pair of nines has about 41 percent equity, which is enough of an edge to three-bet. Three-betting also allows me to further narrow my opponents' ranges because I get to see whether or not they four-bet. Since neither of them does, AA, KK, QQ, and AK are ruled out virtually 100 percent of the time, as well as probably JJ, and maybe TT. While a player sometimes may not four-bet those hands against only one opponent for deception purposes, it is extremely rare (and a big mistake) not to four-bet pre-flop with these hands when three or more players are in.

The flop is very good for my hand given the pre-flop action. I am far ahead of almost all hands my opponents could have. Against K♥Q♥, K♥J♥, Q♥J♥ I have 63 percent equity but against a pair of tens my equity is only 9 percent. However, with no pre-flop cap a pair of tens is unlikely. These hands are the only real threats.

After three-betting pre-flop, I will bet the flop nearly 100 percent of the time. My bet gets a fold from the tight-solid player and is raised by the looser player. While it may seem tempting to call his raise and attempt a turn check-raise, it is much better to three-bet the flop and lead the turn with such a strong hand out of position. This gives my opponent the opportunity to four-bet the flop or raise the turn (allowing me to three-bet) and avoids the risk of a free card on the turn.

After my opponent caps the flop, his range is narrowed significantly: AT, A9, T9, Q♥J♥, TT, Q♥8♥, and K♥Q♥. The turn card is not great for me since it completes the flush. But I am still way ahead of his range and have a good redraw against a made flush, giving me good pot equity.

Once I bet the turn and he raises, my decision is whether to three-bet. Against a tighter player who does not overplay his hands, it's probably best to just call. But against an over-aggressive, loose player, I am willing to risk getting four-bet. When he does not four-bet the turn, being up against a flush becomes unlikely and any non-heart river can be bet with confidence.

Hand No. 16

Limit: $75-$150, five players

Pre-flop: Stox is in the big blind with A♠3♠
Action: Hijack raises, the next three players fold, Stox calls

Flop: (4.5 small bets) K♠T♠2♦ (two players)
Action: Stox checks, hijack bets, Stox raises, hijack three-bets,
  Stox four-bets, hijack calls

Turn: (6 big bets) 5♦ (two players)
Action: Stox bets, hijack calls

River: (8 big bets) K♣ (two players)
Action: Stox bets, hijack calls

Showdown: Stox shows A♠3♠, hijack shows Q♦ T♥

Against one opponent, I will call a raise with ace-trey suited
in the big blind 100 percent of the time. Even against a raiser who
is under the gun at a ten-handed table (who's range is 88+, AJo+,
ATs+, and KQs = 7.4 percent of hands), ace-trey suited has 35.9
percent equity. The threat of domination is somewhat mitigated by
the fact that my hand is suited, meaning that ace-trey suited plays
better on the turn and river than ace-trey offsuit. But this is not a
three-bet situation because the equity generally does not warrant
it, and if an ace flops I will probably only get action that my hand
does not want. So it's better to three-bet with a hand like king-
jack and represent an ace if one flops and have a better chance of
getting paid off when I hit top pair.

The big decision point in this hand is on the flop, which was
good for me. Versus a player who raises 41.2 percent of his hands:
A2o+, K7o+, Q9o+, J9o+, T9o, 98o, A2s+, K2s+, Q5s+, J8s+,
T8s+, 97s+, 86s+, 75s+, 65s, and 22+, my equity is about 50
percent pre-flop. On this flop, my equity increases to 57 percent
against his range, which is an argument for jamming. However,
since my opponent held Q♦T♥, his equity was 54.44 percent, so
I was not in terrible shape. (If he held a spade, it would be 57.5
percent.) But he is definitely not folding middle pair here.

My mistake was four-betting the flop and leading the turn.
Once he three-bets, my hand range estimate for my opponent has

to narrow, and no longer can I assume my equity is more than 50 percent. In fact, it's likely my hand is behind and would prefer a cheap draw. So I'm relatively lucky there was no turn raise.

I also probably could have saved a bet on the river because, after this action, no worse hand is calling and very rarely will a better hand fold in a bloated, heads-up pot like this. At the time, it seemed possible he might have ace-queen or ace-jack, thus the river bet, which is somewhat defensible. But my flop action out of position is a bit too much.

As an alternate line, I could call the flop and check raise the turn, which is more likely to get a better hand, such as a small pocket pair or a better ace, to fold. A third option is to check-call all three streets, planning to check raise if I hit my draw. Ultimately, this last option is best against a showdown-bound, loose-aggressive player. Whereas, it is probably better to semi-bluff by check-raising either the flop or turn against a tight-aggressive player that might fold a better hand.

Hand No. 17

Limit: $150-$300, six players

Pre-flop: Stox is in the big blind with A♠8♦
Action: The first four players fold, small blind raises, Stox calls

Flop: (4 small bets) A♥8♠5♠ (two players)
Action: Small blind bets, Stox calls

Turn: (3 big bets) T♣ (two players)
Action: Small blind checks, Stox bets, small blind raises, Stox calls

River: (7 big bets) K♦ (two players)
Action: Small blind bets, Stox raises, small blind three-bets, Stox calls

Showdown: Small blind shows A♦A♣

In this hand there are a lot of options. My opponent is a winning, thinking player, so I chose a more deceptive approach. Pre-flop, against more of a loose-aggressive player, my default would be to three-bet A♠8♦. Also, I would jam the flop hoping to get extra action and tie my opponent to the pot. Here, I called the flop hoping to raise the turn, thinking my opponent might three-bet the turn with a good ace, especially if the turn brought a flush draw.

Once my opponent check raises the turn, AJ-AK are very likely holdings for him, as are AT, AA, TT, 88, and 55. But it's my opinion my play of this hand was poor. Two better lines would have been to three-bet the turn and call down if he four-bets, or to raise the river as I did and try to find a fold if he three-bets.

When two big hands collide heads-up post-flop, especially in blind battles, second best is going to lose a big pot no matter how it is played. If you are saving money in these spots it means you are not getting enough value in others. It is also a good skill to grit your teeth and put the hand behind you.

Hand No. 18

Limit: $150-$300, six players

Pre-flop: Stox is in the big blind with A♠8♥
Action: The first four players fold, button raises, small blind folds, Stox calls

Flop: (4.5 small bets) Q♣7♥5♥ (two players)
Action: Stox checks, button bets, Stox calls

Turn: (3.25 big bets) 4♠ (two players)
Action: Stox checks, button bets, Stox calls

River: (5.25 big bets) 2♥ (two players)
Action: Stox checks, button bets, Stox calls

Showdown: Button shows J♥6♠

My opponent here plays aggressively, especially when tilting. Thus, I checked and called all three streets hoping to induce bluffs. This line is certainly high variance, but against an opponent who will fire a 3-barrel bluff, it can be optimal.

It was a mistake for my opponent to bet the river, since the only hand I would fold that he does not beat is king-six (but I would likely check raise the turn with that) — all other hands I would have folded on the turn. Against a less aggressive opponent, it might be best to fold ace-high to this river bet since the open-ended straight draw got there on the turn and the flush draw got there on the river. But against this opponent, my ace-high is good more than 1 in 7 times.

Hand No. 19

Limit: $150-$300, four players

Pre-flop: Stox is in the big blind with A♣8♥
Action: Cutoff raises, the next two players fold, Stox calls

Flop: (4.5 small bets) 8♠8♣4♥ (two players)
Action: Stox checks, cutoff bets, Stox raises, cutoff calls

Turn: (4.25 big bets) K♥ (two players)
Action: Stox bets, cutoff raises, Stox three-bets, cutoff calls

River: (10.25 big bets) 3♣ (two players)
Action: Stox bets, cutoff calls

Showdown: Cutoff shows A♠K♠ and mucks.

In this hand, I think playing fast on the flop enabled me to get more action on the turn. Since a possible hand for my opponent is a pocket pair (55-77 or 99+), he may have called my flop raise planning to raise on the next round. Also, he could have made a pair of kings on the turn and thought he improved to the best hand. This is a good example of where it is tempting to wait for the turn to check raise because your hand is strong, but playing this flop fast is better against almost all types of opponents.

Hand No. 20

Limit: $150-$300, six players

Pre-flop: Stox is in the big blind with A♦9♥
Action: The first two players fold, button raises, small blind folds, Stox calls

Flop: (4.5 small bets) A♥Q♥3♣ (two players)
Action: Stox checks, button bets, Stox calls

Turn: (3.25 big bets) 9♣ (two players)
Action: Stox checks, button bets, Stox raises, button three-bets, Stox four-bets, button calls

River: (11.25 big bets) 8♣ (two players)
Action: Stox bets, button calls

Showdown: Button folds

In this hand, if I did not make two pair, my most likely play would be to check-call the turn and river, only betting the river if my opponent checked the turn. Since I did hit two pair, it appears, based on his range that my hand is ahead even after he three-bets the turn. Because I have a read that he gives too much action, he could be three-betting with a just pair of aces, a draw, or a pair plus a draw. Thus, my decision to four-bet even though I was risking a five-bet. (There is no cap heads-up on this particular site.) However, against most players this would not be my strategy.

Hand No. 21

Limit: $150-$300, six players

Pre-flop: Stox is in the big blind with A♥9♣
Action: The first four players fold, small blind raises, Stox calls

Flop: (4 small bets) 9♦6♣5♥ (two players)
Action: Small blind bets, Stox raises, small blind three-bets, Stox
    calls

Turn: (4 big bets) 8♠ (two players)
Action: Small blind bets, Stox raises, small blind calls

River: (8 big bets) Q♦ (two players)
Action: Small blind checks, Stox bets, small blind calls

Showdown: Small blind shows J♣J♠

In this hand, typical strategy for me is to three-bet pre-flop, especially against a loose-passive opponent. Alternately, I will call pre-flop and raise the flop if a nine or an ace comes. I will also raise the flop if my 9♣ is an overcard to two of the cards on the flop, especially if my opponent plays tight post-flop.

Here, my opponent was a fishy calling station, and in retrospect, gave too much action on the turn (unless I took the free showdown on the river) because a flop three-bet from a passive player means he has a strong hand. At this point in, calling down is best since my hand beats some of his nine-x hands and also might improve versus other parts of his range. Actually, I was fortunate he did not three-bet the turn. However, if he makes it three bets my hand should probably hit the muck, which is one of the reasons for my raise.

Hand No. 22

Limit: $150-$300, six players

Pre-flop: Stox is in the big blind with A♦9♦
Action: The first three players fold, button raises, small blind three-bets, Stox four-bets (cap), button calls, small blind calls

Flop: (12 small bets) Q♣Q♦T♣ (three players)
Action: Small blind bets, Stox folds, button calls

Turn: (7 big bets) 9♠ (two players)
Action: Small blind bets, button calls

River: (9 big bets) K♦ (two players)
Action: Small blind bets, button calls

Showdown: Small blind shows A♥K♥, button mucks 9♥8♥

In this hand, the small blind's flop play is interesting and good. The small blind is a solid player, and the button is average post-flop but loose pre-flop.

Because the button is loose pre-flop, I know that the small blind's three-betting range is fairly wide, so I cap with ace-nine suited. The small blind's flop bet is good because it is likely to get a fold from a lot of hands that beat him (i.e. 22-99). If he is behind to a ten, he has good equity. Even though he is way behind to someone with a queen, aces, or kings, betting out with ace-king is strong because the pot is large.

The button's call on the flop is correct because he has a gutshot straight draw and the pot is offering 13-to-1, enough of an overlay to draw to the bottom end of a gutshot even on a paired board. Once he pairs the nine, calling is again a good play.

Given the river is a king, the button can probably safely fold. Even though he is getting 10-to-1, the only hands he beats are 22-88. Against a loose-aggressive player it would be close, but calling here against a tight-aggressive player is a mistake.

Hand No. 23

Limit: $150-$300, four players

Pre-flop: Stox is in the big blind with A♦J♥
Action: The cutoff folds, button raises, small blind three-bets, Stox four-bets (cap), button calls, small blind calls

Flop: (12 small bets) Q♦7♠2♣ (three players)
Action: Small blind checks, Stox bets, button calls, small blind raises, Stox calls, button calls.

Turn: (9 big bets) A♠ (three players)
Action: Small blind checks, Stox bets, button folds, small blind calls

River: (11 big bets) 7♣ (two players)
Action: Small blind checks, Stox bets, small blind calls

Showdown: Small blind shows K♦Q♥

In this hand, the pre-flop decision is very interesting. If we assume the button raises with about 42 percent of his hands: 22+, A2s+, A2o+, K2s+, K8o+, Q5s+, Q9o+, J7s+, J9o+, T7s+, T8o+, 97s+, 98o, 86s+, 75s+, and 65s, and the small blind three-bets about 22.5 percent of his hands: 22+, A2s+, A6o+, K9s+, KTo+, QTs+, QJo, and JTs, I have a small equity edge with ace-jack offsuit:

Button's equity: 30.1%
Small Blind's equity: 33.1%
AJo equity: 36.8%

For the sake of comparison, my equity with various hands would be as follows:

AQo = 39.5%   66 = 34.6%
ATo = 34.1%   KQo = 32.7%
22 = 27.9%   AJs = 39.9%

It is also interesting to look at my opponents' equity if I were to fold:

Button's equity: 44.0%
Small blind's equity: 56.0%

Thus, the small blind suffers a greater loss if I enter the pot, which supports the argument that, if you are going to play against a steal when you are in the small blind, you should generally three-bet.

Because of my equity, folding is the worst option, but is four-betting better than a cold call? With a small equity edge, I get value and gain the initiative from four-betting, which may win me more pots if my hand does not improve since my opponents might fold small pocket pairs on some boards. Further, my hand has reverse implied odds, so it's best to get more money in the pot early. This maximizes my early equity edge and reduces the disadvantages caused by my position and reverse implied odds by increasing the pot size, making the turn and river decisions easier.

As for the turn and river decisions, they are easy since I have position, allowing me to get full value for my hand. If my opponent were to check raise either street, my play most likely would be to call down since the pot is big, but I might fold the river against some players on certain boards.

Hand No. 24

Limit: $150-$300, six players

Pre-flop: Stox is in the big blind with K♦5♦
Action: The first two players fold, cutoff raises, button calls, the small blind folds, Stox calls

Flop: (6.5 small bets) K♠8♦3♠ (three players)
Action: Stox checks, cutoff bets, button raises, Stox three-bets, cutoff folds, button calls

Turn: (6.75 big bets) 4♥ (two players)
Action: Stox bets, button calls

River: (8.75 big bets) 8♥ (two players)
Action: Stox checks, button checks

Showdown: The button folds 5♠5♥

Pre-flop, my hand is the K♦5♦ and the pot is offering me 5.5-to-1 immediate odds, plus the betting action will be closed in a three-handed pot. I call here 100 percent of the time even if both of my opponents play well. In this hand, the cutoff is solid, but the button is weak, making my call even easier. (In fact, in this spot, my money goes in with approximately 90 percent of my suited hands.)

The flop gives me top pair with a weak kicker, and my equity against my opponents' ranges has increased considerably. Also, if I am ahead, my hand is not terribly vulnerable since there is only one overcard to my pair. If one of my opponents has a flush draw, my hand is associated with more risk. But with the draw out there, more action may come my way because my opponents have to include a draw in my range of hands when I play fast.

Many players will bet out in this situation, hoping that the pre-flop aggressor will raise and shut out the button. However, it's my opinion that it's better to check and see what develops. In general, check-raising may get me two bets from each opponent. Even though I may be letting them draw (since they will likely each call an additional bet if I check raise the field), they are being charged the maximum to do so. If I were to bet into the pre-flop aggressor and he raises, my hand will often be behind. Therefore, the only player I beat may be shut out and my strategy will get me heads up with a player that has me beat. Other times when I bet out on the flop, the pre-flop aggressor now has the option to play more correctly by making a good fold.

In this particular hand, checking the flop worked out well. When the cutoff bet and the button raised (which often means a hand like middle pair or a pocket pair less than kings), I was able to three-bet. This shut out the cutoff who could have been drawing live to 5 or 3 outs, and also charged the button, who likely has a second best hand, the maximum to see the turn card.

The turn bet was a basic value bet. On the river, my decision is close and I probably made the wrong one. Against most players, it's best to bet the river for value.

However, since this opponent is over-aggressive, he could have raised the flop with a draw meaning that I should check the river to induce a bluff since the flush draw missed. (A check also allows me to avoid a raise from a slowplayed monster.) But since my opponent's flop raise was likely to shut me out of the pot, it appears that a failed draw is a very small part of his range and I probably missed a river value bet from a worse pair. Given that the eight paired, the check is slightly better because eight-x hands are certainly within an aggressive opponent's range given his flop raise.

Hand No. 25

Limit: $150-$300, four players

Pre-flop: Stox is in the big blind with A♥K♥
Action: The cutoff folds, button raises, small blind calls, Stox three-bets, button four-bets (cap), small blind calls, Stox calls

Flop: (12 small bets) T♣4♦2♦ (three players)
Action: Small blind checks, Stox checks, button bets, small blind folds, Stox calls

Turn: (7 big bets) 3♦ (two players)
Action: Stox checks, button bets, Stox calls

River: (9 big bets) K♦ (two players)
Action: Stox checks, button bets, Stox calls

Showdown: Button shows Q♦Q♥

The button is very loose and aggressive. Pre-flop, I have an easy three-bet with two other players in the pot. If the small blind had folded, just calling would be a consideration. The reason the three-bet gets eaiser with more people in is because ace-king suited has a good equity advantage and three-betting maximizes that equity edge by getting extra bets from multiple opponents. Against only one opponent, ace-king suited certainly has an equity advantage, but the three-bet will only collect that edge on one small bet and loses some deception value. So relative to the deception value gained, the three-bet for equity value is not worth as much against only one opponent.

On the flop, it's an easy call to draw to overcards getting 13-to-1. On the turn, I have a gutshot straight draw and two overcards, giving me up to 10 outs. However, 3 of my outs put four diamonds on board, so not all of my outs are clean. Since I am getting 8-to-1, 5 clean outs are needed to make calling correct, so there is enough of an overlay to call here.

My implied odds are zero, or maybe even slightly positive since my opponent will bet the river most of the time and I can call only when my hand improves. Sometimes folding the river unimproved will cause me to fold a winner or a split a small percentage of the time, but being committed to showdown on the turn getting only 4.5-to-1 effective odds would be a losing play here.

The river pairs my king, and while I am likely ahead, it's my opinion check-calling is the best play, but check-raising is a close second. Check-raising and folding to a three-bet would be a good option because it gets you the maximum value from hands that would bet if checked to but not call a bet. Check-raising in a large pot like this will get some pretty thin calls, and you will probably frequently get called by a worse hand. Lastly, almost all opponents would not three-bet this river without two pair or better given the previous action and your river check-raise. In this hand, my opponent held Q♦Q♥ and likely would have paid off the river check-raise because the pot was relatively large.

The flush draw also gets there on the river, but since the third diamond is a king, that eliminates A♦K♦ and K♦Q♦ from my opponent's range. So the only pre-flop four-betting hands left that make a flush are A♦Q♦ and A♦J♦ (assuming ace-jack suited is a four-betting hand for this opponent).

Hand No. 26

Limit: $150-$300, five players

Pre-flop: Stox is in the big blind with 7♠6♠
Action: The first two players fold, button raises, small blind folds, Stox calls

Flop: (4.5 small bets) 7♣5♥4♣ (two players)
Action: Stox checks, button bets, Stox raises, button three-bets, Stox calls

Turn: (5.25 big bets) A♦ (two players)
Action: Stox checks, button bets, Stox calls

River: (7.25 big bets) 6♥ (two players)
Action: Stox bets, button raises, Stox calls

Showdown: Button mucks A♠K♥

Defending with seven-six suited is pretty standard here. I would even defend with five-trey suited against a solid button stealer for whom a likely range is: 22+, A2s+, A5o+, K2s+, K9o+, Q5s+, Q9o+, J7s+, J9o+, T7s+, T8o+, 98o, 97s+, 86s+, 75s+, and 65s. Five-trey suited has just over 36 percent equity and plays relatively well post-flop. Conversely, a hand like five-four offsuit has approximately 34 percent equity and plays slightly worse post-flop, so be more inclined to muck that hand pre-flop against a solid steal raiser.

Over 317,000 hands at limits $50-$100 and higher, I was dealt five-four offsuit in the big blind when a steal was attempted (steal defined as open raise from the cutoff, button, or small blind) 287 times. My strategy was to defend 41 percent of the time and it cost an average of 0.45 big bets per hand over all 287 trials, a slight improvement over the 0.5 big bet loss from folding everytime.

The 116 times that I put money in the pot, my results was to lose 0.37 big bets per hand. So if anything, loosening up slightly with my defending standards would be okay, at least according to these results. The times I folded are when it was three-bet before the action got to me. For example, if the cutoff opened-raised and the button or small bind re-raised. Also, against a solid-playing, tight cutoff opener, five-four offsuit is often a fold, but it is close.

For comparison, I was dealt five-trey suited in the big blind against a steal raise 82 times and lost 0.7 big bets per hand overall, somewhat worse than the 0.5 big bets per hand loss that would have occurred by folding every time. Using this type of empirical analysis is very valuable, but one of the biggest limitations is going to be variance and sample size. The hands that suffer the most from these limitations are suited connectors both because of their high variance results — making or missing a few big draws can skew the results largely — and their relative infrequency. Of the 82 trials with five-trey suited in the big blind versus a steal raise, I defended 42 times and lost 0.88 big bets per hand. Not a great result, but very easily explained by variance. The table below shows results for similar hands when I chose to defend.

Hand	Trials	Results per Hand
43o	17	-.54
43s	49	-.39
53o	43	-.12
53s	42	-.88
54o	116	-.37
54s	97	+.19
63s	26	-.69
64o	44	-1.04
64s	69	-.09
65o	156	-.29
65s	74	-.38

The following table shows overall results for the same hands, regardless of whether or not I chose to defend.

Hand	Total Trials	Results per Hand	Percent Played
43o	290	-.5	6
43s	103	-.45	47.5
53o	310	-.45	14
53s	82	-.7	51
54o	287	-.45	40.5
54s	118	+.06	82
63s	91	-.55	28.5
64o	291	-.58	15
64s	98	-.21	70.5
65o	283	-.38	55
65s	92	-.4	80

The percent played column should give a rough idea of my defense frequency. There will be some situations where there was a three- or four-bet before me, in which case I would have folded all of these hands, so that is why the percent played number for six-five suited is only 80 percent. There are also situations where a tight, cutoff raiser who plays well opens, causing me to also fold many of these.

From these empirical results, we can draw some absurd conclusions. For instance, five-four suited has performed much better than six-five suited, so you could make the case for defending more often with five-four suited than six-five suited. Since the single most likely card a steal-raiser has in his hand is an ace and five-four suited will make a straight more often than six-five suited when there is an ace on the board, five-four suited is a stronger defending hand than six-five suited. While that argument actually has some merit, the extra pip of hand strength from six-five suited offsets that somewhat. While it is difficult to say exactly which of the two is a better defending hand, it is relatively safe to say that in all situations where you would defend with six-five suited you can also defend with five-four suited and vice versa. Stox played five-four suited 82 percent of the time and six-five suited 80 percent of the time.

Getting back to the hand, the flop is great for my 7♠6♠, giving me top pair and an open-ended straight draw, in case I am currently behind or fall behind on the turn. Deciding whether to cap or call is close. My preferred play is calling. The drawback is that the turn may go check-check because the button was three-betting for a free card and now his ace-x or king-x overcard hand gets a cheap river card. The positive is that some players will keep betting those hands, so I have some bluff-catching equity. Additionally, if I do hit my straight on the turn or the river, I can check raise on an expensive street. Capping the flop and leading the turn is not clearly inferior though, and against over-aggressive, showdown-bound players, it can be a good approach.

On the turn, a lot of hands that were behind me on the flop, just pulled ahead. I am getting 6.25-to-1 and have 13 outs to improve, and sometimes still have the best hand. My outs to a straight are very likely good, certainly the 6 non-club outs are. The 2 club outs might be good, and my outs to two pair might be good as well. So check-raising the turn as a semibluff is just not worth it. For the small benefit of sometimes folding 99-KK, you will get three-bet way too often as well as frequently called down.

I bet the river out of position and out of the lead purely for value, and with the intention of calling a raise. Leading out may cause my opponent to fold, but it may also get a desperation bluff-raise attempt on this board. Ace-x hands almost certainly will call a river bet but very possibly check behind if I do not bet. Overall, the chance of missing value by checking, plus gaining an extra bet when a worse hand raises, outweigh the expected value of checking to get worse hands to bet or to save a bet against a better hand.

Hand No. 27

Limit: $300-$600, five players

Pre-flop: Stox is in the big blind with Q♦J♣
Action: The first two players fold, button raises, the small blind folds, Stox calls

Flop: (4.5 small bets) Q♥7♥5♦ (two players)
Action: Stox checks, button bets, Stox calls

Turn: (3.25 big bets) 5♥ (two players)
Action: Stox checks, button bets, Stox raises, button calls

River: (7.25 big bets) J♥ (two players)
Action: Stox bets, button raises, Stox calls

Showdown: Button shows 6♦4♠

My pre-flop defense is standard. Folding is out of the question, and three-betting is only good against the tightest of post-flop opponents in order to increase my post-flop bluffing equity.

Generally, most players prefer to play fast on the flop with top pair good kicker. But against more aggressive opponents who will almost always bet the turn, waiting to check raise the turn with this type of big, but not huge, hand is often a good play.

Even with the four flush on board, my river bet is for value, especially against an over-aggressive opponent. This seems counterintuitive, but against someone who will bluff-raise, bet/call is usually better than check/call depending on the frequency with which they bluff-raise versus the frequency they will bet after my check. This play should not be used as a default, but only against aggressive players who will bluff raise the river on scary boards. I would estimate this is 15 to 25 percent of all players at the higher limits, but fewer as you move down in limits. Then my default play is to check and call.

Hand No. 28

Limit: $300-$600, six players

Pre-flop: Stox is in the big blind with A♦2♠
Action: The first three players fold, button raises, the small blind folds, Stox calls

Flop: (4.5 small bets) 6♣5♥3♠ (two players)
Action: Stox checks, button bets, Stox calls

Turn: (3.25 big bets) 2♣ (two players)
Action: Stox checks, button bets, stox calls

River: (5.25 big bets) Q♦ (two players)
Action: Stox checks, button bets, Stox calls

Showdown: Button shows A♣4♠

My pre-flop call is close since it is tough to play out of position with this hand, but against a steal raise your equity is relatively good given the odds you are receiving. While you probably suffer from reverse implied odds post-flop, your pre-flop equity is just too much to fold.

	Equity (%)	Win (%)	Tie (%)
Stealer's Hand	54.24	50.42	3.82

Stealer's Hand: 22+, A2s+, K2s+, Q5s+, J7s+, T7s+, 97s+, 86s+, 75s+, 65s, A3o+, K9o+, Q9o+, J9o+, T8o+, and 98o

	Equity (%)	Win (%)	Tie (%)
Stox's Hand	45.76	41.94	3.82

Stox's Hand: A2o

Sometimes with a hand with showdown value, check-calling the flop is better than check-raising. I often do this with ace-high hands that missed the flop and do not have a great draw. Doing this on boards that likely missed your opponent is best because you continue to get value from bluffs. Counter-intuitively, you should play more aggressively on boards that could have hit your opponent since he should also be scared if he missed, and if he connected, you should get information quickly.

Hand No. 29

Limit: $300-$600, six players

Pre-flop: Stox is in the big blind with A♣2♥
Action: The first four players fold, small blind raises, Stox calls

Flop: (4 small bets) K♦6♥5♥ (two players)
Action: Small blind bets, Stox calls

Turn: (3 big bets) Q♥ (two players)
Action: Small blind checks, Stox bets, small blind calls

River: (5 big bets) 8♣ (two players)
Action: Small blind checks, Stox checks

Showdown: Small blind shows A♠T♥

My opponent played very well, and I doubt a river bet would have made him fold. The only decision for me is whether to bet the turn after my opponent checks, or to check behind and call most river bets. Given that my hand was the A♣2♥ and my equity if check raised is pretty small, I like a bet on the turn because folding to a check-raise does not forfeit too much and charging live 6-outers (or getting them to fold) is a plus. If my hand were something like AJ, AT, or A9, a turn check is better because I have more outs when behind and getting check raised is a larger problem.

Hand No. 30

Limit: $300-$600, four players

Pre-flop: Stox is in the big blind with A♥2♦
Action: The cutoff folds, button raises, the small blind folds, Stox calls

Flop: (4.5 small bets) T♥6♣2♠ (two players)
Action: Stox checks, button bets, Stox raises, button calls

Turn: (3 big bets) A♠ (two players)
Action: Stox bets, button raises, Stox three-bets, button folds

After defending in the big blind, a good default play is to check raise any pair or any draw on the flop. However, you should generally check raise less with draws against showdown-bound players, and wait for the turn to check raise more often against over-aggressive players.

My opponent made an interesting turn fold. I think my three-bet is correct given his over-aggressive nature, but an argument can be made for calling and leading or check-raising the river. It is possible my reraise got an ace-x type of hand to fold, but more likely my opponent was on a bluff and was drawing dead.

Hand No. 31

Limit: $300-$600, four players

Pre-flop: Stox is in the big blind with A♥2♠
Action: Cutoff folds, button raises, small blind folds, Stox calls

Flop: (4.5 small bets) K♦8♦2♥ (two players)
Action: Stox checks, button bets, Stox calls

Turn: (3.25 big bets) Q♥ (two players)
Action: Stox checks, button bets, Stox calls

River: (5.25 big bets) J♥ (two players)
Action: Stox checks, button bets, Stox calls

Showdown: Button shows A♦7♠. Stox wins with a pair of deuces

My standard line here is to check raise the flop. However, my opponent is super aggressive and very showdown bound. Given this, he will likely bet all three streets almost regardless of his holding, so my plan on the flop was to call down unimproved.

The more aggressive your opponent, the better it is to check-call all three streets. This particular opponent is in the top 5 to 10 percent in aggression.

The turn is not a great card, but I still beat a good portion of his range. The river is another bad card, but against this specific player, my hand will be best more than 1 in 6 times.

Hand No. 32

Limit: $300-$600, six players

Pre-flop: Stox is in the big blind with 8♥6♠
Action: The first two players fold, cutoff raises, the next two
   players fold, Stox calls

Flop: (4.5 small bets) 9♦6♣6♥ (two players)
Action: Stox checks, cutoff bets, Stox raises, cutoff three-bets,
   Stox four-bets, cutoff calls

Turn: (6.25 big bets) Q♣ (two players)
Action: Stox bets, cutoff folds

   Eight-six offsuit is pretty close to a muck against a tight
player's opening standards in the cutoff, but this player opens
loosely (or plays badly), making this marginal hand worth
defending.
   When I flop a big hand like this, check raise the flop, and my
opponent three-bets, my decision is between four-betting and
leading the turn, or calling and going for a turn check-raise. I
usually four-bet and lead if my opponent is not too aggressive,
because his three-bet usually means either a big hand that will
give action, or he will be more likely to take a free card on the
turn. The more aggressive my opponent is, the more my
preference is to call the flop three-bet and check raise the turn.
   On the other hand, since there is no flush draw on the flop,
playing fast goes down in value. There are two reasons for this.
They are:

1.   My opponent is less likely to have a good draw. And

2.   He is less likely to put me on a drawing hand.

   Ultimately, deciding whether to four-bet and lead the turn or
call and go for a check-raise should be a function of both how
draw heavy the board is — the more draw heavy, the faster you
play big hands — *and* how aggressive your opponent is — the

more aggressive, the better it is to call and check raise the turn. In this hand, since my opponent is not too aggressive post-flop, my decision is to four-bet immediately.

Hand No. 33

Limit: $100-$200, three players

Pre-flop: Stox is in the big blind with Q♥3♥
Action: The first player folds, small blind raises, Stox calls

Flop: (4 small bets) 9♥6♥3♣ (two players)
Action: Small blind bets, Stox calls

Turn: (3 big bets) 4♥ (two players)
Action: Small blind bets, Stox raises, small blind three-bets, Stox four-bets, small blind calls

River: (11 big bets) 5♣ (two players)
Action: Small blind checks, Stox bets, small blind calls

Showdown: Small blind shows 6♣6♦ and mucks

You should defend your big blind versus a small blind steal raise with a very wide range. Queen-trey suited definitely makes the cut, queen-deuce suited would as well.

The flop is good for me, giving me a pair, an overcard, and a flush draw against only one opponent. The flush draw actually makes my play a flop call rather than a raise. I am often ahead, and even when behind, my equity is good. While raising here makes sense from a current equity versus villain's range standpoint, my implied odds are also good, and just calling preserves them. This gives me the option to raise later if I improve, and with basically 14 outs twice, the chances of that are about even money.

Also, since it is a blind battle and the small blind is aggressive, I am more inclined to call the flop. My equity changes dramatically on the turn if the flush card comes, and if it doesn't, I can simply call down. This line shows the most profit when my opponent has overcards that miss, and loses the least versus a better made hand, while still allowing me to raise the river if my flush card comes. If my hand was something like queen-nine, with or without a flush draw, I would raise the flop.

Once the small blind three-bets the turn, a higher flush becomes possible. However, there are also plenty of other hands he would three-bet, including lower flushes, two pair, and sets. I would four-bet even if it were not the cap, but since it is, four-betting is easily the correct play. Additionally, a lot of bad cards can hit on the river — some may kill my action by scaring my opponent, and some may improve my opponent's hand and/or scare me into giving less action. The river bet is a basic value bet, even after all the turn action.

Hand No. 34

Limit: $100-$200, six players

Pre-flop: Stox is in the big blind with Q♠3♠
Action: The first two players fold, cutoff raises, the next two players fold, Stox calls

Flop: (4.5 small bets) J♣4♠2♠ (two players)
Action: Stox checks, cutoff bets, Stox raises, cutoff three-bets, Stox calls

Turn: (5.25 big bets) 5♣ (two players)
Action: Stox bets, cutoff raises, Stox calls

River: (9.25 big bets) A♣ (two players)
Action: Stox bets, cutoff calls

Showdown: Cutoff mucks 4♥4♦

In this hand, my pre-flop decision is actually not that close and depends a bit on my view of the open-raiser. Against a 34.5 percent hand range: 22+, A2s+, A6o+, K4s+, K8o+, Q5s+, Q9o+, J8s+, J9o+, T8s+, T9o, 97s+, 87s, 76s, and 65s, queen-trey suited has about 39 percent hot-and-cold equity and plays pretty well post-flop because it is suited.

After the flop, my equity against that same range is about 50 percent, but once I get three-bet, it decreases considerably. This is a very good spot for a semi-bluff since I can get a number of better hands to fold at some point in the hand. A lot of better queen-x and king-x hands will fold to pressure, and sometimes ace-x hands as well. Playing this flop fast is my preferred line for semi-bluffing rather than attempting to check raise the turn. That approach can be used as a change of pace. Also, you may want to infrequently check-call the flop and lead the turn.

When I make an open-ended-straight draw, in addition to the flush draw, my turn lead without the initiative is an interesting choice versus check-raising or check-calling. It avoids a three-bet, and probably has a similar amount of bluffing equity as a check raise.

The river decision between attempting a check-raise and betting out comes down to an opponent read in most cases. With a hand as strong as mine, it's generally best to err on the side of betting (even though it may give my hand away) because I may get a chance to three-bet. Since the straight did come backdoor and my play already showed strength on the flop, my hand is somewhat concealed. A good hand reader may put me on a marginal value-betting hand that figures a lead is safe because of the scary board. If this happens he may raise as a bluff or for value, both of which are good for me.

Hand No. 35

Limit: $150-$300, five players

Pre-flop: Stox is in the big blind with Q♦7♦
Action: The first two players fold, button raises, the small blind folds, Stox calls

Flop: (4.5 small bets) Q♣8♦5♦ (two players)
Action: Stox checks, button bets, Stox raises, button calls

Turn: (4.25 big bets) Q♠ (two players)
Action: Stox bets, button raises, Stox calls

River: (8.25 big bets) 4♣ (two players)
Action: Stox checks, button bets, stox calls

Showdown: Button shows A♥8♥

In this hand, I did not three-bet the turn because it was my fear any better hand would four-bet and any worse hand would fold. Additionally, I can check raise the river if my flush arrives, even with the full house possible.

Given my opponent's holding of A♥8♥ for second pair, if I had three-bet the turn he might have folded. This play may seem weak-tight, as it looks like a possible better hand is slowing me down, and this is partially correct. I am scared of a better hand almost every time, but missing value bets on my big hands is also a worry. In this particular hand, I think that playing passively on the turn and the river is the best way to maximize my risk adjusted return.

Hand No. 36

Limit: $150-$300, five players

Pre-flop: Stox is in the big blind with Q♥7♥
Action: The first two players fold, button raises, the small blind folds, Stox calls

Flop: (4.5 small bets) Q♠9♦4♦ (two players)
Action: Stox checks, button bets, Stox raises, button three-bets, Stox calls

Turn: (5.25 big bets) 2♣ (two players)
Action: Stox checks, button bets, Stox calls

River: (7.25 big bets) 7♠ (two players)
Action: Stox checks, button bets, Stox raises, button folds

In this hand, I am calling down if my hand does not improve to two pair on the river. Since my opponent is very aggressive, letting him bet maximizes value the times he is on a pure bluff. The drawback to playing hands passively is that if you always check and call to try to induce bluffs and/or lose the minimum when behind, you will invariably win less than the maximum when ahead.

The trick is to ascertain whether it is best to extract money with passive or aggressive play. I do like passive play, especially out of position, because it has the double value of inducing bluffs and minimizing losses. Aggressive play, however, has the double value of getting value from worse hands and folding out your opponent's existing equity. If you get someone to fold 10 percent equity in a pot that is a victory, and something important to consider when you are tempted to play passively.

Hand No. 37

Limit: $150-$300, three players

Pre-flop: Stox is in the big blind with 6♠4♠
Action: Button raises, the small blind folds, Stox calls

Flop: (4.5 small bets) Q♦J♠5♠ (two players)
Action: Stox checks, button bets, Stox raises, button calls

Turn: (4.25 big bets) A♦ (two players)
Action: Stox bets, button calls

River: (6.25 big bets) 7♣ (two players)
Action: Stox bets, button calls

Showdown: Button shows 9♠9♣

In this hand, the pre-flop call is easy. Against only one opponent, I would probably defend versus a button steal down to six-trey suited. Six-trey suited versus a 40 percent stealing range has about 35 percent equity, and it plays pretty well post-flop. Six-deuce suited against the same range has 34 percent equity, so whether or not to defend is a close decision, and if you feel you have a post-flop edge against the stealer, it is worth playing. Six-four suited has about 37 percent equity against the same range and should be a standard call.

It's surprising my opponent does not fold a pair of nines on the turn or river. I guess my read on him was inaccurate. If somehow his cards on the turn were known to me, I would definitely bet. My guess is that he was planning to fold if the river came a king, ten, or spade. If I had chosen to check-call the flop and check raise the turn, or check raise the flop and check raise the turn, it is possible that would have gotten him to fold his

9♠9♣. Hopefully, my overall ranges make his call-down here with a pair of nines a breakeven play at best.

Hand No. 38

Limit: $150-$300, six players

Pre-flop: Stox is in the big blind with K♣T♠
Action: The first three players fold, button raises, small blind calls, Stox calls

Flop: (6 small bets) K♠Q♦9♦ (three players)
Action: Small blind checks, Stox checks, button bets, small blind calls, Stox raises, button folds, small blind calls

Turn: (7 big bets) 3♥ (two players)
Action: Small blind checks, Stox bets, small blind calls

River: (9 big bets) 8♠ (two players)
Action: Small blind checks, Stox bets, small blind folds

In this hand, both pre-flop and flop play present some interesting decisions. Pre-flop, the button open-raises. I would defend my big blind against an average button raise with any king-x hand, but once the small blind calls, it's time to tighten up because I need to win at showdown much more often and my reverse implied odds are worse. King-eight offsuit or better is probably worth a call, maybe king-seven offsuit as well if either player played badly post-flop, and only K9o+ if both played tight and well. Assuming approximately a 40 percent range for the button and a 20 percent range for the small blind (but not the top 20 percent), my hot-and-cold pre-flop equity is 32.0 percent.

The flop is good for me, and my hand is often ahead. Whether to bet into the pre-flop raiser, to check and call, or to check and raise is a tough decision. On one hand, betting into the raiser will give me a better idea of where I stand, but at a high cost because it allows the button to raise a better hand and the small blind to continue only when he has a hand. The coordinated board favors betting into the raiser, putting him to a decision, and getting him to raise, potentially charging the small blind the maximum to draw.

On the flop, the pot is 6 small bets. If I lead the pot will offer 7-to-1 odds, so either opponent is correct to call with 4 or more outs (which is actually a 10.75-to-1 shot, but still a correct call with implied odds). If I bet and the button raises, it presents the small blind with poor odds of 4-to-1 and probably forces him out, but this is not a great result if the button will only raise when he has a good chance to beat me.

Although it is a higher-variance play, my preference is to check raise because it gets more money in the pot and forces my opponents to make mistakes they may not have made otherwise. For example, each time the small blind makes a decision, he faces only one bet, but for the entire street he pays two bets (assuming the button makes the virtually 100 percent standard continuation bet). Even though each decision may be "correct" for the small blind with as few as 4 outs, paying two bets for the entire street is a mistake. Also, with this line, the small blind may make a "loose" check-raise after the button bets. Then, I can three-bet, force the button out, and face the small blind with a tough decision, allowing me to get more money in the pot and thin the field.

Betting into the raiser to thin the field and get information makes more sense in 4 (or more)-handed pots where you benefit more from folds since there are more combined outs to beat you and because the existing pot is larger, making current equity in the pot worth more relative to the action on later streets. In this case, and in most similar 3-handed scenarios, if you check raise and let your opponents see the turn for two bets (one at a time), they will draw out more often, but you will win more money in the long run. The turn and river are basic value bets and I would probably pay off a river check-raise against most players.

Hand No. 39

Limit: $75-$150, three players

Pre-flop: Stox is in the big blind with J♣8♥
Action: The button folds, small blind raises, Stox calls

Flop: (4 small bets) K♥J♠5♣ (two players)
Action: Small blind bets, Stox calls

Turn: (4 big bets) A♠ (two players)
Action: Small blind bets, Stox calls

River: (6 big bets) 8♠ (two players)
Action: Small blind bets, Stox raises, small blind folds

Pre-flop, my strategy is to defend my big blind with almost any two cards — top 85 percent of the hands is a good starting default — against an open-raise from a typical player in the small blind. On the flop, I hit middle pair and likely have the best hand. For that reason, raising for value, especially since my opponent will probably call down-with a wide range, including many ace-high hands makes sense. However, I decide to just call for three reasons. They are:

1. The pot is small, so the value of protecting my hand is relatively low.

2. On this dry flop, my opponent most likely has only 3 outs to beat me if he is behind.

3. This opponent is aggressive, so calling is likely to induce bluffs on the later streets.

The turn card is not good since any ace-high hand just drew out. Raising for a free showdown is an option, but against this opponent, I am not comfortable folding to a three-bet since he may do so as a bluff or semi-bluff. On the river, I got lucky and hit two pair and raise for value.

Hand No. 40

Limit: $300-$600, 8 players

Pre-flop: Stox is in the big blind with J♥8♦
Action: UTG calls, the next player folds, MP2 raises, hijack calls, cutoff folds, button calls, small blind folds, Stox calls, UTG calls

Flop: (10.5 small bets) Q♣T♣8♥ (five players)
Action: Stox checks, UTG checks, MP2 bets, hijack folds, button calls, Stox calls, UTG calls

Turn: (9.75 big bets) A♥ (four players)
Action: Stox checks, UTG checks, MP2 checks, button checks

River: (9.75 big bets) 3♣ (three players)
Action: Stox checks, UTG bets, MP2 raises, button folds, Stox folds, UTG folds

Pre-flop, unless UTG limp/re-raises, I am getting 9.5-to-1 to see a flop, which is enough to try and hit a big hand. Jack-nine offsuit would be an easier call here, and jack-seven offsuit probably goes into the muck. And I would definitely play any two suited cards.

The flop gives me bottom pair and a gutshot straight draw. Although my three jack outs are severely tainted since anyone holding a nine will make a straight, my two eight outs and my gutshot outs are clean the majority of the time. So my estimate is between 4 and 5 outs on average, and the pot is offering enough overlay to call a flop bet. Even though I am not closing the action, UTG is a fairly passive player so it is unlikely he will raise, and there is enough of an overlay on the odds to take that risk.

I am happy to see the turn checked around, giving me a free card. On the river, since the third flush card arrived, there is almost no way my hand is best nor am I getting a better hand to fold, so check-folding is the easy choice.

Hand No. 41

Limit: $150-$300, four players

Pre-flop: Stox is in the big blind with Q♣8♣
Action: The cutoff folds, button raises, small blind calls, Stox calls

Flop: (9 small bets) Q♦7♠2♥ (three players)
Action: Small blind bets, Stox calls, button calls

Turn: (6 big bets) T♥ (three players)
Action: Small blind checks, Stox checks, button bets, small blind folds, Stox raises, button calls

River: (10 big bets) J♣ (two players)
Action: Stox bets, button folds

Pre-flop, getting 5-to-1 and closing the action with queen-eight suited in the big blind is an easy call. The button is a soft spot in the game, so my calling range is wider here, but I would play Q♣8♣ in this situation against two very good players.

The flop gives me top pair without much of a kicker. My preference is to check these flops most of the time and see what the action is before I have to make a decision. Here, my choice is to take the higher variance approach of calling the flop with the intention of raising or check-raising the turn if it is favorable because the button is a weak player and the flop contains no draws. The turn card does make some draws possible, and I am successful with my check-raise. At this point, it's likely my hand is ahead, but it is possible the button has a better queen.

Raising the flop is certainly a viable way to play this hand, but the board was so dry that I can wait to see if an ace or king falls on the turn and try to get a raise in on a safe card. It would be a relatively thin turn raise with top pair medium kicker, but this is steal/defense play and thin bets and call-downs are commonplace.

The river card is not good for me since it completes some straight draws or could have made my opponent two pair if he held jack-ten or ten-seven. My decision is to value bet the river because the button is relatively passive. If my opponent were aggressive, I think check-calling is better because he would be more likely to make a thin value raise, which is best to avoid, and he would be more likely to bluff against no bet.

Hand No. 42

Limit: $150-$300, six players

Pre-flop: Stox is in the big blind with T♣8♦
Action: The first three players fold, button raises, small blind calls, Stox calls

Flop: (6 small bets) T♥4♣2♠ (three players)
Action: Small blind checks, Stox checks, button bets, small blind calls, Stox raises, button folds, small blind calls

Turn: (5.5 big bets) A♥ (two players)
Action: Small blind checks, Stox checks

River: (5.5 big bets) J♣ (two players)
Action: Small blind bets, Stox calls

Showdown: Small blind shows 9♣4♣

Defending with ten-eight offsuit in a three-handed pot is not something I do every time. However, the small blind is the soft spot in the game, so my decision was to play since he was in the pot. The flop gives me top pair, and I check raise the field.

When the ace hits on the turn, there are three reasons for my check:

1. There is a small chance my opponent has an ace and his hand is now best.

2. The small blind is aggressive so checking the turn may induce him to bluff the river.

3. The pot is relatively small so the value of protecting my hand is less important compared to value of inducing a bluff.[26]

On the river, my opponent does bet and my pair of tens is good.

Hand No. 43

Limit: $25-$50, four players

Pre-flop: Stox is in the big blind with Q♣5♣
Action: Cutoff raises, the next two players fold, Stox calls

Flop: (4.5 small bets) A♠5♥5♦ (two players)
Action: Stox checks, cutoff bets, Stox raises, cutoff three-bets, Stox calls

---

[26] Although he still has to bluff quite a bit more often than draw out with a hand that he would fold to make the check correct when you know you have the best hand.

Turn (5.25 big bets) 2♥
Action: Stox checks, cutoff bets, Stox raises, cutoff calls

River (9.25 big bets) Q♦
Action: Stox bets, cutoff calls

Pre-flop, defending with queen-five suited against an open-raise from the cutoff is standard for me. The flop gives me three of a kind, which is obviously a very big favorite to be the best hand. My strategy is to check raise because I think it will get maximum value from most hands. If my opponent has an ace, he will either three-bet the flop or call and raise the turn, both of which will allow me to gain extra bets. If he has a pocket pair and my play is to call on the flop, he may check behind on the turn, causing me to miss bets.

Once my opponent three-bets the flop, I can be fairly certain of three things. They are:

1. He has an ace.

2. Second, he intends to see the showdown. And,

3. He will bet the turn after my check.

Because of these factors, my decision is to call his flop three-bet and go for a check-raise on the turn. This allows me to gain an extra small bet. If I four-bet the flop, he most likely will go into call-down mode thinking there is a good chance my hand contains a five. Also, if the turn card puts a flush draw on board, which it will about 75 percent of the time, my opponent may put me on a draw and three-bet the turn. This would allow me to four-bet, and my opponent will still probably call down with a pair of aces since the pot has gotten so big.

Small Blind Defense Hands

Hand No. 44

Limit: $75-$150, five players

Pre-flop: Stox is in the small blind with 3♦3♣
Action: The first two players fold, button raises, Stox three-bets, big blind folds, button calls

Flop: (7 small bets) J♣6♦6♣ (two players)
Action: Stox bets, button calls

Turn: (4.5 big bets) J♠ (two players)
Action: Stox bets, button folds

Against a button steal raise, I three-bet with all pocket pairs in the small blind (except AA-QQ occasionally). This gives me the opportunity to limit my opponents to just one with a pair and create dead money in the pot if the big blind folds. Also, it allows me to take the initiative and create fold equity for later in the hand.

The flop is good for me, and my pocket pair is likely best. Also, my 3♣ reduces my opponent's outs if he has a flush draw, and gives me a backdoor flush draw if he does not have a club — both small points, especially the first one, but worth mentioning. In general, my strategy is to bet the flop 100 percent of the time when I three-bet pre-flop and just get called by only the original stealer. When my opponent calls my flop bet, his range cannot be narrowed much, especially if he is a bad, loose player. On this flop, he would call with almost all hands with which he would steal. My opponents range here could be any ace, king, or queen.

He also could be slowplaying a six or (less likely) a jack, or playing a flush draw passively.

The turn makes the board J♣J♦6♣6♠, giving me the second nut low. The current pot is 9 small bets (4.5 big bets). Since my showdown equity is 0 percent, if I bet, my opponent needs to fold just under 20 percent of the time for me to break even.

$$.1818 = \frac{1}{5.5}$$

Given my play so far, my opponent could think that I have an ace or high pair. Assuming he will fold all hands worse than ace-high, it is correct to bet because he will have king-high or less much more than the needed 20 percent. If he had called or raised, I would have been done with the hand.

From my opponent's point of view — pre-flop: Once the small blind three-bets pre-flop, the large majority of his hand range includes paired hands and aces. A typical tight-aggressive player would have a pair or an ace about 75 percent of the time.

If I were the button, my decision would be whether to just call or four-bet — folding is not an option getting 6-to-1 in position. First, four-betting with more hands, if that is the cap, makes sense since I can take the initiative without risking another raise. Second, my strategy would not follow the simple formula of just four-betting my best hands.

In this situation, a lot of high-limit players will just call with aces or kings and then raise the flop, or more likely the turn. My approach is to mix up my play, being more likely to call against a solid, thinking player and more likely to four-bet against a loose-aggressive player.

With ace-king, I would four-bet due to my equity edge. And, if my opponent gives action on an ace-high or king-high flop, I will often have his hand dominated. However, with a hand like ace-jack, I would rarely four-bet because if I got action on an ace-high flop, it's not something to look forward to.

On the other hand, a hand like king-queen or king-jack is usually worth going to four bets since that allows me to represent an ace if one flops, but also get paid if I make top pair. AQs, QQ, and JJ are also, in my opinion, worth four bets in this spot.

Finally, I am more inclined to four-bet if my opponent plays tightly post-flop because my fold equity will be larger. If my opponent is loose-aggressive and frequently goes to the showdown — roughly at least 43 percent of the time — it is probably better to call to maximize my positional advantage and implied odds. Even though I have less fold equity against this opponent, my implied odds are higher since they are necessarily inversely correlated.

From my opponent's point of view — on the flop: Assuming the small blind leads, the decision is whether to call, raise, or fold. With a monster hand like JJ, A6, or K6, I would raise the flop hoping my opponent also has a strong hand. Then, if he three-bets, my plan is to usually call and raise the turn. If my opponent were tight, I may just call with (pocket) jacks hoping that he improves on the turn.

With a strong hand like AA-QQ, or a jack, my conclusion would be that my hand was best and raise the flop to protect my holding.

With a flush draw, I would probably just call and raise the turn as a semi-bluff. However, with an ace-high flush draw, my plan would be to call all three streets and raise if a flush card comes — especially when the second jack falls on the turn.

With TT-77 and 55-22, I would call the flop and plan on raising the turn for a free showdown. However, with 55-22, if the second jack hits, my plan would be to fold if my opponent bets again.

With AK, AQ, and KQ (not suited in clubs), I would call the flop. 8-to-1 plus implied odds is enough to draw to overcards.

Ace-ten is also worth a call since it may be the best hand, and even if not, pairing my ten may give me the best hand and I have a (weak) backdoor straight draw. But A9-A2 would be folded unless the ace was the A♣. With the A♣ and any card other than a jack or six, I would call the flop and most likely to go to the showdown. I would also plan on going to the showdown with any other ace-high hand which in my opinion was worth a flop call.

Hand No. 45

Limit: $150-$300, four players

Pre-flop: Stox is in the small blind with 6♦6♥
Action: Cutoff raises, button folds, Stox three-bets, big blind folds, cutoff four-bets (cap), Stox calls

Flop: (9 small bets) 9♠6♠4♠ (two players)
Action: Stox checks, cutoff bets, Stox raises, cutoff three-bets, Stox four-bets, cutoff calls

Turn: (8.5 big bets) 2♠ (two players)
Action: Stox checks, cutoff checks

River: (8.5 big bets) 2♦ (two players)
Action: Stox bets, cutoff calls

Showdown: Cutoff shows A♦A♥

Against an open-raise from the cutoff, my strategy is to three-bet pre-flop with sixes against all but the tightest players. Against most players, I would three-bet any pocket pair, but will muck 22-44 when a tight player open-raises from the cutoff. Small pocket pairs play much better against one opponent, so it is best to force the big blind out and make his blind dead money. On the other hand, a pre-flop three-bet in this spot will get less respect, and when the big blind does call, you are forced to play a small pocket pair out of position for three-bets pre-flop against two opponents, which is not the best situation.

Assuming a tight-aggressive cutoff stealer who raises with about 28 percent of the hands: 22+, A2s+, A6o+, K6s+, KTo+, Q8s+, QTo+, J8s+, JTo, T8s+, 97s+, 87s, 76s, a pair of sixes has about 51 percent equity. I would be willing to three-bet with less than 50 percent equity since it will create an overlay if the big blind folds, and I will sometimes win without a showdown by taking the initiative. Also, my implied odds are important although they are difficult to estimate. On one hand, if I flop a set, they are good. On the other hand, when the board is all overcards to my pair and my opponent semi-bluffs, I may fold the best hand. So on average in this spot, my implied odds are probably close to zero.

The chart below shows the equity of various pocket pairs against a typical cutoff stealer:

22: 44%	77: 53.5%
33: 46%	88: 56%
44: 47%	99: 60%
55: 49%	TT: 64%

Based on the chart, I would usually play fives or better. But a pair of fours is close, and a pair of treys will usually hit the muck, unless I had a big post-flop edge over my opponent. Conversely, if my opponent plays very well, a pair of fours, and perhaps fives, become unplayable.

In this particular hand, my opponent capped pre-flop, so I can narrow his range considerably and it's clear that my equity has decreased. I flopped a set, but there are three cards to a flush out. So my decision is whether to check raise the flop or wait for the turn. Waiting is probably a mistake because there are plenty of cards that can scare me or my opponent. In other words, if ahead my action will be limited because I have to slow down or my opponent does. Even though my equity will change dramatically on the turn, it is still good on the flop since my draw is strong if I am behind. Thus, my decision to jam and hope it gets me more action on the turn.

My opponent is not a good player and tends to play passively, but sometimes shows misplaced aggression, so he could have lots of non-spade overpair hands. After he three-bets the flop, my range for him was: 99+, A♠T♠+, A♠Jx+, K♠J♠+, K♠Qx — 4.1 percent of the hands. Against that range, I have about 66 percent equity on the flop.

The turn card brings a fourth spade, which is not good for me, and now my equity has dropped to 41 percent against his range. Thus, my play is an easy check-call. Once my opponent checks behind on the turn, it's very unlikely he has a spade. The board pairing on the river is nice, but probably unnecessary for me to win. If the board had not paired, my strategy would be to bet-call the river. But the board did pair, so I bet hoping to get a chance to three-bet. Since the only logical hand that beats mine is a pair of nines (which is a possibility), not three-betting would be giving up too much value.

Hand No. 46

Limit: $150-$300, five players

Pre-flop: Stox is in the small blind with A♦7♦
Action: Hijack folds, cutoff raises, button folds, Stox three-bets, big blind folds, cutoff calls

Flop: (7 small bets) J♥5♣3♥ (two players)
Action: Stox bets, cutoff calls

Turn: (4.5 big bets) 5♦ (two players)
Action: Stox bets, cutoff calls

River: (6.5 big bets) 6♣ (two players)
Action: Stox checks, cutoff bets, Stox calls

Showdown: Cutoff shows T♥9♥

The pre-flop three-bet from the small blind with ace-seven suited against a cutoff open-raise is standard for me. I figure to have pretty good equity against the range of a loose cutoff stealer: 22+, A2s+, A6o+, K4s+, K8o+, Q5s+, Q9o+, J8s+, J9o+, T8s+, T9o, 97s+, 87s, 76s, and 65s = 34.5 percent. My hot-and-cold pre-flop equity is 52 percent.

Against a tighter cutoff opener with approximately a 28 percent range: 22+, A2s+, A6o+, K6s+, KTo+, Q8s+, QTo+, J8s+, JTo, T8s+, 97s+, 87s, and 76s, my hot-and-cold pre-flop equity is not much worse, approximately 48 percent and still enough to three-bet with a suited ace that plays well heads-up and post-flop. Hopefully, I can force out the big blind and create some dead money in the pot. On the flop, it's time for my standard continuation bet which is also for value since I still likely have the best hand.

On the turn, I decided to bet. However, a strong argument could be made for checking and calling both the turn and river to induce bluffs, especially against a very aggressive opponent. But he is less likely to bluff against a pre-flop three-bettor, so I elected to bet. If he now chooses to raise the turn my situation is a tough one. Because of the flush draw on board and the aggressive nature of my opponent, I would probably call down but not feel great about it.

On the river, my decision is also tough. The only hands my opponent could hold that I beat are a busted flush draw or a worse ace-high. He probably would not bet the ace on the river and, if he had a flush draw, he probably would have raised the flop or the turn. However, my pre-flop three-bet might have deterred him from semi-bluffing, so I make a very thin call which luckily worked out for me (this time).

Hand No. 47

Limit: $150-$300, five players

Pre-flop: Stox is small blind with A♣8♥
Action: The first two players fold, button raises, Stox three-bets,
  big blind folds, button calls

Flop: (6.5 small bets) K♦8♣4♣ (two players)
Action: Stox bets, button calls

Turn: (4.25 big bets) T♦ (two players)
Action: Stox checks, button bets, Stox calls

River: (6.25 big bets) 5♣ (two players)
Action: Stox checks, button checks

Showdown: Button shows 6♦5♥

In this hand, the button is soft and loose, but not too
aggressive. My strategy would be to three-bet ace-six offsuit or
better here. Since his stealing range from the button is
approximately 40 percent of the hands, my equity with ace-eight
offsuit is about 52 percent. (With ace-six offsuit it would be about
48 percent.)

The flop gives me middle pair, and I make a standard value
bet. On the turn, I have a decision to make because my opponent
will likely raise me with any hand that beats me and some drawing
hands as well. However, against a check, he will likely bet an
even wider range of hands. So I chose the more conservative line
of check-calling, but think that bet-calling is also reasonable. In
either case, I am committed to the showdown regardless of the
river card.

On the river, check-calling seems to be the best way to get in one bet with the least amount of risk. If my opponent had not made a pair on the river, he would have likely bet again.

Hand No. 48

Limit: $150-$300, three players

Pre-flop: Stox is in the small blind with A♠K♠
Action: Button folds, Stox raises, big blind three-bets, Stox four-bets (cap), big blind calls

Flop: (8 small bets) T♣9♠4♣ (two players)
Action: Stox bets, big blind calls

Turn: (4.5 big bets) 3♣ (two players)
Action: Stox checks, big blind bets, Stox calls

River: (6.5 big bets) A♥ (two players)
Action: Stox checks, big blind bets, Stox calls

Showdown: Big blind shows A♦Q♠

The big blind is a good, aggressive player who defends his big blind tenaciously. My pre-flop and flop plays are pretty standard. On the turn, my decision is whether to check-call or bet-call. Even though the pot is large and giving a free card is dangerous, I chose to check-call since my opponent would raise with a wide range forcing me to call to see if I improved on the last card.

The river gives me top-pair-top-kicker, but aces up for my opponent is now a concern. I strongly considered check-raising, but ultimately decided that he would three-bet and win with more hands than he would call with, so my decision was to check and call. This is possibly a weak play that cost me an extra bet. Then again, my opponent might have even three-bet his A♦Q♠, and I might have folded, which would have been a disaster.

Hand No. 49

Limit: $150-$300, six players

Pre-flop: Stox is small blind with A♦T♦
Action: The first two players fold, cutoff raises, button folds, Stox three-bets, big blind four-bets (cap), cutoff calls, Stox calls

Flop: (12 small bets)A♠A♥7♣ (three players)
Action: Stox checks, big blind checks, cutoff checks

Turn: (6 big bets) 4♦ (three players)
Action: Stox checks, big blind bets, cutoff calls, Stox calls

River: (9 big bets) Q♣ (three players)
Action: Stox checks, big blind bets, cutoff folds, Stox calls

Showdown: Big blind shows K♥J♣

In this hand, both of my opponents are loose and aggressive. The cutoff plays about 50 percent of his hands in late position, but plays well post-flop. The big blind plays about 35 percent of his hands overall in 6-handed games.

Once the big blind caps, I would estimate my equity is at least my fair share, or 33 percent. Once two aces flop, this hand is a textbook example of being way ahead or way behind. If behind, I have 3 outs against AJ-AK and 4 outs against a pair of sevens. If ahead, my opponents have at most 3 outs against me.

Given the situation, it is best to play this hand passively on the early streets. Also, because the board is dry, there is no reason to protect my hand. Instead, I want to take the line that extracts the most bets when ahead and loses the fewest when behind.

On the river, check-raising would definitely be a mistake given the big blind's range. Although my hand is strong, his range includes many hands that will fold to a check-raise, a few that will three-bet, and not many worse hands that will call. (Since he capped pre-flop, a worse ace is possible but not likely.) For a check-raise to be correct, the big blind would have to call almost twice as often as he three-bets (assuming I will call and almost always lose to a three-bet, which would be correct against this tricky opponent). Of course, the chance of getting a better hand to fold with a check-raise in this instance is zero.

Hand No. 50

Limit: $150-$300, four players

Pre-flop: Stox is small blind with Q♣T♠
Action: The first two players fold, Stox raises, big blind three-bets, Stox calls

Flop: (6 small bets) 9♥8♦6♣ (two players)
Action: Stox checks, big blind bets, Stox raises, big blind calls

Turn: (5 big bets) 8♠ (two players)
Action: Stox checks, big blind bets, Stox raises, big blind folds

In this hand, I check raise both the flop and turn as a semi-bluff. This is a somewhat fancy play, but has merit in certain situations. First, it is more likely to get a fold from hands like ace-high or low pairs than simply check-raising the flop and leading the turn. Second, it's okay if my opponent checks behind on the turn because it gives me a free card, and a bluff may still be available to me on the river. I am also more likely to make a multi-layered play like this because the standard line of check-raising the flop and leading the turn as a semi-bluff does not have as much fold equity at higher limits in blind versus blind situations where people will generally play more correctly.

This play is an interesting one and is binary on the turn in the sense that a situation is created where there are two possible results to which I am somewhat indifferent, somewhat nullifiying my positional disadvantage. If the turn goes check-check, then I have received a free card for my draw. If my opponent bets, I get to check raise, which is a very strong semi-bluffing line given the flop action. Of course, if it goes to three bets I'm not happy, but this should be more than offset by the times a better hand folds, plus the times I improve on the river to win. Lots of ace-high and king-high hands, in addition to some baby and bottom pair hands, will fold on the turn .

Miscellaneous Hands

Hand No. 51

Limit: $300-$600, six players

Pre-flop: Stox is UTG with 9♣9♦
Action: Stox raises, hijack calls, the next three players fold, big blind calls

Flop: (6.5 small bets) A♣K♦9♥ (three players)
Action: Big blind checks, Stox bets, hijack folds, big blind raises, Stox calls

Turn: (5.25 big bets) J♠ (two players)
Action: Big blind bets, Stox raises, big blind three-bets, Stox four-bets, big blind calls

River: (13.25 big bets) T♥ (two players)
Action: Big blind checks, Stox bets, big blind calls

Showdown: Big blind mucks A♥J♦

Since the big blind just called pre-flop when closing the action in a multi-way pot, I can rule out aces and kings virtually 100 percent of the time. At the higher limits, many players will just call with these hands against only one opponent, but almost everyone knows that you give up too much value by not raising with them when multi-way.

When my opponent check raises the flop, his most likely hand by far is ace-x. He may make this type of play with a draw, but the best possible draw on this flop is only a gutshot. He could have king-nine — unlikely given I have three nines — or a gutshot straight draw QJ, QT, or JT. However, it is very unlikely that anyone but a complete maniac will check raise a gutshot straight draw on this board. Thus, it's virtually 100 percent certain my hand is best. I elect to just call his check-raise with the intention of raising the turn, sometimes a good play when in position with a monster.

On the turn, it's still nearly certain my hand is best, so it makes sense to go four-bets. The river card is scary because it puts four to a straight on board. However, since my opponent will call with any ace in this big pot, I make a thin value bet. Also, given the turn action where my opponent three-bets, the only hand that would possibly do that which contains a queen is queen-ten, which is a very unlikely holding for my opponent. Ace-queen would probably not make a three-bet here. So given the turn action, I bet the river and expect a call from aces-up, the most likely hand by far for my opponent given the action.

Hand No. 52

Limit: $150-$300, six players

Pre-flop: Stox is in the hijack seat with A♣A♥
Action: UTG raises, Stox three-bets, cutoff folds, button four-bets (cap), UTG calls, Stox calls.

Flop: (13.5 small bets) 7♥2♣2♥ (three players)
Action: UTG checks, Stox checks, button bets, UTG raises, Stox three-bets, button calls, UTG four-bets (cap), Stox calls, button calls

Turn: (12.75 big bets) 3♦ (three players)
Action: UTG bets, Stox calls, button calls

River: (15.75 big bets) 5♦ (three players)
Action: UTG bets, Stox calls, Button calls

Showdown: UTG shows Q♠Q♥, button folds A♠ K♠

   In this hand, UTG is a solid, big winner and the button is very loose and aggressive in the wrong spots. Thus, after he caps pre-flop, his range is still very, very wide.
   The flop is great for me. I am way ahead of everyone unless someone has a pair of sevens or a deuce. I could completely rule out either opponent having a deuce if they were both rational players, but deuces and ace-deuce suited are both in the button's capping range.
   The pre-flop action makes it less likely that one of my opponents has a flush draw. But even if one does, I have the ace of hearts and I hold one of his outs, and have a re-draw to a better flush if the turn brings a heart.
   The flop action is somewhat complicated. The standard play is to check to the pre-flop capper, as is done here. When UTG check raises, it's not a worry since he would do so with a marginal hand to shut me out in this big pot. I three-bet to try and shut out the button and/or charge my opponents the maximum to draw, since getting a fold from even small equity hands has good value because of the size of the pot. Conversely, my opponents will call very thin here specifically because the pot has gotten very large, which is also good. Getting three-bets from a 10 percent equity hand is much better than getting two. After the button calls and UTG (who is a good player) caps, I put a pair of sevens relatively high on his list of hands along with KK, QQ, or (maybe) K♥Q♥. So I decided to play passively on the turn and the river, which may have cost me a little value but resulted in some nice overcalls. (Notice the river overcall with ace-king.)
   Once the button just calls on the turn, it's almost certain that he does not have a deuce. Thus, the only hand to be concerned about is a pair of sevens from UTG.
   I ended up getting turn and river overcalls from the bad player. If I had raised somewhere there would be risk of getting three-bet from UTG and, at the same time, shutting out what I

thought was my best customer. So while there is still a good chance I am ahead, raising here both shuts out the third player who made marginal overcalls and allows UTG the option to three-bet. So even though my hand is strong, not getting in a raise on the turn or the river was correct.

Hand No. 53

Limit: $100-$200, 9 players

Pre-flop: Stox is MP1 with A♠J♦
Action: The first two players fold, Stox raises, the next player folds, hijack (poster) calls, cutoff three-bets, button and small blind fold, big blind calls, Stox calls, hijack calls

Flop: (12.5 small bets) T♠7♠2♠ (four players)
Action: Big blind checks, Stox checks, hijack checks, cutoff bets, big blind calls, Stox calls, hijack raises, cutoff three-bets, big blind four-bets (cap), Stox calls, hijack calls, cutoff calls

Turn: (14.25 big bets) T♦ (four players)
Action: Big blind bets, Stox folds, hijack calls, cutoff folds

River: (16.25 big bets) 4♠ (two players)
Action: Big blind bets, hijack calls

Showdown: Big blind shows Q♠J♣, hijack folds 6♠3♠

In this hand, I flop the nut flush draw on an all-spade flop. With four players in, having lots of action on the flop is great. Although the heavy betting increases the chances that two-pair or a set is out, I will still win more than my fair share of pots — probably around 25 percent.

The board-pairing T♦ on the turn was not a good card for my hand. If I was up against a set, ten-seven (possible), or ten-deuce (not likely), my draw is now dead. However, that alone is not reason enough to fold because the pot is offering a big overlay.

On the other hand, the turn card will very often kill some of my outs when my opponents are holding a ten or an overpair. Also, my implied odds are now probably close to zero. Finally, when it was my turn to call a turn bet, there was a decent chance that one of my opponents would raise behind me, and I would have to call a second bet because of the huge overlay that will be available at that point. Based on all of these factors, I chose to fold. In this hand it turned out to be a mistake, but let's look at this decision a bit more closely.

On the turn, it's almost a certainty I am behind given the board and previous action. There are 9 spades left in the deck out of 46 unseen cards, so my odds to river a flush are 37-to-9 or approximately 1 in 5.[27] With the turn card pairing the board there is a chance I am now drawing dead and a chance it will cost me extra bets to see the river since there are two players to act after me. At the time of my decision the pot is offering me 15.25-to-1 to draw to my 4-to-1 shot, but given the previous action I made the incorrect judgement that the chance my hand was behind was simply too large when combined with the possibility of getting raised and three-bet.

Hand No. 54

Limit: $75-$150, seven players

Pre-flop: Stox is hijack with A♦K♥
Action: The first two players fold, Stox raises, cutoff calls, button calls, small blind calls, big blind calls

---

[27] Actually less since there was a good chance I was already up against a flush.

Flop: (10 small bets) Q♥3♣3♦ (five players)
Action: Small blind checks, big blind checks, Stox bets, cutoff folds, button raises, small blind folds, big blind folds, Stox calls

Turn: (7 big bets) 9♣ (two players)
Action: Stox checks, button bets, Stox calls

River: (9 big bets) K♠ (two players)
Action: Stox checks, button bets, Stox raises, button calls

Showdown: Button mucks Q♠J♠

In this hand, I make a standard open-raise with ace-king offsuit 2 seats off the button. There are 4 callers, including both blinds. The flop is not great for me, but there is a chance it missed all my opponents as well. I considered checking, but elected to bet.

After the button raises, the pot is offering 13-to-1 closing the action, making this an easy call. At this point, I am pretty sure the button does not have a trey, since he would have probably just called with players to act behind him. Since the board has no draws and my opponent would have three-bet pre-flop with a pair of nines or better, it appears he has a queen or a lower pocket pair, 22 or 44-88.

The 9♣ on the turn probably did not help my opponent unless he held queen-nine suited (possible) or a pair of nines (unlikely). His most likely hand by far is queen-x since lots of suited and/or connected queen-x hands would have overcalled pre-flop. After my check, he bets, and I am getting 8-to-1 to draw to my overcards. If it was certain that all 6 of my outs were clean, I would need 6.7-to-1 to break even. As it is, 8-to-1 provides a slight overlay to compensate for the times an ace or king comes but my hand still loses. Also, my implied odds are positive since I will fold 100 percent of the time I miss and, when my hand improves, it will often win an extra bet or two. Thus, with implied odds, I am getting somewhere between 9- and 10-to-1, making this a call. Thankfully, a king comes on the river and it allowed me to win 2 big bets by getting in a check raise and being called by a worse hand.

Hand No. 55

Limit: $150-$300, six players

Pre-flop: Stox is UTG with Q♦J♦
Action: Stox raises, hijack three-bets, the next three players fold, big blind calls, Stox calls

Flop: (9.5 small bets) J♣T♣5♦ (three players)
Action: Big blind checks, Stox checks, hijack bets, big blind raises, Stox three-bets, hijack four-bets (cap), big blind calls, Stox calls

Turn: (10.75 big bets) T♦ (three players)
Action: Big blind checks, Stox checks, hijack checks

River: (10.75 big bets) K♦ (three players)
Action: Big blind checks, Stox checks, hijack bets, big blind folds, Stox raises, hijack calls

Showdown: Hijack mucks A♦K♣

When the hijack three-bet my raise from under the gun, it appears he has a strong hand (99+, AQs+, or AQo+). The flop gives me top pair with a decent kicker, but it is still a concern that the hijack has me dominated with an overpair. I check the flop to see what develops. When the big blind check-raises, he could be trying to shut me out with a hand like middle pair. I three-bet because my hand may be best and it forces the hijack to define his hand. When he caps, I figure to be behind, but have the odds to see the showdown since he could be jamming the flop with ace-queen or ace-king, probably with a club.

Once the turn gets checked through, I am virtually certain that the hijack has either ace-king or ace-queen, since he would have bet any other possible holding. The river gives me a flush, which is a heavy favorite to be the best hand, and the K♦ is a very good card because it is likely to have hit the two hands which my opponent probably has, ace-king and ace-queen. It is also very unlikely that either of my opponents has a full house given the turn action. In addition, for one of my opponents to have the nut flush, he would have to have A♦2♦-A♦9♦, which is not probable given the pre-flop and flop action.

Since the hijack has ace-king or ace-queen, the king on the river just gave him top-pair-top-kicker or a straight, both of which he will bet if checked to, but may not raise if I bet. Thus, my decision is to go for a check-raise since he will have to pay it off with either hand because the pot is so big.

Part Seven

Quizzes

Quizzes

Introduction

We have chosen the following quizzes to highlight what we consider to be the most important concepts in this book. We believe this will help you develop a systematic method to observe different situations and come to correct conclusions on your own. Even though this may lead to some redundancy, we feel it is well worth the effort.

For example, there are many quiz questions which involve defending your big blind and re-stealing. This is because they are two of the most important keys to winning in tough hold 'em games. By repeatedly looking at several situations at the margin, you will develop skills to make the correct decisions at the table, even in tough situations.

As always, there may be room for debate about some of the answers. In fact, if you have a specific read on an opponent, like he is badly tilted, it may be correct to take a different approach than we suggest. However, we have provided answers that, with the general reads given, we are confident are the best play to be made the vast majority of the time.

Big Blind Defense Quiz

This quiz is designed to test your big blind defending ranges and to give you a framework for evaluating them on an ongoing basis. The matrix below gives you 56 different hands in the big blind and asks whether you would call or fold given the specific characteristics and position of the pre-flop raiser. We do not cover whether or not you should three-bet because most of these hands should almost never be three-bet pre-flop, and it is so dependent on your opponent's post-flop play, that it would be nearly impossible to provide answers. This exercise examines stealing and defending ranges closely, but also adds defending ranges versus a legitimate, non-steal raise. It is important to have an idea of what types of hands are playable against legitimate raises against only one opponent from the big blind as well.

There are 8 opponent profiles in the table below, giving the matrix a total of 448 decisions. We could have made this matrix even larger, but hopefully this is enough to give you a good start.

The 8 player profiles are as follows:

1. A solid raiser under the gun (UTG) in a 6-max game (i.e. 3 seats off the button). This range is approximately 15.5 percent of the hands: 44+, A7s+, K9s+, Qts+, J9s+, T9s, 98s, A9o+, and KQo.

2. A tight raiser in the cutoff (CO) (i.e. 1 seat off the button). This range is approximately 20.4 percent of the hands and is tighter than what we consider optimal from that position. You probably will not encounter this type of player too often, but they do appear periodically. The range is: 44+, A6s+, K9s+, QTs+, J9s+, T9s, 98s, A7o+, KTo+, and QJo.

3.   A solid raiser from the hijack (HJ) (i.e. 2 seats off the button). This is the range of a typical tight-aggressive player and is approximately 22 percent of the hands: 33+, A4s+, K7s+, Q9s+, J9s+, T8s+, 98s, 87s, A7o+, KJo+, and QJo.

4.   A solid raiser from the cutoff. This range is approximately 28.5 percent of the hands: 22+, A2s+, K7s+, Q9s+, J8s+, T8s+, 97s+, 87s, 76s, A5o+, K9o+, and QTo+.

5.   A tight raiser on the button (BU). This range is sub-optimal at approximately 28.5 percent of the hands: 22+, A2s+, K7s+, Q9s+, J8s+, T8s+, 97s+, 87s, 76s, A5o+, K9o+, and QTo+.

6.   A loose raiser in the cutoff. This is a wide range, approximately 39.7 percent of the hands: 22+, A2s+, K2s+, Q5s+, J7s+, T8s+, 97s+, 86s+, 75s+, 65s, A3o+, K8o+, Q9o+, J9o+, T9o, and 98o.

7.   A solid raiser on the button. This range is approximately 39.7 percent of the hands: 22+, A2s+, K2s+, Q5s+, J7s+, T8s+, 97s+, 86s+, 75s+, 65s, A3o+, K8o+, Q9o+, J9o+, T9o, and 98o.

8.   A loose raiser on the button. This range is really wide at approximately 49.9 percent of the hands, and there are plenty of players at the higher limits who play this loose when folded to on the button: 22+, A2s+, K2s+, Q2s+, J5s+, T6s+, 96s+, 86s+, 76s, 65s, A2o+, K5o+, Q7o+, J7o+, T8o+, and 98o

The answers are given on the page following the quiz:

	Solid UTG	Tight CO	Solid HJ	Solid CO	Tight BU	Loose CO	Solid BU	Loose BU
	15.5%	20.4%	22.0%	28.5%	28.5%	39.7%	39.7%	49.9%
A2s								
K2s								
Q2s								
Q3s								
J2s								
J3s								
J4s								
J5s								
J6s								
J7s								
T2s								
T3s								
T4s								
T5s								
T6s								
93s								
94s								
95s								
96s								
85s								
86s								
74s								

	Solid UTG	Tight CO	Solid HJ	Solid CO	Tight BU	Loose CO	Solid BU	Loose BU
	15.5%	20.4%	22.0%	28.5%	28.5%	39.7%	39.7%	49.9%
75s								
63s								
64s								
65s								
52s								
53s								
54s								
42s								
43s								
32s								
A2o								
K2o								
K3o								
K4o								
K5o								
K6o								
K7o								
K8o								
K9o								
Q5o								
Q6o								
Q7o								

	Solid UTG	Tight CO	Solid HJ	Solid CO	Tight BU	Loose CO	Solid BU	Loose BU
	15.5%	20.4%	22.0%	28.5%	28.5%	39.7%	39.7%	49.9%
Q8o								
Q9o								
J7o								
J8o								
J9o								
T7o								
T8o								
T9o								
97o								
98o								
87o								
76o								

The answers to this quiz are done on a simple hot-and-cold equity simulation. We recommend that if you have more than 35 percent equity versus the raiser's range, you should call. If you have less, you should fold. However, it should be noted that you should also consider how well your opponent plays post-flop, but only to a limited extent. If your opponent plays poorly post-flop, you may want to play hands that have approximately 34 percent equity or greater. Conversely, if your opponent plays very well post-flop, you may want to require 36 percent equity or greater to continue. Finally, in very close decsisions, how willing your opponent is to go to the showdown should guide your decision of whether to defend. If your opponent is showdown bound, you should be more inclined to play hands that have some showdown value, such as ace-high or king-high hands. On the other hand, if your opponent does not go to the showdown too often, you should be more willing to play suited and connected hands that may flop a good draw with which you can semi-bluff.

How did we arrive at 35 percent equity? Against one opponent, that seems to be about the right estimate given the average final pot size and our empirical results. Most hands with equity in the high 30s do well when defending, and most hands in the low 30s do poorly, losing more than the 0.50 big bets per hand that results from simply folding pre-flop. In the table, if a particular hand has 35 percent equity or more against the raiser's range the equity number is in bold, which means you should generally defend with it. If the equity number is not in bold, it is under 35 percent, and you should generally fold.

	Solid UTG	Tight CO	Solid HJ	Solid CO	Tight BU	Loose CO	Solid BU	Loose BU
	15.5%	20.4%	22.0%	28.5%	28.5%	39.7%	39.7%	49.9%
A2s	**0.393**	**0.423**	**0.426**	**0.451**	**0.451**	**0.488**	**0.488**	**0.488**
K2s	**0.355**	**0.366**	**0.376**	**0.386**	**0.423**	**0.423**	**0.423**	**0.446**
Q2s	0.340	0.347	**0.353**	**0.363**	**0.363**	**0.391**	**0.391**	**0.407**
Q3s	0.343	**0.351**	**0.356**	**0.368**	**0.368**	**0.394**	**0.394**	**0.413**
J2s	0.327	0.333	0.340	**0.352**	**0.352**	**0.371**	**0.371**	**0.379**
J3s	0.331	0.337	0.344	**0.358**	**0.358**	**0.374**	**0.374**	**0.384**
J4s	0.334	0.340	0.349	**0.364**	**0.364**	**0.380**	**0.380**	**0.390**
J5s	0.341	0.346	**0.355**	**0.366**	**0.366**	**0.385**	**0.385**	**0.394**
J6s	0.344	0.346	**0.357**	**0.369**	**0.369**	**0.388**	**0.388**	**0.398**
J7s	**0.355**	**0.354**	**0.365**	**0.382**	**0.382**	**0.402**	**0.402**	**0.412**
T2s	0.316	0.326	0.334	0.342	0.342	**0.359**	**0.359**	**0.363**
T3s	0.320	0.329	0.337	0.348	0.348	**0.362**	**0.362**	**0.368**

	Solid UTG	Tight CO	Solid HJ	Solid CO	Tight BU	Loose CO	Solid BU	Loose BU
	15.5%	20.4%	22.0%	28.5%	28.5%	39.7%	39.7%	49.9%
T4s	0.323	0.332	0.342	**0.354**	**0.354**	**0.368**	**0.368**	**0.373**
T5s	0.327	0.336	0.346	**0.354**	**0.354**	**0.371**	**0.371**	**0.374**
T6s	0.342	0.348	**0.360**	**0.369**	**0.369**	**0.386**	**0.386**	**0.390**
93s	0.308	0.324	0.328	0.340	0.340	0.347	0.347	**0.355**
94s	0.308	0.324	0.331	0.343	0.343	**0.350**	**0.350**	**0.358**
95s	0.326	0.340	0.347	**0.355**	**0.355**	**0.366**	**0.366**	**0.371**
96s	0.341	**0.353**	**0.361**	**0.370**	**0.370**	**0.380**	**0.380**	**0.386**
85s	0.338	0.348	**0.350**	**0.362**	**0.362**	**0.371**	**0.371**	**0.373**
86s	**0.353**	**0.360**	**0.364**	**0.376**	**0.376**	**0.386**	**0.386**	**0.387**
74s	0.327	0.337	0.339	**0.354**	**0.354**	**0.362**	**0.362**	**0.366**
75s	0.344	**0.354**	**0.356**	**0.366**	**0.366**	**0.377**	**0.377**	**0.379**
63s	0.323	0.335	0.337	0.346	0.346	**0.353**	**0.353**	**0.358**
64s	0.336	0.349	**0.352**	**0.362**	**0.362**	**0.369**	**0.369**	**0.374**
65s	**0.352**	**0.364**	**0.367**	**0.374**	**0.374**	**0.383**	**0.383**	**0.387**
52s	0.318	0.332	0.332	0.339	0.339	0.349	0.349	**0.352**
53s	0.331	0.346	0.346	**0.355**	**0.355**	**0.362**	**0.362**	**0.368**
54s	0.343	**0.359**	**0.360**	**0.370**	**0.370**	**0.377**	**0.377**	**0.383**
42s	0.310	0.326	0.326	0.335	0.335	0.344	0.344	0.349
43s	0.323	0.339	0.339	**0.351**	**0.351**	**0.356**	**0.356**	**0.364**
32s	0.305	0.321	0.320	0.329	0.329	0.337	0.337	0.343
A2o	**0.357**	**0.390**	**0.392**	**0.419**	**0.419**	**0.458**	**0.458**	**0.484**
K2o	0.318	0.330	0.340	**0.350**	**0.350**	**0.389**	**0.389**	**0.413**

	Solid UTG	Tight CO	Solid HJ	Solid CO	Tight BU	Loose CO	Solid BU	Loose BU
	15.5%	20.4%	22.0%	28.5%	28.5%	39.7%	39.7%	49.9%
K3o	0.322	0.333	0.343	**0.356**	**0.356**	**0.392**	**0.392**	**0.419**
K4o	0.325	0.337	0.348	**0.362**	**0.362**	**0.398**	**0.398**	**0.424**
K5o	0.333	0.343	**0.355**	**0.365**	**0.365**	**0.407**	**0.407**	**0.432**
K6o	0.339	0.346	**0.360**	**0.371**	**0.371**	**0.415**	**0.415**	**0.443**
K7o	0.341	0.345	**0.361**	**0.377**	**0.377**	**0.422**	**0.422**	**0.457**
K8o	0.345	**0.350**	**0.370**	**0.384**	**0.384**	**0.433**	**0.433**	**0.472**
K9o	**0.358**	**0.368**	**0.391**	**0.407**	**0.407**	**0.463**	**0.463**	**0.497**
Q5o	0.317	0.323	0.332	0.341	0.341	**0.373**	**0.373**	**0.390**
Q6o	0.323	0.326	0.336	0.347	0.347	**0.379**	**0.379**	**0.379**
Q7o	0.323	0.322	0.332	0.348	0.348	**0.384**	**0.384**	**0.405**
Q8o	0.338	0.338	0.349	**0.364**	**0.364**	**0.400**	**0.400**	**0.429**
Q9o	0.348	**0.354**	**0.368**	**0.377**	**0.377**	**0.423**	**0.423**	**0.453**
J7o	0.320	0.318	0.329	0.347	0.347	**0.368**	**0.368**	**0.379**
J8o	0.336	0.334	0.347	**0.364**	**0.364**	**0.384**	**0.384**	**0.403**
J9o	0.346	**0.350**	**0.363**	**0.378**	**0.378**	**0.404**	**0.404**	**0.427**
T7o	0.319	0.321	0.333	0.348	0.348	**0.365**	**0.365**	**0.367**
T8o	0.335	0.337	**0.351**	**0.363**	**0.363**	**0.379**	**0.379**	**0.388**
T9o	0.342	**0.351**	**0.368**	**0.377**	**0.377**	**0.395**	**0.395**	**0.411**
97o	0.317	0.326	0.335	0.349	0.349	**0.359**	**0.359**	**0.363**
98o	0.332	0.341	0.349	**0.364**	**0.364**	**0.374**	**0.374**	**0.380**
87o	0.329	0.333	0.338	**0.354**	**0.354**	**0.364**	**0.364**	**0.364**
76o	0.325	0.331	0.335	0.347	0.347	**0.358**	**0.358**	**0.358**

Pre-Flop Play

Quiz No. 1

In a 6-handed game, you are dealt the A♥7♣ on the button. A loose passive player limps under the gun, and the next two players fold to you. Should you:

A. Call
B. Raise
C. Fold

Answer: B. You should raise. Ace-seven offsuit has a good equity edge against a loose limper's range and by raising you have a good chance to get heads-up post-flop against the loose-passive player. Isolating the loose player has a lot of value since he will "chase" post-flop, paying to draw to 3 to 6 outs when the pot odds do not justify it. Also, since he is passive, you will have a very good idea of the strength of his hand if he plays back at you post-flop, allowing you to make easy decisions.

Quiz No. 2

In a 5-handed game, a loose-passive player open-limps under the gun. You are next to act in the cutoff with A♠2♣. Should you:

A. Call
B. Raise
C. Fold

Answer: C. You should fold. Even though your hand might have a slight equity edge against the limper's range, it is not strong enough to play. There is too great a chance that one of the three players left holds a hand that has you dominated, such as a better ace or a pocket pair. Even if you raise to isolate (which may force one of the players left to act to fold a better hand), they may realize what you are doing and relax their calling and/or three-betting standards. You should wait for a better hand before you take a shot at the limper.

Quiz No. 3

In a 6-handed game, you are dealt 8♦7♦ on the button. A loose passive player limps under the gun, and the next two players fold. Should you:

A. Call
B. Raise
C. Fold

Answer: A. You should call. Even though you have a significant equity disadvantage against the limper's range, the favorable implied odds and the fact that you have position make eight-seven suited playable here. Also, against a passive player, you will have a good idea of where you stand if you flop a marginal hand, like a pair of eights or sevens. Since your hand has no showdown value, you do not want to raise to isolate the loose-passive player. By raising, you also seriously diminish your favorable implied odds, since you will have to pay at least two bets to see the flop. Furthermore, raising to take the initiative does not have much value against a player who makes loose calls and most likely goes to the showdown too often.

Quiz No. 4

In a 6-handed game, you are dealt 6♠5♠ on the button. A loose, passive player limps under the gun, and the next two players fold to you. Should you:

A. Call
B. Raise
C. Fold

Answer: C. You should fold. Even though you have position and good implied odds, six-five suited is simply too weak to play. The main reason for this is that when you flop a pair of sixes or fives, your opponent will be more likely to have a better pair, and even when you are ahead, he will almost always have at least 6 outs to beat you. If there were more than one limper, you could definitely call because your implied odds will be greater.

Quiz No. 5

In a 6-handed game, you are dealt the J♥T♠ on the button. A loose-passive player limps under the gun, and the next two players fold. Should you:

A. Call
B. Raise
C. Fold

Answer: C. You should fold. Even though you are only a slight underdog against the limper's range and you have position, your hand is too weak. Because your hand is not suited, your implied odds are not as favorable. If there were more than one limper in the pot, you could definitely call because your implied odds will be better.

Quiz No. 6

In a 6-handed game, you are dealt 5♣5♠ on the button. A loose-aggressive player open-raises from the cutoff. You estimate that he is opening with about 35 percent of his hands from this position: 55+, A2s+, A4o+, K3s+, K8o+, Q5s+, Q9o+, J7s+, J9o+, T7s+, T9o, 97s+, and 87s. Should you:

A. Call
B. Three-bet
C. Fold

Answer: B. You should three-bet. Even though you are a very slight underdog against the cutoff's range (50.1 percent versus 49.9 percent), you have a great opportunity to fold out the blinds and get heads up, thus creating an overlay for yourself with the dead money from the blinds. Also, you will have position on the cutoff which increases your post-flop expectation.

Quiz No. 7

In a 6-handed game, you are dealt A♦9♥ on the button. A loose-aggressive player open-raises from the cutoff. You estimate that he is opening with about 35 percent of his hands from this position: 55+, A2s+, A4o+, K3s+, K8o+, Q5s+, Q9o+, J7s+, J9o+, T7s+, T9o, 97s+, and 87s. Should you:

A. Call
B. Three-bet
C. Fold

Answer: B. You should three-bet. With ace-nine offsuit you are a favorite against the cutoff's range — 54 percent versus 46 percent. Plus, you have the potential to create dead money from the blinds. There is a slight risk that you are dominated if the cutoff has nines or better, or a better ace. However, that risk is somewhat mitigated by the fact that you have position. Also, your equity edge is significant enough to compensate for the times you are dominated.

Quiz No. 8

In a 6-handed game, you are dealt K♣J♣ on the button. A loose-aggressive player open-raises from the cutoff. You estimate that he is opening with about 35 percent of his hands from this position: 55+, A2s+, A4o+, K3s+, K8o+, Q5s+, Q9o+, J7s+, J9o+, T7s+, T9o, 97s+, and 87s. Should you:

A. Call
B. Three-bet
C. Fold

Answer: B. You should three-bet. With king-jack suited you are a favorite against the cutoff's range — 53.1 percent versus 46.9 percent. Plus, you have the potential to create dead money from the blinds. There is a slight risk that you are dominated if the cutoff has JJ+, AK, AJ, or KQ. However, that risk is somewhat mitigated by the facts that your hand is suited and you have position since they improve your implied odds.

Quiz No. 9

In a 6-handed game, you are dealt K♠Q♣ on the button. A loose-aggressive player open-raises from the cutoff. You estimate he is opening with about 35 percent of his hands from this position: 55+, A2s+, A4o+, K3s+, K8o+, Q5s+, Q9o+, J7s+, J9o+, T7s+, T9o, 97s+, and 87s. Should you:

A. Call
B. Three-bet
C. Fold

Answer: B. You should three-bet. With king-queen offsuit you are a favorite against the cutoff's range (52.6 percent versus 47.4 percent). Plus, you have the potential to create dead money from the blinds. There is only a very slight risk that you are dominated if the cutoff has QQ+, AK, or AQ. Your equity edge is too big not to three-bet.

Quiz No. 10

In a 6-handed game, you are dealt 7♠7♦ on the button. A tight-aggressive player open-raises from the cutoff. You estimate that he is opening with about 25 percent of his hands from this position: 66+, A2s+, A7o+, K6s+, K9o+, Q8s+, QTo+, J8s+, JTo, and T8s+. Should you:

A. Call
B. Three-bet
C. Fold

Answer: B. You should three-bet. With a pair of sevens you are a slight favorite against the cutoff's range (50.8 percent versus 49.2 percent). Combined with the potential to create dead money from the blinds, you definitely have enough equity to three-bet. Also, you will have position on the cutoff which increases your post-flop expectation.

Quiz No. 11

In a 6-handed game, you are dealt A♣8♣ on the button. A tight-aggressive player open-raises from the cutoff. You estimate that he is opening with about 25 percent of his hands from this position: 66+, A2s+, A7o+, K6s+, K9o+, Q8s+, QTo+, J8s+, JTo, and T8s+. Should you:

A. Call
B. Three-bet
C. Fold

Answer: B. You should three-bet. With ace-eight suited you are a very slight underdog against the cutoff's range (50.05 percent versus 49.95 percent). But with the potential to create dead money from the blinds, you have enough equity to three-bet. There is a risk that you are dominated if the cutoff has a pair of eights or better, or a better ace. However, that risk is somewhat mitigated by the facts that your hand is suited and you have position since they improve your implied odds.

Quiz No. 12

In a 6-handed game, you are dealt K♥J♥ on the button. A tight-aggressive player open-raises from the cutoff. You estimate that he is opening with about 25 percent of his hands from this position: 66+, A2s+, A7o+, K6s+, K9o+, Q8s+, QTo+, J8s+, JTo, and T8s+. Should you:

A. Call
B. Three-bet
C. Fold

Answer: B. You should three-bet. With king-jack suited you are a very slight underdog against the cutoff's range (50.1 percent versus 49.9 percent). Plus, you have the potential to create dead money from the blinds. There is only a slight risk that you are dominated if the cutoff has JJ+, AK, AJ, or KQ.

Quiz No. 13

In a 6-handed game, you are dealt Q♠J♠ on the button. A tight-aggressive player open-raises from the cutoff. You estimate that he is opening with about 25 percent of his hands from this position: 66+, A2s+, A7o+, K6s+, K9o+, Q8s+, QTo+, J8s+, JTo, and T8s+. Should you:

A. Call
B. Three-bet
C. Fold

Answer: C. You should fold. With queen-jack suited you are an underdog against the cutoff's range (54.8 percent versus 45.2 percent). But even with the potential to create dead money from the blinds, you do not have enough equity to three-bet. There is a significant risk that you are dominated if the cutoff has JJ+, AQ, AJ, KQ, or KJ. Even though your hand is suited and you have position, your equity disadvantage makes this a fold.

Quiz No. 14

In a very tight ten-handed game, you are dealt A♣A♥ UTG. Should you:

A. Call
B. Raise
C. Fold

Answer: A. You should call. In a very tight game, there is a good chance your raise from early position will cause everyone to fold, winning you only the blinds. This is not a good outcome since your expectation with aces is much higher than the blinds. (This is also true for kings.) Also, if someone raises in middle or late position you will be able to re-raise, creating a big pot and pushing your tremendous equity advantage. However, in order to balance this play (if balancing is necessary because this is your regular game or you have played with these players before) you should also limp-re-raise from early position with other hands such as, 77-88, KQs-KTs, QJs-QTs, and JTs, depending on the situation.

Quiz No. 15.1

In a ten-handed game, you are dealt 8♦8♠ UTG. Should you:

A. Call
B. Raise
C. Fold

Answer: A. You should call. A pair of eights is not strong enough to open-raise when you are 7 seats off the button. However, it has decent equity and very favorable implied odds. Also, being out of position is not a much of a disadvantage with a hand like eights since you will usually only continue past the flop when you hit a set. Finally, calling here provides "cover" for the times you attempt to limp/re-raise with aces or kings.

Quiz No. 15.2

You call with your 8♦8♠ UTG, two tight-aggressive players limp behind you in middle positions, a loose-aggressive player raises on the button, and both blinds fold. Should you:

A. Call
B. Reraise
C. Fold

Answer: B. You should reraise. With a pair of eights, you are a favorite against the button's range. Also since the two limpers are tight, there is a good chance that they will both fold to your three-bet. This will get you heads up with the button and create a significant amount of dead money in the pot.

Quiz No. 15.3

You call with your 8♦8♠ UTG, an aggressive player raises behind you in middle position, the button cold-calls, and both blinds call. Should you:

A. Call
B. Three-bet
C. Fold

Answer: A. You should call. Even though you likely have a small equity edge with a pair of eights, since you are out of position, you should just call to keep the pot small. Also, if you did three-bet, you will not force any players out because they will have to call only one more small bet to see the flop (unless of course the original pre-flop raiser four-bets which will make you a significant underdog to his range). Furthermore, since the pre-flop raiser is to your immediate left, by just calling you maintain good relative position and will most likely be able to check raise and trap the entire field those times a third eight does comes.

Quiz No. 16.1

In a ten-handed game, you are dealt the Q♥J♥ UTG+1 and the player UTG folds. Should you:

A. Call
B. Raise

C.   Fold

Answer: A. You should call. Queen-jack suited is not strong enough to open-raise when you are 6 seats off the button. However, it will have very good equity in a multi-way pot and very favorable implied odds. Calling here encourages other players to enter behind you and also provides "cover" for the times you attempt to limp/re-raise with aces or kings.

Quiz No. 16.2

You call with your Q♥J♥ UTG+1, three tight players call behind you, the small blind calls, and the big blinds raises. Should you:

A.   Call
B.   Three-bet
C.   Fold

Answer: B. You should call. Even though your hand has a significant equity edge against your opponents' rainges, you should just call because, if you three-bet, you may shut out the tight players to act behind you by forcing them to call 2 bets cold. Furthermore, since the pre-flop raiser is out of position in the big blind, he is more likely to have a big hand. By three-betting, you may end up heads up as a significant underdog.

Quiz No. 16.3

You call with your Q♥J♥ UTG+1, two loose players call in middle position, an aggressive player raises on the button, and both blinds call. Should you:

A.   Call
B.   Three-bet
C.   Fold

Answer: B. You should three-bet. In a hand where 6 players are likely to see the flop, Queen-jack suited has a significant equity edge so you should reraise for value. Also, it is unlikely that your three-bet will shut out the limpers to act behind you since they are loose and will want to see a flop in this big pot.

Post-Flop Play

Quiz No. 17.1

In a six-handed game, you open-raise with 8♣7♣ on the button and only a tight-aggressive player in the big blind calls. The flop comes A♦9♦4♠, and the big blind checks. Should you:

A. Check
B. Bet

Answer: B. You should bet. Since there are 4.5 small bets currently in the pot, your opponent needs to fold 23 percent (or more) of the time for this bet to be profitable. Even a tight player will defend his big blind with a fairly wide range, and, since he cannot have overcards on this flop, he will fold a good portion of his hands to your bet when he does not flop a pair or a good draw.

Quiz No. 17.2

You bet the A♦9♦4♠ flop with your 8♣7♣, and your tight-aggressive opponent calls. The turn is the 3♣, and he checks. Should you:

A. Check
B. Bet

Answer: A. You should check. Since your opponent called your flop bet, you can be fairly certain that he either has a pair or a flush draw. If he has a pair, he is most likely going to see the showdown since you open-raised from the button. If he has a flush draw, he very often will check raise the turn forcing you to fold your eight-high. It is time to give up on this hand unless you improve on the river.

Quiz No. 18.1

In a six-handed game, you open-raise with J♠T♣ on the button and only a loose-aggressive player in the big blind calls. The flop comes A♦9♦4♠, and the big blind checks. Should you:

A. Check
B. Bet

Answer: B. You should bet. Since your opponent is loose, he likely defended his big blind with a very wide range of hands — probably close to 100 percent. Therefore, he will completely miss the flop more than the requisite 23 percent of the time. Moreover, he may make a loose peel on the flop and fold if you bet again on the turn. (See the next question for more on this.)

Quiz No. 18.2

You bet the A♦9♦4♠ flop with your J♠T♣, and your loose-aggressive opponent calls. The turn is the 3♣, and he checks. Should you:

A. Check
B. Bet

Answer: B. You should bet. Since your opponent is loose, he could have called your flop bet with a wide range of hands (for example, hands with two backdoor draws or hands with two overcards to the 9♦ on the flop and a backdoor draw). Since the turn is a complete blank, it is likely that he will give up on these hands if you bet again. Furthermore, with 3.25 big bets in the pot, you need your opponent to fold 31 percent of the time for this bet to be immediately profitable. It is actually less than 31 percent because that does not include the times your opponent calls with a pair of nines or lower and you spike a jack or ten on the river to improve to the best hand.

Quiz No. 19

In a six-handed game, you open-raise with J♠T♣ on the button and only a tight-aggressive player in the big blind calls. The flop comes 8♦7♠2♦, the big blind checks, you bet, and he calls. The turn is the K♥ and he checks. Should you:

A.   Check
B.   Bet

Answer: B. You should bet. Since the flop in this hand contains three low cards, your opponent could have called with a fairly wide range (such as, two overcards or one overcard and inside straight or backdoor draw). When the K♥ hits on the turn and you bet again, your opponent will be forced to fold enough to make this bet profitable.

Quiz No. 20

In a six-handed game, you open-raise with the Q♠6♠ on the button and only a loose-passive player in the big blind calls. The flop comes 8♦7♠2♦, the big blind checks, you bet, and he calls. The turn is the K♥, he checks, you bet, and he calls. The river is the A♣. Should you:

A.   Check
B.   Bet

Answer: B. You should bet. Since the flop is fairly coordinated (containing both flush and straight draws), there is decent chance that your opponent had a drawing hand, which missed, and will fold to a river bet. Since there are 5.25 big bets in the pot, you need him to fold hands that beat you more than 16 percent of the time for this bet to be profitable.

Quiz No. 21

In a six-handed game, you open-raise with T♠9♦ on the button and only a loose-passive player in the big blind calls. The flop comes 8♦4♠2♣, the big blind checks, you bet, and he calls. The turn is the Q♥, he checks, you bet, and he calls. The river is the A♣. Should you:

A.   Check
B.   Bet

Answer: A. You should probably check. Since the board is very uncoordinated, it is likely that your opponent had a pair or ace-high (which has now made a pair) when he called your turn bet. Also, it is likely that your opponent will call a river bet with any pair since he is loose. It is time to give up and check the river.

Quiz No. 22

In a five-handed game, you open-raise with A♣7♦ on the button and only a loose and very aggressive player in the big blind calls. The flop comes 9♠5♥3♦, the big blind checks, you bet, and he calls. The turn is the K♣, and he checks. Should you:

A.   Check
B.   Bet

Answer: A. You should check. Since your opponent is very aggressive, there is a good chance he will bluff the river. Also, because your opponent is loose, he could have called the flop bet with a wide range (including overcards and inside straight draws). This actually increases the probability that he will bluff the river since he will hold more hands with which he knows he cannot win at the showdown. Even though your opponent may have 6 outs to beat you, the pot is not that large, so it is less important to bet to protect your hand. But if you bet, a very aggressive opponent may check raise bluff the turn, which may force you to fold the best hand. Finally, your opponent may already have made a pair, and checking the turn allows you to take a free card those times you are behind.

Quiz No. 23

In a five-handed game, you open-raise with A♣7♦ on the button and only a loose-passive player in the big blind calls. The flop comes 9♠5♥3♦, the big blind checks, you bet, and he calls. The turn is the K♣, and he checks. Should you:

A. Check
B. Bet

Answer: B. You should bet. Since your opponent is loose, he called your pre-flop raise and flop bet with a very wide range of hands. Thus, it is likely that your ace-high is still best. Also, there is very little value in checking to induce a river bluff against a passive opponent. Furthermore, if he check raises the turn, you can be almost certain that you are drawing very thin and should fold. In this case, it is better to bet the turn and check behind on the river (assuming you do not improve your hand).

Quiz No. 24.1

In a six-handed game, you open-raise with 2♣2♠ in the cutoff and only a loose-aggressive player in the big blind calls. The flop comes 8♦7♥4♦, the big blind checks, you bet, and he calls. The turn is the Q♣, and he checks. Should you:

A. Check
B. Bet

Answer: B. You should bet. Since your opponent is guaranteed to have at least 6 outs against you (and in some cases 15 or more outs), you should bet to protect your vulnerable hand. If your opponent were super-aggressive (i.e. would bluff the river 100 percent of the time), you may want to check to induce a bluff. However, it is very rare that you will find an opponent this aggressive.

Quiz No. 24.2

You bet the turn with your pair of deuces on the 8♦7♥4♦Q♣ board, and the big blind check raises. Should you:

A. Fold
B. Call
C. Raise.

Answer: A. You should fold even though there is a chance that your opponent is semi-bluffing and you may have the best hand. If you are behind, you are drawing to at most two outs and do not have odds to continue. Furthermore, it is quite a parlay for you to currently have the best hand and for your opponent to not improve to beat you on the river. Getting effective odds of 7.25-to-2 is not enough to call down.

Quiz No. 25

In a four-handed game, you open-raise with the T♣T♠ on the button and only a loose-aggressive player in the big blind calls. The flop comes K♦9♥4♠, the big blind checks, you bet, and he calls. The turn is the 9♣. Should you:

A. Check
B. Bet

Answer: A. You should check. With this board and your pair of tens, it is far more likely that your opponent has 3 or fewer outs to beat you. Thus, checking the turn to induce a bluff is less risky. Also since your opponent is aggressive, there is a good chance that he will bluff the river with a hand worse than yours.

Summary

Limit hold 'em is a game of small edges and relative values. If you are good enough to get most of the small edges going your way, you will do well. However, if you destroy that value by periodically neglecting some of the big stuff — it sounds crazy, but most players do, at one point or another in their career, neglect the big stuff — it does not matter how well you take care of the small stuff. This final stand alone chapter is a reminder of what we consider the "big stuff" and some of it may be repetitive, but it is important and worth repeating. A big part of being a winning player in limit hold 'em is consistency, not only in how you play your hands (consistently unpredictable), but also in how you approach the game, strive to improve, select tables and seats, and avoid playing in situations when you are not at your best.

Table and Seat Selection

It has been said that you can be the tenth best poker player in the world but still lose money if you choose to sit with the nine players better than you. Furthermore, the difference in variance and expectation is large when you can correctly choose the best games, and it doesn't take much time to do it. Often, which table and seat you choose is the single most important decision you make in a session.

In order to have some basis upon which to select your tables, you will need to have a reasonable read on some or most of the opponents who play in your games. Assuming you are a regular, this is relatively easy to accumulate over time. However, if you are at a new casino or poker site, or at a new limit, you may have to spend some time watching the game to develop reads.

The process of observing play online is easy, and we suggest that you plan changes in sites and limits ahead of time and spend a small amount of time doing some advance scouting of the players you will be playing against. The issue is a bit more complex in a live casino because it is more time consuming to observe players, you have much less control over table and seat selection, and the frictional costs associated with the entire process are much greater.

On average, the level of play for a given limit of live poker should be lower than the corresponding limit of online play, so this should somewhat compensate for your reduced ability to practice good table and seat selection. However, playing live is a bit more expensive because of a higher average rake and dealer tipping. Our suggestion for live play is to get the best seat you can, and if you find yourself in a terrible game, get on a different list or structure your day so you can play when the games are better.

Bankroll Management

The world of high-stakes poker is filled with players who have little or no regard for money itself, much less bankroll management. Many of them play poker well, and a few of them have run hot enough to solidify a long-term place at the highest limits. Conversely, many of them ran hot for a short period of time, but ended up on the rail because they played above their bankroll.

It is tempting to watch some of these players and think you can emulate them. While it is possible to reach the top in this fashion, it is certainly not advisable on any type of risk-adjusted basis. It is easy to look at the best players in the world and think you can play with them, and maybe you can, but copying the bankroll management style of some of them is not something we advise.

Like many things in poker, you are walking a tightrope, trying not to fall off on either side. There is some level of game and limit selection that optimizes your earn while minimizing your risk of ruin based on your bankroll, playing ability, and risk tolerance. A pro who takes money from his bankroll every week to pay for living expenses should play more conservatively than someone playing for recreation who has income from other sources. The same pro also needs to be realistic about what he needs for expenses and whether his current bankroll allows him to play safely at a particular limit and easily cover his expenses. If his lack of bankroll forces him to play too low, he will not be able to pay his bills. If his expenses are so high that he stretches his bankroll to play higher limits, it may work for a while, but sooner or later a bad downswing can cripple his cash reserves.

Psychological and Tilt Control

It is human nature to attribute success or failure to things over which you have control. It is poker's nature to often bestow success or failure to chance, regardless of ability. These two realities do not mix well, and we caution people against getting too emotionally excited with their winning sessions or, conversely, too down about their losing sessions. Often, for very long and unbelievable periods, players will experience abnormal wins or losses due to variance. It is a reality of poker that winning players can lose big and losing players can win big for fairly long periods of time.

From a psychological standpoint, you should not exacerbate the situation anymore than exists on its own. When running good, you should not necessarily feel you have a license to jump up two limits from your normal game. To the contrary, you should always think long and hard about all the ramifications of moving up even one limit. When running poorly, you certainly do not have a reason to move up any limits at all. Unbelievably, many players, including many good ones, do this in an attempt to get unstuck. You should not be among them.

Lifestyle and Happiness Factors

Being a poker pro can sometimes be the most rewarding experience and sometimes an awful one. You may even go from one extreme to the other in a period of hours. Smoothing out these emotional highs and lows is not easy, but a bit of self-knowledge, forethought, consistency, and introspection can help to ease the periodic pains. Anytime you win a big hand, we suggest you mentally store the hand in your memory — maybe you got lucky and came from behind to win a monster pot. File those hands away for the times you are being hard on yourself. If you get very unlucky in a hand or a session, try and remember the times you were the beneficiary of the luck factor.

This book has been mostly about the little things, but if the big things are not done correctly then doing the little things will not mean very much. Bankroll management, tilt avoidance, and game selection are important. Make sure you get those right. If you cannot, it will not matter how well you play your hands.

Index

NOTES